ESCAPE FROM FAILURE

The linchpin to transcending the devastating impact of Black gangsterism is asking for and a willingness to forgive the transgressions of one's enemies for their war-time behaviors.

STEVEN R. CURETON

ESCAPE FROM FAILURE

WILLIAM V. FIELDS

Cupidity Press
Carson, CA

Escape from Failure

William V. Fields

Escape from Failure is a work of fiction. Names, characters, places, and incidents are the products of the author's imagination or are used fictitiously. Any resemblance to actual events, locales, or persons living or dead, is entirely coincidental.

Escape from Failure Copyright © 2011

Cupidity Press

All Rights Reserved.

Dedication

This book is dedicated to Devin Brown, Leonard Deadwyler, Eula Love, Margaret Mitchell, Susie Pena, Ralph Miller, Rodney King, Donovan Jackson, Michael Byounes, Darrick Collins, Steven Eugene Washington, Ruben Walton Ortega, Eddie Felix Franco, Marcus Smith, Richard Ray Tyson, Jule Dexter 3rd, and all victims of police violence, gang violence, domestic violence, mental violence, physical violence, sexual violence, racial violence. Lastly, this book is dedicated for all the sincere community activist and nonprofits who want to see a better way of living for the kids in their communities who give of their time and resources daily without any recognition I thank You!

Acknowledgement

My Brother Corey "KP" Fields, we don't always see eye to eye, but you have always supported my growth and writing I trust your opinion because I know you want hesitate to keep it real with me and for that I thank you and love you. Continue to build little bro!

Table of Contents

Dedication 1

Acknowledgement 2

Focus Lost 5

Chapter 1 Finally 6

Chapter 2 Oder by Law 13

Chapter 3 Things Change 23

Chapter 4 A Ladies Touch 28

Chapter 5 Ones We Live With 38

Chapter 6 Boys in Blue 44

Chapter 7 Home 55

Chapter 8 Concrete La Jungla 67

Chapter 9 Friends Become Strangers 78

Chapter 10 Gang Life 98

Chapter 11 Gang Land 105

Chapter 12 Harsh Realities 112

Chapter 13 Unacceptable 119

Chapter 14 No Lesson 126

Chapter 15 Lesson learned 134

Chapter 16 Hot Tea 144

Chapter 17 Last Breathing 150

Chapter 18 Let Down 154

Chapter 19 Churches 159

Chapter 20 El Pecho 171

Chapter 21 Silence is betrayal 181

Chapter 22 Tragedy 193

Chapter 23 Self-Hatred 207

Chapter 24 Two ears one mouth 221

Chapter 25 Old Ties 236

Chapter 26 Green Light 244

Chapter 27 Red Light 252

Chapter 28 Target 260

Chapter 29 Regroup 266

Chapter 30 Grow 271

Focus Lost

Rotating periscopes attached to my sockets a steady consumer coming out of my pocket.

C.R.E.A.M mentality still runs rampant get it embedded no matter what happens.

Born to lead, but choose to follow. Normal symptoms when one's brain is hollow unwise choices leave me wobbled steadily reaching for that bottle, for in its nectar I find relief dragging me further from my beliefs. Juiced up chasing dreams that never belonged to me, caught in a continuous image of what the media depicts of me. No thoughts in my mind when I need them to be reason learning never appealed to me.

Squinting my eyes, I focus my vision realizing now that the thoughts I harbor weigh on every decision. Sad when you are any age off in prison. Triggering me to clean my lenses to perfect my precision knowing life is hard that's a given as knowledge of self becomes the way to write my life's revision.

Nevertheless, my focus is no longer lost knowing to succeed I must build my mind to the point of exhaust.

Chapter 1

Finally

"You sure that's him I'm not trying to waste no bullets on no smokers or has-beens." Uzi said tucking his 357 python into his brown khakis.

"Cuzz I'm positive, I just did a violation with him in CMC where he was pushing a line on the homies." Tall Can said while adjusting his red beanie.

"Pull over on the side street behind his car we'll catch him when he comes out the liquor store. We can post against the gate. I'll shoot him in the head while you give it to him in the body." Uzi said as Baby Uzi pulled behind their victim's brown 83 Cutlass Supreme.

Stepping out of their black 97 Honda Accord Uzi and Tall Can made their way to the side gate of an apartment building which set adjacent to an alley on the corner of Figueroa.

Usually they would have stood out in the Blood neighborhood, but they were flamed up, so they blended into the environment well for their current mission.

"Hey Uzi, you see those kids over there playing jump rope in that yard?" Tall Can asked as he looked down the alley in the other direction at some smokers digging through a graffiti dumpster.

"Yeah, I see them, but it does not mean anything once they here the gun shots they'll start running anyway or continue playing. Besides, they hear gun shots all the time it probably wants even stop them from playing."

"I'm just putting you up on the kids, so no bullets hit them."

"Cuzz, fuck them kids I'm not trying to hear that soft shit. Go join a non-profit if you want to help save the kids, I gangbang."

"Let me get five packs of Cherry berry blunt wraps too." B-Down told the Asian cashier as he paid for the blunt wraps along with the twenty-four pack of MGD for his set day on October 9. He had been out twenty-six days and was feeling damn good after pulling eight in the pen.

Being away so long had its benefits and draw backs. For one he was the new swipe in the set which meant all his home girls new and old wanted to give him a piece before he got sucked up by the street life. Plus he was looking good with his twenty inch arms that set apart from a pumped out wide chest, but mostly the females were on his extra-long hair which he wore in nine French braids that set against the middle of his upper back. The drawback of course was he had to start from scratch with everything including meeting new Y.G. homies who had only heard about him, but that was the least of his worries, he was going to get a chance to see his eight year old daughter who he hadn't seen since his baby momma received thirteen years for consecutive shoplifting. Since she had gone to jail his daughter had to be raised by her parents who lived in Arizona, but also had family that lived on Imperial and Vermont which they came out every month to see, luckily his daughter was out in L.A this weekend so that he could see her.

 Bending the corner B-Down quickly noticed the two Black males leaning against the gate not too far from his car.

"What's up blood?" Uzi said.

"Just *bicking it*." B-Down replied.

"Dogg you need help with those brews?"

"Naw I'm *bool*, I got it blood." B-Down replied as he reached in his pocket for his car keys with his right hand.

Opening his trunk, he placed his beers inside before he could close it, he was thrown off guard by a question from Uzi.

"Blood you got a bigarette on you?"

"Naw, blood I don't smoke." Turning back around to close his trunk B-Down heard the sound of sneakers screeching behind him, but it was too late as Uzi placed the 357 Pythons nose to the back of his head squeezing the trigger all in one fluid motion. The blast of the revolver knocked the back part of his

Escape from Failure

skull along with his forehead into the hood of the trunk beating the upper part of his body which quickly followed.

The thickness of B-Down's braided hair muffled the normally loud python, causing little to no reaction from the kids a few homes up. What did catch their attention were the multiple shots from Tall Can's 45 automatic handgun that pumped bullet after bullet into his hunched over deceased body.

Uzi had done this numerous times before and walked away with no regard for what he had just done. With Tall Can right behind him they walked a few feet to their awaiting car which Baby Uzi already had up and running.

While opening up the passenger door Uzi felt eyes on him, when he turned to meet the gaze he saw that it was coming from the children a few feet from them leaning over their gate watching the entire last part of their mission. Without much thought Uzi tossed his 357 into the passenger seat and grabbed his AK 47 that had a hundred round drum attached to it lying against the side of the passenger seat. The kids didn't think much of the man coming towards them in a red t-shirt and hat with a big gun by his side and before they realized his intentions he had opened fire on them killing them all in a matter of seconds with a few sweeps of the AK which ended up hitting more of the house then anything.

Back in the car Uzi lit a cigarette as Tall Can set in shock at what he just saw. He had heard stories about how crazy Uzi was, but he just realized he was in the presence of pure evil.

"Cuzz you just killed three kids." Tall Can said hysterically.

"Tell me something I don't know any other quick facts."

"There was no reason for that."

"Says who?"

"Says me, you just murdered some little Black kids for no reason."

"There was a reason they saw my face."

"But they were just little kids they wouldn't have been able to identify you."

"Whatever, besides, they would have turned Lanes anyway."

"Cuzz, that don't sit well with me."

"Then you probably want be feeling this either. "Uzi said reaching his arm into the backseat with his 357 pointing directly at Tall Cans head pulling the trigger. The close range of the hollow tip bullet split his forehead as if an axe had gone through it as his body flipped forward.

"Damn cuzz, now we have to burn the car. Soft as nigga talking about, I killed some kids, nigga please we just killed a man, the producer of kids.

***

"After a five-year investigation ten Los Angeles Police Officers belonging to the 77th Street C.R.A.S.H. division have been charged with a string of unlawful arrests, murders, attempted murders, and various other crimes that span over a 20-year period. There will definitely be a public outcry equaling that of the Rampart corruption scandal that happened to the city many years ago." This is Pat Harvey reporting for KCAL 9 News.

Askari was paralyzed in body and soul by the news report he had just seen; he had been following the case for the last year since it started to appear in the Los Angeles Sentinel. For a while he had thought the investigation on the corrupt police officers would just be swept under the rug like so many suspect shootings, beatings, and arrests. Yet he sat galvanized at the possibility that many of his peers would once again have an opportunity to walk the streets with their families, but most importantly he thought about the twelve years he had been incarcerated and how it could now be coming to an end.

 Fantasies of his freedom crossed his mind frequently in the beginning of his term, but after seeing countless board extension, legislatives for three strikes ignored, and appeals denied he had simply put his problems in Gods hand choosing in the meantime to dwell in his on comforts and understanding of life and the way it was supposed to be. Like so many others he had come to accept life in prison as the way it was with a small amount of hope that every human being needed to survive day to day that there would eventually be a light at the end of the tunnel that would set him free. For many years he had known mental freedom quite well, it had been physical freedom that had become foreign to him over the last decade yet now he felt a feeling that had only visited him in dreams and while watching the Discovery channel.

This feeling made his eyes slightly water as he stared off into the air that had been his for far too long it was after all a breathless air that lacked life all together. He felt a slight since of shame that he had even allowed himself to have such a foolish feeling he seen this type of scenario played out too many times with the same results, but that inner hope was always there no matter how much he denied it. Nevertheless, he reacted like he always did when confronted with such feelings and thoughts bury them inside.

The next day the prison yard was filled with the same gleefulness that usually followed the news of early release bringing with its facts and fiction of what was said the night before on the case regarding the police. Askari just continued his daily routine letting the echoes of what was going to be slide in one earlobe and out the other.

It was Tuesday and the sun were shining bright on the inmate's skin as they all tried to adjust to the sun that had been denied to them for three months due to a lock down. For some it took a little more adjusting then others to gain their composure reason being there were a lot of youngsters on the yard serving life sentencing for a for all type of crimes, but the majority being murders and robberies gone wrong. This disturbed Askari a lot, because he was seeing a cycle of wasted young misguided life thrown away year after year. The ages ranged from 18 to 26 years old and the numbers were increasing. With so many youths placed in prison he often wondered what would eventually happen to neighborhoods without any male influence. From what he had heard there was an increase in lesbianism on the streets do to the fact that the male influence was so in decline, women had started to take on the role of the missing soon to be link. A day did not pass that he did not hear my bitch just left me for another bitch escaping a youngster's lips. Just a few years back the average inmate had to worry about another male taking his place, but now they had double trouble with the women being Involved. So much had changed yet so much remained the same. The death rate in California had dropped over the last couple of years, but the only reason being that the system had locked up the majority of the line pushers from the different sets throughout L.A. county nevertheless brothers were still killing brothers as the new crop of gang members were being born to single mothers in the ghetto.

The rise in black on brown killings were still increasing in Compton, Watts, SGV, Pomona and throughout the L.A. area basically every Black gang was having some type of friction with a Hispanic gang over money, territory, misunderstandings or just skin issues. This information was constantly being reported on the news of what was taking place between the two races everyday which did nothing but fuel the tension in the prison environment as well as the county jail.

Most blacks didn't realize the low number of blacks until they reached the jail system then it eventually dawned on them that they needed each other at the end of the day especially when faced with a seven to one ratio in a riot. The word nigga still sounded like fingernails being dragged across a chalk board in his ears whenever he heard it especially when said around different races. He had just gotten two youngstas from 83 Hoover who came from another yard placed next door and they seemed to be having a competition on who could say nigga the most in one day; there had been a lot of bed moves since the last riot which basically meant there would be a whole lot of chaos on the yard for the next few months. Askari would eventually get around to meeting his new neighbors and possibly give them some knowledge in the meantime. One of the youngsta kind of reminded him of his protégée K-Stone who had moved on to the physical freedom that eluded so many inmates. Even though he heard from him once a month he still missed being around his comrade who he lived through vicariously in the form of pictures, letters, and phone calls.

November 3, 2008 the world felt a united anticipation as they stood by on all levels of the social ladder waiting on Tuesday to come bringing with it the results of who would be their next president. Emotions were running high in Beverly Hills at Nate'n Al were younger Jews were discussing the possibility of Obama wining and what it would do for their taxes while their matzo ball soup cooled downed; over on Hyde Park behind some rundown apartment building the Rollin 60 Crips were initiating two brand new teenage members; a little further down on Crenshaw Eso Won book store was serving Pearl-gray tea from the Coffee Bean and Tea leaf as a group of people out in the community ranging from early twenties to late eighties discussed how they could continue to keep the interest of politics fresh in the community after Tuesdays presidential results while informing the community how they could help make the president's job much easier ; Down in East L.A amongst the hustle and bustle Hispanics leaned against their vendor vehicles after a long prospers day making sure their Obama stickers were still intact while talking in their native tongue about what their children's health care benefits would be like under Obama's policies. In prisons across California conversation ranged from "who cares who wins I got life", "It would be righteous to see a familiar face in the White House", and "That nigger better not win", but mostly inmates were concerned with the passing of Proposition 9 which would take away the little rights they had managed to hold on to. To the inmate it really did not matter who won on the free world if Proposition 9 was passed. For that reason, the prison system was on high alert because of talk of a possible riot on staff if the 9 Bill did pass. Furthermore, there was talk in the air that if Obama did win the Skin Heads and Aaron Brother hood were going to launch a full-scale attack on all Black inmates within the system. There was also talk about the Blacks doing a similar attack if McCain won the presidency. Tensions were just high all around the board throughout the prison complex and the world at large with the recession getting worse, but even with all the distress there was a ray of hope awaiting one inmate in the form of a letter within a mail bag.

Chapter 2

Oder by Law

Sergeant Waters a 35 years old white male who appeared to be younger because of years adherent to his military training and dieting, set hard pressed in his office revealing years that hardly showed, but were secretly hid in the skin surrounding his dark blue eyes that usually set aloof in a deep puzzling stare. Sitting in his chair jaw clinching back and forth he knew he would have to talk to the chief and request some favors for the officers under his command after reading the continual coverage about the scandal that seemed to be reported on daily. Crumbling up the Los Angeles Times he reached for his log in sheet to see what time Rodriguez, Vasquez, Lee, Cleveland, and Pikes shift ended. He needed to debrief with them before the public started to ask for them to be removed from the streets, but most importantly before their behavior could be linked back to him for cosigning their rogue behavior which was now coming to light.

Chief Anthony L. Williams was a short man in his early sixties with a thick Boston accent that became more pronounced when he became angry or irritated with a person or situation that he deemed not to be going along with his beliefs. His latest irritation stemmed from the entire recent backlash his department was receiving because of his officers policing strategies that had brought violent crime down 50% since he became chief of the department in 2002. He felt that the People of L.A were too finicky in their thoughts, one minute they wanted crime down the next minute they were complaining about how it was done they were never happy and it was starting to grow old more so the L.A weather was starting to make his white skin peel causing him to have a reddish look whenever he went out to speak; all in all he missed the cool temperature of his home town. He was just about to phone his wife when he heard a knock at his door.

"Come in." Chief Williams said stepping from behind his desk to the front of it.

"Chief, am I free to speak?" Waters asked closing the door behind him.

Escape from Failure

"Of course, but not here, we'll go to the usual place to discuss the issue that I believe you came to speak about.

"Yes, I will meet you there at the usual time". Waters replied while seeing himself out of the chief's office.

The Pantry downtown was a one stop eating place for cops of various division as well as the criminals they arrested; so it was the perfect spot to have meeting on current issues without seeming too suspicious more so everyone was usually in and out of the place not having much time to see who was who let alone speculate on what certain individuals were talking about. Chief Williams and Waters frequented the Pantry only when it was time to discuss a major shift in the department. The whole situation with the police corruption was nothing more than an irritation to them and the department at large; like most things people would shut their mouths once they were paid.

"So how much do you think this one is going to cost us?" Waters asked before taking a sip of his coffee.

"About 3 million, we'll pay different amounts to different individuals and the rest we will send through the motions until they take whatever we throw their way. Besides, you know how these people are, all they are going to spend their money on is clothes, cars, and jewelry so a few thousand here and there should do the trick. Just make sure you have your officers review any suspect arrest that can come back to haunt them, that way we will know to whom to give what.

"Done, so what about the media's coverage, they are bringing up a lot of questions?"

"Waters, the only concern you should have right now is that your officers don't get their noses dirty while we work to clean this situation up. The media is like fleas on a dead carcass once the meat is all gone, they will move on to the next piece of flesh. Right now, let us just stay posed. I do not know If you heard, but the Inglewood police department just killed some homeless man a couple of hours ago, so it will not be long before the next story is overshadowing our department. Lastly, never forget we have one of the most powerful unions and Sacramento is at our call when need be." With that Chief Williams paid for their coffees and slices of lemon pie and adjusted his jacket before walking out the restaurant with sergeant Waters close by his side. Outside the restaurant both men shook hands before making their separate ways to their vehicles.

***

"Shots fired in the alley of 84th and Hoover!"

"We are approaching the scene." C.R.A.S.H officer Hector "Hard Toes" Rodriguez replied to the officer on the other end of the intercom. Rodriguez was a 28-year-old proud Mexican-American that had thick black hair that rested on his head like a panther giving him the appearance of a greaser with a slight resemblance to Elvis Presley, but with a sharp chin that played on his Aztec roots. Rodriguez grew in F13 neighborhood which was also claimed by the 76 East Coast Crips who had been at war for quite a while over some drugs. Growing up he was no stranger to gang violence and the strain it put on the community, he had been a victim himself of both The F13 and the East Coast Crips. The East Coast had robbed him numerous times when he went to Gompers Elementary, while the F13 would pressure him to join so that he could get help to fight against the *mayates* which was a derogatory term used to describe Blacks; when he refuses to join he faced getting robbed by them too. It was not until his parents moved to Gardena that he escaped the constant harassment of both gangs. Time went by and Rodriguez eventually joined the L.A.P.D and with hard work got assigned to the C.R.A.S.H unit, a day did not go by that he did not remember the *jacking* and beat downs he received from not only the Blacks, but his own kind as a child. It was his goal to rid the streets of gang's period so that no kid would have to endure what he had to endure growing up.

"Vasquez it would sure help if they gave us a description of the suspects or a make on any cars that might have been involved with the shots fired?" Rodriguez said pulling to the side of the alley.

"They probably assume we know the description of the suspects any way. "Vasquez said in his thick accent slamming the door of the car. There's no one in the alley, let us just ride someone will pop up."

Luis "V" Vasquez was 32-year-old product of two immigrant parents who came from Guatemala he was raised in Diamond 13 neighborhood which was

Escape from Failure

situated in East L.A., although he was not a member he was cool with the local gang members until he found out that they were taxing his father's small tamales business which was hardly making enough to feed the family of four. He was angered that the gang who he considered his friends were taxing his father and taking food out of his families mouth; so he went to confront the gang members against his families wishes and was put in the hospital for a month from stab wounds; when he returned home he found that his father was made to pay double as long as he stayed in the home so at the age of sixteen he was forced to leave home and find his own way. It was a struggle at first going to school and trying to find work to support his self he eventually had to drop out and work full time washing dishes and buffing tables at a small restaurant not far from his old home; occasionally he would see his parents, but he rarely spoke to them not wanting to bring trouble upon them again. At the age of nineteen he enrolled in a G.E.D program at Trade Tech College downtown an eventually enrolled in the college to take general education not really knowing what he wanted to do with his life. Being on campus opened him up to a myriad of possibilities he even met his future wife their taking classes too. Nearing graduation, he had started to work campus security at the college and liked the respect he was given when he put on the uniform. While performing his duties one day he came across four Hispanics smoking weed in the bathroom, when he tried to radio it in, they beat him up while taunting him calling walkie talkie cop. Lying beaten up against the plastic trash can Vasquez had nostalgia of when he was attacked by the Diamond 13 it was then amongst the graffiti bathroom walls that he decided that he would join his own gang the L.A.P.D. His first four years in the department were hard, but he stuck with it, his Latin roots gave him deep acne scars which layer like craters on his cheeks more so his shape would not define no matter how much he exercised especially with his short stature he did so in an effort to set his self apart from any stereotypes he was always the one to enforce the law on suspects so that his collogues would not view him as a race sympathizer.

Driving North up Hoover towards the 65 Menlo's Rodriguez hit the brakes quickly when Vasquez inform him that another C.R.A.S.H car had some 18st gang members hemmed up against the wall of the liquor store.

"Fuck here comes faggot ass Hard Toes and V." Puppet said looking over his shoulder.

"Well fellas what do we have here, a couple of South Centrals finest wall destroyers." Rodriguez said pushing up the two suspects against the wall. "I see you out hanging with your girlfriend Cartoon Today Puppet?"

"That's not my fucking girlfriend." Puppet responded; his chest now pressed against the wall of the liquor store by Vasquez while Rodriguez continued to talk.

"So, if he's not the girl friend then you must be the bitch, Cartoon is you the man of the relationship?" The reason I ask is because I always see your names graffiti up and down Figueroa, Manchester, and Hoover so I figure they have to be a couple or something to guys always together doing everything together it just makes me wonder what else are they doing together. Every time we hem you up you are together and never with any home girls, so I assumed that one of you were the home girl. So, tell me which one of you is the bitch in the relationship and we will let you on your merry way."

Cartoon looked to Puppet to see if he was going to answer the question. Both stood in silence thinking to their selves that they were getting tired of the four pack harassing them which was a term their homies used to describe the four C.R.A.S.H officers that patrolled their neighborhood.

"Sure, taking you ladies a long time to answer the question. They must be lesbian fellas because either one wants to step up to claim their panties. We might have to check their gender then before we take them to the station." Rodriguez said pulling his leg back about to kick Puppet in between the legs.

Right before he could do so they received a call that four Black males in white t-shirts were approaching the alley way on 84th.

"Next time ladies, you will be going to *Los Hemelos* for an overnight stay." Rodriguez said getting in his squad car.

Escape from Failure

Using their training the two squad cars descended on the four Black youths with the precision of a scalpel, corralling them up against a chain link fence that set adjacent to the alley.

"A 40 Cal will catch you before you get to the corner boy, but please be my guest."

Cham "Jackie Chan" Lee said egging one of the suspects on. Lee had grown up in Long Beach in the neighborhood claimed by the Insane Crips and Asian Boy Crips and unlike his partners he was an active member of the Asian Boys for a year until his parents moved to Torrance. Reluctantly he went to Torrance High School ditching whenever possible to go back to his old neighbor to get high with his homies smoking purple Kush and drinking night train wine with blue berry Kool-Aide so that it made their mouths blue like their rags. Lee was ready to leave his home and go live on the streets with his homies until he was hit by the reality that they were going home at night to be with their families after hanging in the streets all day; his part time banging was just that, part time, the reality that he would actually have to fend for his self was not very alluring. Lee's parents had money and he realized that he did not have to live fist over fist, it sounded good in theory, especially when him and his homies would get high and drunk, but the actuality of living in the streets was not ideal to him. Although after leaving the gang Lee felt a slight depression, he missed the bond with his fellow members and the gun play too it had even crossed his mind to join the military, but the thought of being away in another country dodging missiles and I.E.Ds did not necessarily appeal to him, but joining the L.A.P.D did so at the age of 23 he joined the L.A.P.D and within 3 years he had been recommended to the C.R.A.S.H division by fellow officers who quickly picked up on his uncanny ability to solve crimes and know the mind of gang members. 4 years with the unit had proved to be all it he thought it would be, shit talking and busting heads.

"Wise decision boy, I thought I was going to get a chance to use these new hollow tips, damn maybe next." Lee said closing in on the right side of the suspects to create a protective perimeter while Officer Vasquez did the exact formation on the other side securing room for Rodriguez and Pikes to close in through the middle on the four Black males for a pat downs and warrant check.

"Any of you ladies hear anything about shots being fired by this alley?" Rodriguez asked while patting down his first suspect who had on a long white T-shirt that had been washed a few times, but still looked new because it was ironed with a crease residing in the middle, his baggy blue jeans with the picture of a tiger ready for attack on his right back pocket had a few rime stones missing as well from constant wear giving the appearance that he might be concealing a weapon, but he wasn't. All the search yielded was a couple of Newport cigarettes that he probably had purchased at the gas station up the street, an old California I.D that looked like it had been washed a few times with the jeans he had on, and five bus tokens. After searching his first suspect he placed his I.D. in a small pocket that rested on the front of his uniform while commanding the suspect to stand against the wall with his hands on his head before moving on to the next suspect. The second suspect yielded the same possession as the first minus the two cigarettes; he also had on a similar outfit the only difference being his jeans were a lighter blue overall it was clear that the two suspects hung together regularly, at least that is the assumptions Rodriguez had made while he gave the same command to the second suspect that he gave to the first while also placing his I.D. in his pocket. Taking a few steps back Rodriguez waited on Officer Pikes to finish up the pat down on the other two suspects knowing Pikes was going to give is usual thorough search.

Roger "Dike" Pikes was 35 years old white male who was raised in the Midwest the thought that came to most people's minds when they laid eyes on him was that he was a corn feed white boy from the south. Standing a little bit over six feet tall Pikes straight laced demeanor gave off the impression that he was taller than he was. His tact for details was unmatched by his partners, his suits were always extra starched to bring out the darkness of his uniform more, so his boots were always had a military shine. Pikes kept his hair noticeably short which gave the impression that he was bald headed, but his sharp line could be seen when up close. After serving six years in the marines Pikes moved to Los Angeles to join the L.A.P.D there was no reason, he just wanted to see some new scenery. Pikes had been a C.R.A.S.H officer

Escape from Failure

longer then all his partners and took pride in his work which he felt was getting the bad guys off the street.

"Okay sir, you are clear just stand over to your left near your friend so that I can search the last guy then you guys can go after we run your names for warrants and parole violations." Pikes was always respectful of suspects no matter what they were into he treated everyone equal and expected the same but knew that some people did not know better so they could not do better. On his fist suspect he found nothing but old loose tobacco with a mixture of cigar tobacco and weed stems in his right basketball short pocket his left pocket was empty, but the finding of the weed stems let Pikes know that the suspect was a weed smoker leading him to check his socks and shoe for any rolled up blunts; his hunch turned up one half smoked damp blunt sitting in the suspects sock the fourth and final suspect was clean plus he had on just a pair of basketball shorts with no shirt making the search go quicker the one before him. After running their names all the suspects came back clean with no records.

"Well ladies you all came back clean this time which means you can go, but know we now know your names so if we catch you around here claiming Hoover or hanging with them you are going to jail. Hoover has a gang injunction on them, so it is illegal for them to function together as well as do other gang related activities together." Rodriguez walked back over to the two suspects he had patted down and through their I.D.s on the cement for them to pick up.

"What ladies is there a problem." Rodriguez asked looking at the Blacks males aggressively.

"Yeah, there is a problem, why did you throw our I.D.s on the ground instead of giving them to us." One of the Black males asked.

"It was an accident you; should not be so sensitive about everything it could cause you problems in the future. Maybe you should ask your little friends about me because you must be new around here." Rodriguez said turning his back on the boys and returning to his car.

"Here you go sir." Pikes said to the last suspect he had searched before approaching the first suspect he had searched.

William V. Fields

"Unfortunately, I am going to have to write you a ticket as well as take you in to the station for possession of a controlled substance and withholding information from the police." The suspect was in shock as he complied with the officer's commands interlocking his fingers behind his back ready to be hand cuffed.

"You really going to take me to jail for a half smoked blunt, that's some bitch shit Pikes." The suspect was familiar with Pikes and felt he was a bitch and that is why those who encountered him referred to him as Dike on the streets because he went by the book to the point that it was stupid to them.

"Don't forget I asked you if you had anything on you and you told me no."

"Man, I just forgot it was in there wasn't anybody lying to you."

"Regardless, you are guilty so you are going to jail, keep yapping and I will charge you with disrespecting a peace officer." Pikes said lowering the suspect head into the car. Securing the scene, the officers sped off in the direction of the 77th division on Broadway leaving the three youth in the distance.

"Which one of you is going to call Brian's mom to let her know he is in jail?" One of the youths asked the other.

"I'll call her and let her know she won't be happy about this."

"Yeah, I know now he'll have a record, which will probably make him join 74."

"You think he will join Hoover now?"

"Most likely, especially now that he will have a record. He's been kicking it with them lately anyway."

"Hope fully he don't, fools be getting killed once they start banging anyway or killing somebody else and getting life."

"Let's get off this corner before we get shot; besides the only thing that is bothering me right now is constantly getting harassed by the police."

"Yeah I feel you on that it is really starting to play out, I wish there was something we could do to make them leave us alone."

"Me too, but what, we just niggas."

"I don't know, but something needs to change, I just wish they would try to help us instead of looking down on us and disrespecting us every time they run across us."

"Nigga they don't want to help you, their job is to lock you up, don't you know it is ordered by law that we get locked in the prisons that were built."

"I don't know about all that Steven, but I do know things need to change."

"Change them then."

"I would if I knew how to."

Chapter 3
Things Change

"Too long Mr. Franks, too long. From your response I gathered that you preferred a face to face visit versus a written correspondence and phone calls and I fully understand your preference for a more personal conversation; after a little over ten years of incarceration I would also be highly skeptical of virtually everything and everyone. We have waited a long time for this day to come, yet even now as I sit here with you it is unbelievable to me and I am an appeals lawyer. Regardless, to all my rambling the main thing of importance is that you will be getting out of prison soon preferably within the next few months. As you know through reading the newspaper or watching the news the officers that were being investigated kept their jobs and were suspended temporarily for re-training. There were also various sums paid to particular victims including yourself which is one of the other reasons I was in full agreement to come see you."

Askari listened intently to his appeals lawyer who he had known for about 8 years, but only talked to face to face two times. Even though he worked with Askari through the years he always felt that the lawyer did not give his all because he thought Askari was guilty. The only reason he had an appeals lawyer anyways was because his mother had paid for it and assigned all her assets after she had died to pay for his continual work on the case until the money ran out which only took five years then that's when it became harder and harder to catch up with his lawyer, yet he held no ill will towards the man people were entitled to have their beliefs about whomever they choose; what mattered the most was that he would be turning in his CDC number very soon not the fact that his lawyer could have gave a damn weather he was released or not, in fact the only reason he showed up in Askari's opinion is that he thought he would probably get some type of sympathy money from him, but as he talked on he found that his assumption were correct more so the only reason he had written him was because the LAPD had contacted him thinking he was still working on Askari's case.

Escape from Failure

"Enough small talk Mr. Franks, the LAPD not only contacted me about your release, but they have agreed to pay you 2.3 million to just walk away and not alert the media about what happened to you or this agreement."

"Walk away without a word." Askari muttered to himself.

"I did not quite catch that Mr. Franks." Askari's lawyer said slightly irritated.

"Because there was nothing for you to catch, I need to read over the document first before I can give you an adequate answer." Askari said bring the document closer.

"But of course, Mr. Franks, why wouldn't you, but I assure you everything is on the up and up I read over the details myself and I feel it to be a wise decision."

"Opinions vary depending on the acquirements of the individual in a particular situation."

"Yes, I see Mr. Franks." The lawyer said confused not knowing what he meant by his response, yet he felt slightly insulted, but could not understand why.

"Are you alright Mr. Franks? You seem a little solemn for a man who is about to be released after so many years furthermore you are going to be a millionaire.

"Perception is completely owned by the eyes of the watcher who choose to see what they want, thus capturing what they feel to be beauty or happiness in the lenses of their eyes as well as life experiences." Askari said looking up from the document to look into the lawyer's eyes.

"Yes of course, we often see what we want to see."

After reading over the document twice Askari felt it left little to question it was straight to the point. The money was a nice incentive he was expecting just to get a reduced sentence at the most his immediate freedom. Through the years his mental keenness was steadily growing greater which lead him to take the offer instead of trying to drag it out in court wasting any more of his life to the case that gave him a life sentence in prison. He signed the paper without a word sliding it over to his lawyer.

"That concludes are business Mr. Franks I will get this document over to the appropriate people tomorrow, here is your copy."

"I appreciate you taking the time to come down as well as your patience."

With that Askari walked to the door of the visiting room to await a correctional officer to come escort him back to his cell. This would be his last escort on the level four yard or better yet any prison yard and it felt unreal because it was a new experience for him so he did not have a definition for the feeling whatsoever he just knew it gave him a feeling he could not quite identify. Regardless of his new circumstances Askari still maintain the mentality that he was in prison it was no time to get loses it was not over until he walked out the gates of Delano II.

Tiny 3Stone and Young Football could be heard doing burpees in their cell which set right next to Askari's cell. Walking down the tier Askari gave them a fist in the air as he passed by to his cell. Before he could get situated, they were both in the vent asking him who came to visit him on a Monday when visits were not run until the weekends.

"They are kicking down doors already Askari, they can't wait for a nigga…. I mean a brother. My bad Askari you know I am working hard on the N word." 3Stone said speaking through the vent.

"Actually, it was my lawyer who came to see me not a woman."

"What he is talking about?"

"My release young brother…it will be soon."

"That is groovy, we need men like you on the streets; make sure you tell them lil Nig… I mean brothers that this gang banging is garbage. I can't even get a homie to put minutes on my phone or send me a fifty-dollar package it is ridiculous groove."

"Definitely 3Stone, I will enlighten them to what lies in store for them when they are loyal to a gang."

"That's real because this lifestyle is super boo- boo, between me and Football we have over a hundred years and I can't help, but think that this is it for us, I

Escape from Failure

mean this is how my life is going to end, I am only twenty-two years old Askari and it is over for your boy."

"Honestly, Brother I must disagree with you on it being over, because life is what you make it no matter what situation you may find yourself in. Find a way to be free mentally and the rest will follow. In correlation to that I will leave you a few of my books and personal writings so that they may help you not only find yourself, but to also find solace in your current situation."

"That would be appreciated groove; I need something to get my mind right because the working out for hours at a time is only taking a little bit of the edge off."

"The physical can sedate the mind for only so long for physical exercise is for the physical you, thus mental exercise is more congruent for what you need to quail your mental anguish."

"Life is going to be different around here after you leave Askari, you the only Black who tried to teach me and Ball something."

"Replacement is always in motion, so when I leave their will be a replacement just make sure you are keen, aware, and focused so that you can align yourself as you did with me."

"*Fo sho*, I stay focused so that will not be a problem. Well Askari I will catch you later I have to make a call."

***

Benito "Shy Rock" Hernandez was a 32 years old Mexican American who grew up in South Central L.A. and belonged to the 18st gang since the age of nine. His father was the lead singer in a mariachi band and his mother worked a food truck that rested in the alley which sold a variety of items. His parents named him after Mexico's president Benito Juarez who championed the poor in 1861 and refused to rule under a monarchy. Much like his name sake he also rebelled against any authority he felt went against his true nature or fellow Mexican, so he had taken great pride in the mission *La Eme* had bestowed upon him to restructure his fellow *Surenoes* on the street. With Antonio Villaraigosa remaining mayor of Los Angeles and Sonia Sotomayor attaining a seat on the supreme court becoming the first Hispanic to do so and only the third woman out of 111 justices before her it was only obvious to the Hispanic people that they were indeed moving forward to seeing the first Hispanic President in the near future; what was once talk was now slowly becoming a reality and with this new reality *La Eme* knew it was time to switch gears to a more tangible goal in the form of politics, instead of sending their homies to the prisons it was now time to send them to college so that they could be in better position to sit in a seat of power when the gears turned permanently in the favor of the Mexican people an impossible task if they remained strictly to street level crimes. Being a *Carnal* gave Shy Rock the power he needed as well as the backing to accomplish not only his goal, but *La Emes*.

Shy Rock took a deep breath as he lay across the bottom bunk on his stomach with his state blue shirt tightly rolled up underneath his chin. He was waiting for count to clear so that his celly Grumps could finish his collage of Maria Felix clutching a rifle against her chest with a seductive grin on her lips similar to the one he had kept the last few days as he neared the end of his twelve-year sentence in Pelican Bay State Prison.

Chapter 4

A Ladies Touch

"I had a *bool* time last night, it was *bool* how you put that little function together for my B-Day, I wasn't expecting nothing like that, I thought you was going to come through with a few sacks and some Patron, but you caught a bitch off guard with the surprise party like I be seeing on movies and shit". Toy Box said caressing Tiffany's hair as she lay between her legs up against her breast.

"You know I always like to show out for your babe; besides, you only turn 25 once in your life, mightiest well party up on all your milestone years".

"That's real talk the way niggas be getting killed out here nowadays it is best to live each one as if it was the last, because a bitch never knows when it will be her time to be taken out or to be the taker that's why I stay with the 45 glock for a bitch or Crip nigga".

"Toy Box have you ever had to kill anybody before, I hear you talk about it, but I always wondered if you have ever actually killed someone just because"?

"Bitch is you wired, or something don't be asking me any shit like that, what's wrong with you, Tiffany you need to seriously stay in your place and mind your own business. Asking questions like that will get you killed".

"I've asked you not to talk to me like that numerous times Toy Box, why do you continue to do it especially after we had such a good night."

"Look when you act stupid, I act stupid, it is just that simple, you don't want me talking to you like this stop doing and saying things that get me wound up". With that Toy Box reached for her red dickie khakis; once they were on she stood up off the bed and tighten her red initial belt that spelled out I.F.G. Sitting back on the bed Toy Box laced up her red chuck Taylors with the skinny red lace which she preferred over the thick red laces that gave the shoes a puffy look.

William V. Fields

Much like she preferred her laces skinny she also liked her clothing to fit nice and tight to show off her curvaceous thick frame that had never been caressed physically by a man for Taniesha "Toy Box" Green always knew that she was into women since the 8th grade when she use to ride her bike up to Darby park in Inglewood to hang with her homies from Inglewood Family Blood. Her click was 92nd street and she represented the gang as well as her lesbian lifestyle to the fullest. Too often she would get the typical harassment and assumptions to why she preferred women over men, but as she got older, she heard less and less of the stupid questions regarding her choice of lifestyle.

At 25 years old she had heard all the questions that could be asked of one in the life such as did she get molested as a child by a woman or man by counselors at her schools or was she possessed by a demon by religious people or was she going through some type of phase by her family members. There were always questions from some curious motherfucker who figured they had her all figured out, but known of their assumptions were correct at the end of the day for that is all they were, assumption from individuals who were so caught up with her being lesbian that they seldom asked why she gang banged, which wasn't surprising because must didn't even believe she gang banged because she was the typical pretty lighted skinned thick chick with long ink black hair from out of Inglewood. The only thing that through the stereotype off was she did not have green eyes and instead of being dung out by local and surrounding gang members she did the digging with her strap on which she duded Luther.

"So, what do you have planned for the day Toy Box"? Tiffany asked rubbing her hands alongside the straps of her black tang top while sitting behind her on the bed"?

"Shit you know, get this money the best way I know how to blood ain't nobody going to feed a bitch out here especially with this recession going on it's like a modern day jungle out here in these streets and a bitch got to fend for herself amongst these hungry as niggas and bitches in the streets". So, I will catch up with you later this week after I get my issue out here in these streets". Toy Box said reaching for her car keys.

"Be careful, Toy."

Escape from Failure

"Don't worry about that that's why I keep the four-fever close by. "With that Toy Box tucked her Glock 45 into her waist band and headed out the apartment buildings towards the underground parking to get in her 98 green Tahoe truck. All that was playing through her mind was the bank robbery her and her homies had been plotting on for the two weeks they were supposed to hit the bank at the end of the week and she couldn't wait times had been tough for her the last few months since her mom had passed and she had to move in with her sister and her two kids. The little bit of money she did have put up went towards her mother's funeral, so she was unable to keep up the payments on her mother's apartment alone. Living with her sister was cool, because she was not all in her business if she kept her high when she got high. Being it was a two bed room apartment she had to sleep on the couch which had been in the family since her mother was a teenager; the cushions were so thin that the springs could be felt and heard every time she sat or slept on the couch causing her to make a pallet on the floor most nights to sleep on to avoid getting impaled by one of the springs sharp edges on various parts of her body. The first thing told herself she was going to buy was a new couch for her sister with her cut of the money, even though she planned on moving out she wanted to get the couch just in case times got hard again which they often did at least she would have a decent place to lay her head without worrying about losing an eye or getting stabbed in the thigh by some punk ass spring in a couch. Besides, she had been stabbed already in the arm a few years back by some bitch from Legend Crip while she was fighting a murder case with two of her homeboys. The slash across her upper arm was a constant reminder that anybody could get caught slipping if they were not on their toes or became too arrogant.

A few days had gone by and Toy Box was sitting down in the kitchen getting her hair put into a wrap by her sister, tomorrow would be the make or break day and she needed to look the part to catch the tellers off guard.

"So, what you getting all hooked up for?" Toya asked her younger sister.

"Just switching it up that's all, sometimes you just got to switch it up on these niggas out here in the streets."

"It is a trip seeing you with your hair pressed out like a girl I am so use to seeing you with it in pig tails or a pony tail that I forgot how pretty you can be. You were always the prettiest one of us both, but you never seemed to care about your looks. Anyways I know if you every have any kids they will be beautiful."

"Kids, you know I will never have kids; besides, I have my niece and nephew if I ever feel like taking care of some kids."

"There's no feeling like having your own kids Taniesha."

Toy Box shuttered at the sound of her government name coming off of her sisters lips she hated her name and she knew her sister knew, but just as much as she had her government name her sister hated her gang name. She just knew it was time to leave especially with all the having children talk. Personally, she thought bitches were stupid for getting pregnant by niggas that did not take care of not only them, but their kids. Half the niggas she knew just had kids for no reason at all and most only did it to tie a bitch down anyway. What was funny to her was that her sister was telling her to have kids when her punk ass baby daddy did not even take care of her niece and nephew. If and when he was every out of jail he would only come by to have sex with her sister and beg for money and once he got his beat up as cutlass fixed which he had been driving for 10 years he would be right back in his set trying to tell some other young nigga how he should be living his life. That is one of the reasons she could not stand niggas, because they were just sorry when it came down to protecting their families. They would tell a bitch whatever she wanted to here to get what they wanted that is why it was always sickening to her to hear them boast about turning her out and making her love dick. Niggas focused too much on their dicks and Toy Box knew this was their constant down fall that's why it was so easy to jack niggas because they always thought that they were all that all the time when really they weren't shit, but little boys that would do anything for some pussy.

The sun was casting a golden light around the Los Angeles Forum as Toy Box made her way up Manchester to meet her homies; she was rapping Lil Kim's versus on the Quiet Storm as she neared Iceman's apartment building where they held the majority of their meetings. Pulling up behind a couple of cars she noticed a few that belonged to her homies and one she had never seen before. Walking to the front gate of the apartments she noticed Iceman finishing off a blunt.

"What up blood, I almost didn't recognize you for a minute I thought you were one of the little *breezies* that stayed up in here."

"That's *bool* then that means I will through everyone else off too tomorrow."

"Yes, yes that's the point to through them off their game and then hit them before they realize what's going on."

"How long have ya'll been here?"

"About an hour, but it is time to go ahead and get it *bracking*."

With that said Toy Box and Iceman walked upstairs to his apartment where two more of her homies were sitting on the couch while an individual she had not seen before sat at the countertop smoking a cigarette.

"What's up Toy Box blood?" G-slim and Red flag said simultaneously.

"Just *bicking it,* that's all." Toy Box said making her way to the smaller of the two couches in the apartment.

"A Toy Box that's the homie Uzi right there from 74 Hoover, he the one that put us up on the bank."

"What's up with you?" Toy Box said in a reluctant voice.

"Nothing much, just chilling waiting to make it go down." Uzi said scanning Toy Box face. He had heard about her reputation in the streets before and how fine she was, but seeing was believing because different individuals considered certain aspects as beautiful, but the hype was true she was definitely bad too bad she was on pussy was all he kept telling his self it just meant he would have to try a little harder to bust her down in the bedroom that's all.

After the formal introduction was complete, they all set around a card table that was positioned in the middle of the apartment with hand drawn drawings of the inside of the bank on top of it. It did not take long for Uzi to start laying the plan down to them and telling each one their position in the bank robbery. The entire meeting took about an hour with little question asked by anyone at the table because most of them had hit numerous banks before, so it was nothing new.

William V. Fields

"So, we will meet here in the morning about 5am to get on the 10-east freeway to Redlands to hit the new Chase bank they just opened up out there." Uzi said rolling up the drawings he had brought. Uzi didn't like that they had to drive an hour out of L.A. to go hit a bank, but he knew mostly all the banks out towards his way were all burnt out or had super security devices which prevented bank robbers from getting in without a struggle. Nevertheless, he was going to get the money one way or another the recession was making it hard on the day to day hustler to get by everybody wanted a deal of some kind or a hook up so it was better to just go back to full time robbing which was more of a risk, but yielded greater rewards. The morning air was crisp, and the streets were quite as Toy Box inhaled the last thoughts of anxiety about what she was about to do in a few more hours. It had been a long time since she had been up so early in the morning to do anything in fact the last time, she could remember she was up this early was when she was in elementary school. Oh how the times slips away she thought to herself it wouldn't be long before she was pushing thirty years old and would be considered old by all the new little young twenty-year-old bitches coming up that's why it was imperative that she hit this lick is what she kept rehearsing to herself every time the thought of getting caught crossed her mind. Fuck it though she thought before coming to the rest of her thought, because she knew her fuck it though phrase was just another way to block out her common sense to do what was right in life. Whenever a situations was getting out of hand and she felt herself losing control she would be like fuck it though in her head and do the exact opposite of what she knew to be right in her heart, just to gain a small morsel of control of her life back, it was sad, but at times it was all she had in the world the only phrase that kept her sane when all else was chaotic around her. Thus was her life at this moment standing in the cold with a pistol tucked in her waistband and a fuck it though imprinted in her mind as she came out her temporary solace amongst the others who lay asleep in the numerous surrounding apartments around her for her sleep was a continuous one that kept her dreaming for a better life that would pull her away from a mentality that was dragging her down day by day. Her destiny came in the form of a gray Astro van whose white muffler smoke seemed more pronounced in the cold air, the smallest things were always evident to her right before doing something extremely violent she was still trying to figure out why, but wasn't giving it much thought as she let herself into the van.

Inside the van everybody had their game face on and their weapons close G-Slim and Red Flag both had Smith and Wesson M&P15A's with extended clips, Ice Man had a Kel-Tec sub rifle 2000 that looked like it came out of an old war movie, Uzi had a Kmini-14 with an extended clip that looked like it never ended, and Toy Box had her 40 Glock with a 35 round clip. The whole scene looked like an old A Team episode, but it was far more deadly there were no actors in this van just killer who would kill anything and any one for a come up. They were unaware of people having to go home to their families it was a concept that they were completely oblivious to, they only knew come up at any cost and whoever was in the way was meant to be killed or wounded depending on the severity of the situation. By the time they arrived in Red Lands traffic was starting to get going and kids were on their way to school unknowing of the terror that encamped within their community. After all it was a nice little town that rarely experienced violence expects probably at the local movie theater when a rated R movie was playing. Toy Box had been out to see the bank only once and it was late in the afternoon she really did not realize until now that it sat directly on a main street. Pulling up into the parking lot she could see out the back window that there were only a few people in the bank so far. The way the bank was set up there were multiple booths on the right hand side so it was G-slim and Red Flag job to secure the right hand side while Uzi got the volt which also lay against the right hand side of the bank. Ice man's job was to secure the middle while Toy Box hit all the registers. Toy Box was the first one to go inside so that she could feign filling out a deposit slip only to pretend to leave something in the car so that she could let the others know how many people were in the bank.

"So, what does it look like in their?" Uzi asked with a look of eagerness. "It's about fifth teen people in there, five within the booths to the right, six tellers, and three customers being helped."

With nothing more said they were all out the van Toy Box leading the pack. G-Slim and Red Flag quickly took their positions splitting off amongst the booths that lined the right side of the wall before the few workers that were working realized what was taking place they were gripped with fear and cold gun

William V. Fields

smoke reeking barrels to their faces, their instinct leads them to the ground before the gun totters could mutter the words. As Becky a new cashier came up from her register counting money she was met by a black blurry object which she would later figure out was a gun across the bridge of her nose blood came spewing out immediately as she tried to gain some type of mobility before hitting the floor, but it was too late Toy Box was making her rounds of what seemed to be 20 registers.

"Come on Bitch open them all!" Toy Box demanded as she held Becky by her collar from register to register. While Toy Box was working on her last few registers Ice man was manning the floor, but he had one concern about the back rooms that sat right behind the registers. It had been less than 40 seconds and they had taken the entire bank over with no resistance. They all came to attention once Uzi came out the volt with a Santa clause bag full of money and for the first time Ice man had seen him smile. That was the queue to leave and they all made their way out the bank as calmly as they had walked in. No matter how seasoned they were none of them could hold back the excitement to what they had all done to them it was the equivalent of completing a four-year degree and walking the stage, but instead of crossing the stage of USC or UCLA they were crossing the stage of every nigga that had a ghetto dream of coming up the easy way and their diploma as well as hard work was in the sack of money they had just taken. The van was already running when they came out side and started to pile in, they were just pulling out the drive way when a cruiser came pulling in they knew what had to be done, but who was going to do it was the only question robbing was one thing, but killing or even trying to kill a cop was an entirely different ball game. While they were pulling out the cop car was pulling in Uzi could see that the cop was in the car by his self, so he knew he had time to get him before he radioed in the vehicle. The driver of the van knew the protocol after all it was Baby Uzi so when Uzi gave the hand gesture to stop he did and Uzi bust out the back of the door Mini-14 blazing with deadly accuracy shattering the back side window causing the officer to run into a nearby tree at that point the officer was unconscious and Uzi seeing no movement returned to the van which quickly sped off towards the freeway. The entire time they were driving to the freeway a white Mazda was following behind them; about thirty minutes away from the scene they exited the freeway somewhere in Fresno were the white Mazda took them all except for baby Uzi to another location. While they were headed to the other location Baby Uzi was followed by a Beige Honda Accord to a location somewhere off the 60 freeway where he burned the van in the mountains before meeting back up with the others.

Once they counted three hundred and fifty thousand just out the vault bag they were all sitting around listening to personal rap songs that often came to their minds when they dreamed about a lick like this G-Slim had C.R.E.A.M from Wu-Tang playing in his head, Red Flag had various Relative songs playing through his mind, while Ice man had Jay-Z's Dead presidents flowing through his head, and Toy Box mind was being taken over by Gucci Manes Get money. The only one that didn't have any music on his mind was Uzi, the only thing that was going through his mind was should he take all the money, but that meant he would have to shoot it out with them all, even though it was a cool come up three hundred and fifty thousand to the head would be better than having to split it six ways. He still was debating on rather he wanted to split it when his attention was caught by the news report on the T.V.

"In the early morning hours four gunman and a woman robbed the Chase bank in Red Lands, not only was the robbery extremely violent, but one of the suspects opened fire on a police officer as he arrived on the scene with a high power assault rifle nearly killing the officer who is now in the hospital recovering from minor injuries. Officer Clive's has more." "Yes these bank robbers are extremely dangerous and will be pursued to the fullest extent of the law anyone with information is asked to call the number at the bottom of the screen, lastly there will be a reward for the apprehension of these individuals."

"You hear this shit, they always talking about what they going to do when they have no clue to who did the shit." Uzi said repositioning his mini-14 on his lap which was aimed at the door. Nobody in the room replied to Uzi's comment they were silent waiting on the next move that would put an end to the day's robbery. Toy Box main concern now was when they were going to get back to Inglewood. She didn't really care that much for Uzi and it wasn't because he was from the other side, but because he seemed to be too extra out, he put a lot on it for no reason she thought, but even that wasn't the reason it was just something about him that did not sit well with her and she didn't want to be around him too much longer if it wasn't necessary. In life she had learned that some people use or have a phrase they rely on occasionally for various reason, these people were many including herself, but for the many there were few who not only knew a phrase, but lived by it, Uzi fit the few she had run across and it was clear that he embodied the fuck it mentality with a strange sense of loyalty the type of loyalty that got others killed.

Chapter 5
Ones We Live With

He was composed naturally without much thought, years confined can do that to a man. His thoughts were a drift much like the mild Smokey wind that lay across his face causing his eyes to slightly water as he stood a few feet from the entrance of the prison that was his captor for far too long. Yes, Askari was physically free yet he stayed perfectly still as his cab driver waited for him a few feet away on the dirt road in which he could feel every grain of dirt twisting beneath the bottom of his shoe. Still he refused to take a step until he gathered his thoughts, each move he made from this point on had to count as well as mean something, so he waited until the thought he was waiting on appeared. Time was of no importance to him at this stage in his life, but the decisions he made were, for he had to live with them and so it was he knew what he had to do as he set afoot to the cab on his way to L.A. His hand lay securely atop his pile of composition books that were tightly wrapped in a plastic bag inmate typically used for *pruno* while he peered at the passing trees through the back seat window that was slightly rolled down causing a crisp cutting sound to take over the majority of the ride as the driver did 75 miles per hour all the way to the Grey Hound station where he was to meet his long time comrade. Askari stood still as his pupils scanned the station it had been quite a while since he had been around so many people at one time and smelt so many combinations of smells intermingled together, they were pungent yet sweet to nostrils that had smelled nothing, but depression, negativity, and death for the last decade; these were the smells of life and he relished in them. Before a nearby seat could be reached in the corner, he saw his comrade coming through the front entrance and from his quick movement in his direction he realized he must have seen him too.

"It's been a long-time brother." K-Stone said standing in front of his comrade Askari shaking his head. He was still dealing with the fact that his friend was standing in front of him, a friend he had been communicating with strictly by letters and monitored phone conversations.

William V. Fields

"Yes, brother it has, and I see you have been staying solid, the photos you have been sending me through the years have done you no justice."

Without further delay the two comrades embraced each other, their love for each other was that of brothers. After all it was Askari who had taught K-Stone all he knew and set him afoot to a better life in which he felt permanently indebted.

"Glad you are out comrade we need strong brothers like you out here to set positive examples."

"Indeed, I intend to invoke change how ever possible, but we can talk about that over nourishment."

"I take that to mean you are hungry brother?"

"Yes, quite the observant one I can see."

"Well I figure you would want some worldly food after being away from it so long, so I have a place in mind over in West L.A. that I know you will feel."

Over the years Askari had read about the quality of German vehicles and the effects fresh leather could have not only on ones nostrils, but skin as well; like most things he figured the descriptions were gross exaggeration of companies trying to make a buck off of consumers, but not even he could deny the comfortable interior and solid handling of his comrades BMW. ASkari knew there was a difference between being materialistic and appreciating quality even though the two were often confused by most especially those that occupied the ghetto he uses to play in as a child. Too often parents would buy expensive outfits and shoes instead of taking the money and putting it towards a family outing , thus is the reality still where the parent know their children's favorite name brand, video game and rap song, but are completely unaware of their educational strengths and weaknesses until it is too late which forces an outsider like a teacher to have to step in an act as a surrogate parent to a child that has probably never had a stable adult in their life just a bunch of surrogates filling in for someone else who wasn't doing what they were supposed to be doing. Loss of focus was routine in a material world so much so that it made Askari feel slightly guilty about enjoying the simple luxury of riding in a vehicle that society deemed for the elite; it hadn't been

Escape from Failure

24 hours and he had already sold out to the powers that be his conscious was telling him, but he knew that not to be the case for he realized that he was breaking his on rule of not enjoying the moment.

"Feels weird at first, but you will adjust to it soon. Stone said noticing Askari staring out the window with a glazed look. It took me about two months before I was slightly adjusted and even then, I was super paranoid for a few years. Honestly, you will never fully adjust, you just learn to function amongst others and stay out the way of possible bad situations. Knowing the type of individual, you are you want have a problem avoiding foolish people and situations.

"Scars are inescapable in warfare, this is something that I have come to live with K-Stone my first few years in prison I truly believed that I would leave unscathed by it all, but life and experience has taught me well, there is always a price to pay for change desired and acted upon."

"I like that; you can elaborate on it more in the Sushi bar." With that Askari and K-Stone proceed to the Inside of the Sushi bar leaving the car with the valet.

"Feels strange sitting in a chair, even, I had grown so accustomed to sitting on those metal stools every day that I completely forgot what it felt like to relax my back against a chair." Askari said while taking in the entire vibe of the restaurant which was nothing like he had expected a sushi restaurant to smell like. There was not a scent of fish in the air although the station where the chiefs were preparing the rolls was adjacent to their table. "So, what do you typically order K-Stone?"

"Tempura, California rolls, and sometimes the eel depending on what I have a taste for, but for you I recommend the Tempura and the salmon rolls just to get you use to the basics of the sushi experience."

"Seems like your frequent sushi bars frequently, so I will go with your suggestions it is always good to listen to those more experienced in an area then one's self."

"I agree brother, if only more individuals were so wise typically people want to go against the grain as if doing so makes them a man or woman when in actuality it creates confusion which leads to division amongst movements that could have otherwise coincided together to complete a goal."

"Yes, yes I agree completely with you K-Stone it is this rebellious spirit that prevents our people from moving forward, more so it is the main reason we find ourselves stagnant on issues we should have solved years ago. It is really sad that we are dealing with police brutality, poor education, and broken homes in our communities that steadily keep rising."

"What is terribly sad is that we just do not get it, if we continue to define ourselves as niggas and bitches the rest of society, we never respect us a people it is just that simple. I get tired of our people steadily looking for the solution for our problems from someone else, this theory that someone else will come and save us is the main way of thinking that is holding us back it is time that we start to check our own and make personnel comments to better ourselves and those around us, but it has to start with family first. One of the most sickening thing that I saw during the Obama election was the amount of support our people put behind him financially peoples grandmothers, grandfathers, aunts, and uncles sent checks, went into their saving, organized fundraisers, and took up offering at the church to get this man in office, but these same people never spent a dime to promote the education or ideas of their own children, grandchildren, nieces, nephews, and local Obama's in their community who were beating the streets daily to make a change."

"That's deep, but so true people rarely value the talent right in front of them and sadly our people lead the race in placing doubt in our own while building up another Jesse; Jackson was the paradigm for that in 2009 during the election. The hatred we harbor for one another is so deep it really is not surprising that we covertly and overtly hate on one another while promoting others to get on the hatred as well then act astonished when police, law makers, and other minorities prey on us, kill us, and treat us like less than human beings. Until we stop sending out the mixed messages to society about our people the cycle will continue and every few months there will be a crying mother on T.V. or in the newspaper telling their story of sorrow of how their kin was assaulted or killed by another."

"So, you actually feel that a change can be made if we as a people start to police ourselves? It sounds good on paper, but in reality few want to change because they feel there is nothing wrong with their behavior or those of their peers; I know this personally from my work in the community the three years I have been out. I hit the streets with a passion to make a change then reality set in that everybody doesn't want to change for the reasons I said before and for the few that are receptive my work was diluted by the ever corrupt values of the community that kept tearing down the values that I had instilled within the children the few hours a week I had spent with them."

"It sounds like you hit a stumbling block with your work in the community; did you ask yourself how you could overcome the block that was preventing you from progressing?"

"Of course, and I am always open to suggestions as you know."

"Yes, I know and I have more than a suggestion, but a plan that I have been working on for the last five years. It is a little extreme, but I feel it is necessary for change we have been speaking about tonight."

"Extreme how, did you create a new form of intervention that's going to curb the one that the non-profits are using currently?"

"Not necessarily, what I plan to do will not involve your comrade at least not on the front line. I like the life that you have acquired for yourself out here and to be honest brother you are more needed then you know, but what I speak of has been spoken about in the back of alleys and in the depths of penitentiary yards for last forty years by all type of street organizations. I am going to go to war with the police department as well as the court system."

"I have to ask what you plan to accomplish by doing that, besides death, destruction, and chaos."

"All this is true, but there will be a method to the madness. For years we society has been preaching stop gangs and violence, yet violence is the only thing that stirs a response from the media and those in a position to pass legislation. When I take the ills of these youth which has become a cancer in our community and unleash it in their communities there will be immediate change. I am not talking about doing a kamikaze, but training up the best soldiers from each set throughout Los Angeles, Compton, and Watts. I will stir up the nest while you collect the honey so to speak, this will be violence for a purpose we will only attack those that have attacked our communities and people."

K-Stone had heard talk like this before from intoxicated home boys who had been harassed by the police in one way or another, but it never really moved anything in him because he knew they were just talking out the *side of their neck* and were basically speaking out of anger and frustration. Askari was speaking out of neither; the fact that he had spoken on it let K-Stone know that it was going to happen Askari was the type that didn't waste his time entertaining thoughts that he wasn't going to act on. Things were going to change drastically in Los Angeles soon and he only hoped it would be for the better.

"You want be seeing me for a while comrade I plan to leave for South Africa within the month to go explore another part of the world and gather some perspective on the new business venture I have been working on. There has been an increase in exports in South Africa lately making it a good time to get items in bulk for substantial lower price."

"What type of business are you thinking about putting together?"

", I had mentioned the idea to you when we were called up together, but it probably slipped your mind, I am going to start a cleaning service that employees strictly gang members and felons. By going to Africa, I will secure a vendor for the products and clothing I need to get started."

"Sounds like a solid plan Askari, I can't wait to see how it unfolds."

"Me too, this life we live is definitely what we make it out to be. Are decision being ones we must live with rather they are wise or just wise in our own eyes."

Chapter 6

Boys in Blue

"Omar Jackson is wanted for three gang related murders in the Athens area. He is believed to be armed and extremely dangerous so we will be on extreme alert when we raid the house tomorrow morning supposedly it is his grandmother's home so there might be small children inside as well as other bystanders. Unfortunately, we have seen situations like this before, so we need to get in fast and safe without causing too much damage. We will deploy from the station around 3 a.m. giving us enough time to surround the house before the locals begin to wake up. Gentlemen let us make this a clean safe hit we don't need any more bad press right now." With that said sergeant Waters shuffled his paper work together before stepping down from the podium headed towards his office annoyed that he had to raid a murder suspects grandmothers house, he had no respect for these gangsters that used their families as shields for their criminal behavior especially when weapons and children were involved.

"This asshole finally put the nail in his own coffin after all these years Rodriguez thought to him." He had known Omar or better yet O-Dogg as he was called by the 76 East Coast Crips for years all the way through high school when he use to pocket check him on his way home from school nearly every morning and that was before he even started claiming a gang once he actually joined 76 street he always threaten to kill Rodriguez because he secretly convinced himself that he was from their rival F13, but that never happened because he went away to camp for strong armed robbery and life went on. Despite the years being far in between since their childhood the disrespect of having his pocket entered by another person on the daily along with death threats that he took seriously pissed him off he wanted to put a bullet in Omar's head if he got the chance to slapping the cuffs on him meant nothing. He could just feel his muddy boot up against his face tomorrow morning smashing it into the mud in his front yard. Tomorrow could not come soon enough for him.

William V. Fields

"Rodriguez, you ready to head out to breakfast?" Vasquez asked with Lee and Pikes standing nearby.

Yes, is not that the ritual before we go do a raid, I wouldn't want to break a ritual."

Roscoe's Chicken and waffles was always packed on Manchester and Main and today was no different even cops had to wait sometimes, but rarely and if so, only for a few minutes.

"About how long is the wait?" Pikes asked the younger Black woman who usually did the sitting.

"About fifth teen minutes how many people are in your party?"

"Four." With that Pikes returned to his three partners in the small shopping center where Roscoe's sat adjacent to the corner which some considered a blind spot in which one could get shot. The 87 gangsters knew about this blind spot well for the 83 Hoovers had used it numerous times to come shoot at them, especially on August seventh. Manchester and main was consider to be the eastside especially once you crossed main street where you found yourself surround by the majority of the eastside Crip and Blood gangs as well as Hispanic gangs the area was drenched in gang violence, poverty, and hopelessness, but still people called it home making a living no matter what, with a few actually making it out along the way. Jewels like Roscoe's and other eateries could be found throughout the city yet those that stayed near them were mostly the recipients of their pleasures while outsiders who lived only blocks away had to phone in orders or have their women to pick up an order because it was in the wrong set yet individuals from around the world not even from the area came enjoyed the sites and eateries without a problem. Thus, was the way of the ghetto treat others better than you treat your own; nothing as nice as a Black gangster giving a white stranger directions or information.

Stuffing waffles in their mouths the officers knew they had a drawn-out day before the raid which was how it always was. The anticipation of it all was something that could never get use to after all it wasn't promised one would come out alive it was rare officers lost their lives in line of duty, but it happened enough for one to be cautious.

Escape from Failure

"That was great they didn't have this type of food where I came from." Pikes said wiping the fried chicken crumbs off the side of his lips."

"They didn't have a lot of things where you came from like Mexicans and gangs so now you are getting to experience a whole new world good and bad." Rodriguez said reaching for his wallet.

"Why is everything race and gangs with you Rodriguez?"

"Because everything is race and gangs haven't you figured that out yet, are you still thinking your back home on the farm tending various animals? Since you can't relate to gangs and race let me put it to you in farm language we cops are the pigs here to clean up everybody's shit the Blacks and the Mexicans are the sheep all the same yet you have different breeds nonetheless they are easily lead easily divided then you have the chickens and ducks that make up the other various groups around here along the other animals that make up the farm life."

"So, you're saying that I am a duck or chicken Rodriguez?" Lee asked jokingly.

"Why yes you do have a similarity to a duck now that you say so." Rodriguez said laughing.

"Rodriguez, I seriously think your childhood warped your perception of the world as well as people and hopefully one day you will see things differently." Pikes said standing up from the table."

"That was a great quote Dr. King. You are so in touch with your inner self, live out here a few more years and then see what you have to say. Let us all give Pike a round of applause.

"Lay off of him you know he has a different way of doing things then us." Vasquez said as they all got up simultaneously to head to the door.

Vasquez had lived in the city of Inglewood seven years with his wife Lupe and their two 5year old twin daughters Maria and Anna. Inglewood was a predominantly Black community for several years; Vasquez marked a generation of Mexican Americans who were moving into the affluent community which also harbor some of most notorious gangs in its outskirts. Inglewood was known to most that were familiar with the area as a Blood city or *bity* depending on who you were asking it laid claim to the Inglewood Family Bloods, Neighborhood Piru, Avenue Piru, Centinela Park Bloods, and Crenshaw mafias. Although it was known as a Blood city there were a few Crip sets which included the Legend Crips, Imperial Village Crips, Tonga Crips, and the 102 Raymond's. Also, amongst the Crips and Bloods you had the Inglewood 13. Outside of the Crip and Blood beef the two sets rarely had friction with the I13 outside of fist fights after school at the local high schools Inglewood and Morningside. Overall it was a solid community when compared to the others that surrounded its borders the main reason being it was mostly middle class families that lived in the area with a plethora of Black owned business quite as kept it is probably one of the few Black communities still in existence it was definitely one of the draws that brought Vasquez to the community it was still one of the few were kids could play outside without worrying about being shot down. Often, he would not see his daughters for weeks at a time because of his busy schedule so on these rare occasions he would pick them up from school early and take them out for ice cream at the local 31 flavors. While there he would listen to all their stories that had been built up in his absence; these times were his most precious because his mother and father rarely got the chance nor could afford to do such things that were normal to him. Between him and his wife they made about one twenty a year, yet they lived very modestly helping both sides of their families. As he set, they are with his two beautiful daughters he could not help but think in between laughs that he wanted to be able to do this all his life.

Rodriguez also stayed in Inglewood in a gated community called Carlton Square which was right off of Manchester next to the old sports arena which the city rarely used anymore as a teenager he and his family went a few times when the Circus would come into town. Rodriguez liked staying in the gated community mostly for the privacy everybody mostly kept to themselves which was the way of the community in some regards. He could bring his women in as he pleased without anybody seeing them as they came and left because he stayed in a cul-de-sac on the property. Usually on his days off he would hit the gym or just sleep for hours to prepare for another grueling schedule. Normally he would work all the over time he could to help pay for his mortgage it was not cheap staying in Inglewood especially a gated community, but he did alright for himself. He still was pumped about giving it to Omar so he decided to call up this chick he had met at some club in downtown a few weeks ago to see if she wanted to come have a private secession after a second thought though it would make more sense to just chill and play some games on his PS3 he wouldn't want to be too wore down having to be down at the station at three in the morning.

Lee loved when he got some time off and could go down to the local pool halls in his city to shoot. Especially before a raid because he felt like it helped with his aim when shooting an assault rifle. There were not too many people out of his division that lived in Gardena probably because it was so many different groups of people living throughout Gardena which was home to a few Crips gangs those being the Shotgun Crips and the Paybacc. The City wasn't as populated with major gangs as most cities the two major Hispanic gangs were the G13 and the C13 which beefed heavily with the Paybaccs for years when their beef started it was rare for Blacks and Hispanics gangs to beef so there was no real alarm about it reason being it was seen as an anomaly. Although Gardena was not that big of a city it did have individuals with money spread throughout most of them Asian the next city over was Hawthorne which plagued by many gangs. Hawthorne was more like a refuge for various gang members to go live when they wanted to be close to their sets but did not want to live in their sets which came from the thinking don't shit where you eat. Between Gardena and Hawthorne Lee intertwined with the locals few if any knowing he was even an officer and he liked it that way. He was cool with everybody, so he blended well. The only problem he found with the two cities was you could run into your local street thug to someone wanted by the F.B.I you could never guess because the cities were wide open for any type of illegal business drugs, prostitution, and robbery. Lee mostly moved through life no real purpose nothing really moved him except being out of control.

Pikes had grown to like the city of Carson it reminded him of his little town in a lot of ways it was mostly quite around the city outside of a few shooting and car chases here and there. The 190 East coast Crips were the major set in Carson so there were not that many gang issues in the city outside of situations that took place at a party or something. Carson was also one of the few Black communities that still thrived in a place where kids could still walk the neighborhood and go to the local parks to play without much worry of getting shot. Pikes felt secure in Carson it was patrolled the Sheriff department who ran a very tight shift on who came and left their city. Carson was also near the city of Torrance which was a nice size city with a variety of different cultures it was also home to a few big malls which generated a lot of money in the area along with other small business that could be found throughout the area. Pikes loved good food and people they always reminded him of home so it was no surprise that on down time such as a day before a raid he would hold up in a Boston market. Loneliness also came with eating alone a loneliness that could only be cured by having a family a thought that constantly plagued his mind.

Ms. Jackson had been living on 76th place for over forty years and in those forty years she had seen very few changes in the community none being for the better and this saddened her deeply, but she just didn't know what to do, so she prayed that the Lord would help her people every day to take away the spirit that made them kill each other as well as destroy their own community. She often wondered why the Lord let this destruction goes on for so long, yet this wondering did not last long because she knew better then to question the Lord about his creations and decisions. It had been a while since she had set on her porch and just enjoyed her community; sitting watching her grandchildren play in the front yard under the sprinklers put a smile on the old woman's face that had been absent with all the homicides that engulfed the community monthly. In her prayers which were few she also prayed for a day when her people wouldn't rejoice over just losing only three lives in a week, it was sick to her that it had gotten so bad that a little death was better than a lot.

Then the frown returned that normally resided on her face as she heard the loud offending lyrics booming from a dark blue Magnum shattering all peace that was present and around the neighborhood as it turned the corner then the embarrassment hit deep when she saw that the driver of the vehicle was her grandson who she hadn't seen in a few days returning home. Ms. Jackson always wondered where she went wrong with the raising of her son that produced her

Escape from Failure

Grandson: she knew it was not Omar's fault that his daddy was in and out of jail leaving him to be raised by his grandparents who were too busy and old too keep tabs on a young impressionable Black male.

"Omar, you know I've told you about pulling up to the house playing that music loud a thousand times and where you coming from with your shirt off showing all those tattoos?"

"Ma why you trippin, I forgot besides, I'm just running in and out." Omar said moving fast past his grandmother to get to his dope stash in his room. "All right ma, I'm gone I will see you later tonight."

"Omar do I really need to see you're behind every time you leave the house?" Ms. Jackson asked as Omar walked down the stairs towards his car with his t-shirt slung over his left shoulder ignoring her all the way to his car.

"Yeah nigga I'll be over there in a minute I had to coast by the pad to pick it up." Omar had to say nigga a minimum of a thousand times a day just to feel like a nigga. He was getting tired of his grandma sweating him about his music being too loud when everybody else was bumping their music in the hood too. She didn't understand that a nigga like O-Dogg had to beat when he was coasting poor grandma and her street ignorance that's why a nigga like O-Dogg was hustling to get out the house so he wouldn't have to hear her nagging anymore at 29 years old.

"Damn, this punk ass phone is always losing reception when I get over here." Omar said to himself as he tried to call his boy to come outside to pick up some pills.

"Damn it took you long enough." Feet said opening O-Doggs passenger door.

"Look nigga I'm here, besides, I'm not trying to hear all that shit."

"You should take like twenty off for me having to wait." Feet said with a grin on his face.

"You acting like one of the dudes right now, why you trying to work me down to the bone. See its niggas like you that make a nigga like me have to raise the price on shit."

"Stop crying here's all your bread, speaking of the dudes what's cracking on getting some tonight?"

"You don't even have to ask me, but we have to go in your ride they know mine now."

"Cool."

Between 2 a.m. and 4 a.m. the streets of Los Angeles were as still as they get, even the stray dogs and cats were tucked away under some underpass or barely living piss smelling bush recuperating with the rest who lived in and around the community without shelter. Traffic was minimal as the raid unit drove up the backstreets to Ms. Jackson's home in their BATT-XL black tactical truck which held twenty armed men securely because of its resistance to .50 Cal ammunition. The ride was silent all the way to the house there was no need for conversation as they arrived a few feet from the home in which they were about to invade. The house was old so they were aware that it would creek once they were on the porch, but that would be the only give away. They knew that Omar was in the house because of information received from an informant the department had been using. Twenty feet from the house the tactical unit filed out the back of the truck in black fatigue with their 6.5-pound Smith and Wesson M&P15A tactical assault rifles into the formation that they had been trained around the house, there were five windows around the that needed to be secured. Lee and Vasquez covered the side window on the left side of the house the bathroom windows were smaller, so they needed a man for each, Pikes secured one and another officer secured the other. The two front windows were secured by four officers who sat in tactical squat positions to get better aim in case someone tried to come out the window. Five officers were in a line formation in front of the door the first one carrying a huge shield ready to kick in the door with Rodriguez right behind him ready thirty minutes ago, his adrenaline was pumping and his fingers were sweating from the black combat gloves as his trigger finger caressed the trigger.

The signal was given in the form of a hand gesture to enter the house and soon after the boot meet the old wood of the front door which didn't give much resistance or sound coming unhinged instantly to the first officers surprise because sometimes it took two quick kicks to get the job done. Once inside the officer yelled for everyone to stay down on the ground while they made their way to the back of the house to the room Omar supposedly occupied. There were four pre-teens inside the house and they were detained by the other officers and brought outside the house in plastic cuffs when Ms. Jackson awoke from all the commotion she didn't know what was going on, she assumed someone had broken into the house and reached for her .38 revolver she had since she bought the house in her nightstand, but before she could retrieve it her hand loosened from the handle as something came over her telling her not to get the gun. The instant she retrieved her hand she was blinded by the flash light that lay atop of the assault rifle and thrown to the ground by nearby hands that instantly placed the plastic cuffs on her that tightly cut into her old wrinkly skin cutting straight to her brittle bone and their she laid with her face pressed into her own carpet with a boot in her back pr4essing up against her and ruined nightgown that her deceased husband had bought her on their last anniversary before his passing. Omar heard the commotion and knew that it was a raid. A nigga like him always talked about what he would shoot it out if the police came kicking in his door, but like most things it sounded good on paper. It did not take long for him to go with option B to just surrender after all a nigga like him was not that stupid to shoot it out with the police just other niggas like himself. So he stayed in bed pretending to be asleep and seconds later what he had braced himself for, happened, the police came kicking in his door Rodriguez leading the pack with the butt of his gun cracking down on Omar's head instantly splitting it seventeen stitches wide.

Omar was nearly unconscious by the blow to the back of the head which sent a gush of blood water falling down his entire face into his mouth which lay open moaning from the pain that was exacerbated by Rodriguez's boot to his mouth which flipped him over on his back where he was met by another blow from the butt of Rodriguez's rifle to his mouth knocking out a few of his upper front teeth as well as him. Seeing that Omar was unconscious the other officer flipped him over on his stomach and cuffed him up with plastic cuffs dragging his limp battered bloody body down the hall way to the front of the house where the rest of his family lay on the front yard on the wet grass restrained, fearful, cold and ashamed while the officers hi-fived and congratulated each other on their success.

The oldest granddaughter who was fifth teen pleaded with the officers to take the restraints off of their grandmother who was laying on her side in the wet grass crying silently out of hurt and shame of being humiliated like this in front of her home as well as neighbors who had started to come out the house in bath robes and sit behind their screen doors watching after hearing all the commotion. Coming from the side of the house Pikes instantly took notice of Ms. Jackson spiraled across the grass and went to pick her up.

"Are you alright Ms.?"

Ms. Jackson was silent for a minute she actually didn't know how to respond to the question which should've been clear; normally she would have responded yes she was alright even though that wasn't the case, but under these circumstances she replied no.

"What can I help you with?"

"The restraints are cutting off my circulation."

Pikes did not hesitate to cut the restraints with his Seal pup knife as he watched Ms. Jackson take a long breath of relief shaking her hands in the process. Her hands were still throbbing from the tightness of the restraints as she looked around at all her grandchildren lined up across the grass and then her eyes enlarged as she focused her vision on Omar's blooded body laid against the gate in the dirt.

"Is my grandson dead?" She uttered not really wanting an answer.

"No, there is an ambulance on the way right now to take him to the hospital."

"Do they normally take this long to come?"

"It all depends on how far they are and what's taking place in the area."

"What the hell are you doing Pikes, you released a suspect?" Lee asked walking up behind Pikes and Ms. Jackson.

"She's not even the suspect Lee more so she is an old woman."

"Old ladies can pull triggers too. In fact, they found a loaded revolver in her nightstand that she could have easily killed one of us with do not be foolish Pikes. Always keep your guard up these people will kill you.

After hearing about them finding a gun in Ms. Jackson's nightstand Pikes started to second guess himself about relieving her of the restraints, yet his morals over rid the doubt of leaving an old woman in that condition. Two hours had gone by and the tactical unit were gone the same way they came in fast and silent with Omar in custody and the Black community still in disgust over how they were treated by their own law enforcement agencies.

Chapter 7

Home

Getting tickets to Africa was more difficult than Askari knew it took him about two months just to book a flight to Africa in which he first had to take a flight to London which would take him to Johannesburg and from there he would catch a flight to Cape Town where he had reservations at the Protea hotel sea point. The taxi rides to the L.A.X was smooth with traffic being light until they arrived within the zone of the airport. Askari was traveling extremely light all he was taking with him was his passport, clothes on his back, iPod touch, and a book on African translation. His clothing was simple beige khaki pants, black Stacy Adams matching belt, and a long sleeve shirt that complimented the rest of his attire covered by a black thigh length pea coat. The last time Askari was at an airport he was a teenager going to Egypt with his uncle back when security was a lot more lax then the 9/11 tragedy occurred and with it the entire process of flying it all reminded him of being back in prison with the only thing missing was bend over and cough. After putting his shoes back on he made his way down to the waiting area passing a few stores before stopping at one to get some Earl Grey hot tea while he waited on his flight.

Darkness offered little insight to what laid beneath the airplane as it departed into the night sky towards London. After hearing the all clear electronic devices Askari put on his head then ran his finger across his iPod to select the shuffle command for his jazz collection. He had picked up on technology rather fast it all just made since to him plus he always had time to practice especially when he had to sit in Kaiser to get his shots to even come to Africa. Waiting was no problem to him he had been waiting all his life it seemed for something to happen that would make him say now I get it, but that moment hadn't happened yet and he wasn't quite sure it ever would yet that is what kept him going all these years even the prison years the answer to why he was even born.

It felt good to stretch his legs once the plane landed in London he had gotten a little sleep while on the plane ride from L.A.X. Night fall was still with the passengers as they stepped off the plane to get refreshments before taking back off to Johannesburg. Stepping out the restroom Askari was headed to get another hot tea before the plane boarded again when he was greeted by a lovely smile that seemed to take away all thoughts except joy standing in front of him in line.

"Hello, my name is Carole." She said extenting her hand out.

"Nice to meet you my name is Askari."

"That's a different name it sounds like something a scholar would be named; do you mind me asking what it stands for?"

"Of course, not it means warrior in Swahili."

"Great, are you African, I don't hear the Accent?"

"No, only in blood I am from Los Angeles."

"That's great, me too, what part might I ask?"

"I am all over the place right now, but I was raised in the Athens area as a child, what area did you grow up in?"

", I am originally from Texas, but I moved to Los Angeles when I was nine teens to go to USC for social work and Journalism. While going there I stayed off campus in the general area."

"So, where you are you living now?"

"Downtown Los Angeles, near the fashion district in a loft and I love it."

"Well it seems like we are both a long way from home."

"Yes, I guess so depending on how you chose to look at the situation."

"Indeed, I feel you on that. It was nice meeting you Carole I have to board my plane and I am sure you do too." With that Askari shook her hand and proceeded to walk towards his plane with Carole right be sides him. I see we are going in the same direction?"

"Yes, it seems that way. Could it be we are both going to Johannesburg?"

William V. Fields

Askari waited briefly before answering his gut was not giving him any strange feelings about Carole, but his minded was always reading in between the lines. What were the odds that he would meet an attractive Black woman from the United States in London going to Africa too? Plus, she was not on the plane with him which means she either was already here or she took a flight in from somewhere else which he needed to find out.

"Seems like we are both going in the same direction, so where did you fly in from?"

"Texas, in went out there to see my parents before I came all the way out here to do a story on women being raped in Nigeria because the locals believe that it will cure their aids if they have sex with a virgin. One of the victims stays in Johannesburg so I have to interview her."

"That's amazing that you are shedding light on such a sickening ignorance I would like to talk some more about it on the plane if you don't mind sitting next to a brother."

"Askari it would be a delight." Carole said following behind across the platform into the plane.

"So, I have to ask who you write for?"

"Currently I report for CNN as well as write for a couple local papers on various issues affecting the community."

"That's nice, what made you get interested in that type of journalism?"

"Honestly, I have always liked to investigate and find the truth behind why things happened instead of just taking someone else's word for it. Growing up Dallas I was exposed to many libraries where I could go and look up any and everything, I wanted plus my parents encouraged me to explore new things."

"I find that fascinating whenever I hear parents exposing their kids to the world and not setting limitations on them, what type of work do you parents do?

"They are both retired doctors my mother was a pediatrician and my father was a dentist."

Escape from Failure

Carole was the first woman that Askari had spoken too in over fifth teen years this long and in depth, yet he felt like he knew her all his life like they grew up next door to each other as kids. She was educated, smart, funny, and beautiful, but most importantly she was just a nice person which was hard to find, especially in a Black woman. Normally there would have been some type of awkward vibe or standoffishness between the two. Usually women he assumed from his previous experiences thought that all a man wanted was to see them bent over some item therefore making friendly conversation near impossible between the sexes. Never one to be ashamed of his past life he was ashamed of the social stigma attached to someone who had been to prison he couldn't help, but think that it would create the awkwardness that was now nonexistent in their conversation flow.

"Askari, it seems you know a lot more about me then I know about you, what brings you out this far?"

"Vacation, I came to enjoy the beaches of Cape Town for a few weeks as well as check into some clothing and cleaning chemicals I need for my business."

"Interesting, what type of business do you operate?"

"A cleaning service that cleans homes, businesses, parks, and hotels that cannot afford a full staff to work permanently."

"So, you next question is going to be what sparked your interest in that line of work."

"People will always need their homes and establishments cleaned. More so I learned as a young man not to follow the crowd and never be fearful of getting my hands dirty. The part of town I grew up in consisted of working class people, but even amongst the working class the person who cleaned home was nearly invisible to everyone else; no one ever paid much attention to the cleaning person which wasn't a bad thing in my eyes because they were always the underestimated. Think about the last time you talked to a cleaning person."

"Sounds like my next story all I would need is a title. I can honestly say that I have never paid much attention to the people that keep are city clean. So how many times have you been to Africa?"

"Actually, this is my first time to the continent, although I have read a lot over the years in various books so in thought I have been here countless times."

"I see the reason I asked is because you are the first person, I have met that has come down here for business. Normally I run into professors bringing their students down or someone looking for a life changing experience down in the mother land. With you it is different though the look in your eyes says you are on a mission of sorts."

"Interesting what else do my eyes say Carole?"

Carole hardly knew Askari, but she was intrigued by him. It was as if he came from another world which was strange to her because she had met many different types of people throughout her young and adult life yet this man ignited her curiosity to want to know him better and why his eyes held a pain his demeanor didn't exude. Even amongst the occasional smile at one of her jokes she knew smiles were not common to this man who spoke her name as if he had known her all his life with not the slightest bit of uncomfortable flow when he spoke to her.

"They say that you are lonely and need a friend to make you laugh, smile, and relax sometimes."

"That's amazing that you see all of that in my eyes, so I guess you are that friend to bring all these things into my life?"

"Depends on if we stay in contact after this encounter or we just walk away as if we had never met going are separate lives like most people often do not taking advantage of a promising future that lay before them in a chance encounter."

"Walking away from you physically would be easy, but mentally impossible for you have already made an impression that could never be forgotten even if I tried. It is rare to find a unique spirit encased by a beautiful vassal. I am encouraged to have you as a friend if nothing more."

Before Carole could respond to Askari's comment her thoughts were interrupted by the flight attendant announcing that they would be landing in Johannesburg within the next five minutes.

"Askari your words are sweet. Here is my card give me a call when you arrive back in the states so that we can meet up at Starbucks so that I can hear all about your trip."

"I'll be looking forward to it Ms. Perkins."

Carole's smile spread from her inside to her face as she gathered her bags from up above their seats and made her way down the hall looking back one more time and waving to Askari before walking off the plane. Askari's smile did not resonant on his face as usual, but there was a warm feeling in his chest that had not been felt since his youth.

With the exception of meeting Carole, the trip to Cape Town had proved to be draining to even someone like Askari who was in incredible shape and he was glad to be at the hotel which was located on Arthur's road a main street to all the local areas he would need to visit for his business. Once inside his room he poured some bottled water into the coffee pot which was located not far from the door to make him some tea before going to sleep. While the water heated up, he checked the room over to get familiar with the lay out. After retrieving a Styrofoam cup near the coffee pot, he filled it with tea and preceded outside on the balcony that overlooked the city he would setting fourth into the net day.

Thoughts of Carole came from nowhere as he stood waiting on his tea to cool; he could visualize her round lips talking to him as he sipped his tea and listened to her voice that he had captured in his mind. Sadly, he could not capture how it felt to touch a woman in a sexual manner it had been that long since he had held a woman that the feeling had escaped all recollection.

The Athlone newspaper which was one of the few English written newspapers in the continent was slid underneath his door when he awoke very well rested. Shortly after reading the newspaper and getting caught up on all the politics of the area he dialed up his business contact he was supposed to meet at 12 noon not far from his hotel.

Cape Town was bustling as he imagined since it had the second largest population in Africa, people were everywhere much like downtown Los Angeles in the garment district trying to sell things they had grown, crafted, or stolen nothing new just a different part of the world.

William V. Fields

Through his research online Askari came across Jelani Chemicals & Fabrics which sold their name sake wholesale to the public and small mom and pop stores in the region through them he would order uniforms and cleaning supplies for his business Personal Touch. Once he reviewed their better business rating, he gave the head office a call to set up a meeting which they were eager to do.

He was already at Ma Ma Africa a popular restaurant in the heart of Cape Town which had a few American dishes on their menu. True to form he arrived early before his scheduled meeting with Kagiso a representative of C&F. The restaurant was a standard size location with low brown colored ceilings surrounded by pictures of nature. The tables were long and narrow which was something he had never seen before, but he thought it was nice the way everything had tied into each other. Overall, the restaurant had a calm feel to it. From the dress and the briefcase, he knew it was Kagiso walking into the restaurants entrance.

"Hello Kagiso, I appreciate you taking the time to come and greet me." Askari said pulling out the chair for Kagiso after shaking her hand.

"No problem Mr. Franks did you have a hard time finding Ma Ma's?"

"No, it was actually quite easy with the directions you had given me."

"Good, so is this your first time to our country?"

"Yes, it is, but I have always had a desire to come visit and since I had business out this way, I told myself what better reason to come then now."

"Well definitely take the time to go to Table Mountain before you go there are a few restaurants that serve ostrich steaks you can get there by cable car so make a day of it. Here is your paperwork along with the contract you have with C & F and lastly your receipts for the items you have purchased."

"Thank you so much, now that the business part of my trip is over, I can start my vacation. By the way are there any places that I should be aware of or stay away from?"

"Everywhere is basically safe just stay away from Sea point at night it is red light area where a lot of mugging takes place. Besides that, your vacation should go worry free."

"I appreciate the insight and I will stay clear of that area."

"Unfortunately, I have to leave to another appointment, but I have preordered you some dishes on the company for flying to see us."

"Not a problem I understand and thanks for the meal."

After the meal Askari made his way back to his hotel to put up his paperwork and get a map so that he could navigate his way to Sea point later that night. There was a ghetto over there that he had heard about, so he wanted to check it out. Nighttime came around quickly so it seemed and Askari was ready to hit the streets of Cape Town up until night fall, he was out and about picking up more traditional attire of the area so that he could blend more easily. Cruising through the streets of Africa was much like most cities alive with the night life which seemed to dwindle more and more as they made his way down to Sea point which seemed to resemble the eastside of Watts more than anything. Sitting at a stop light he noticed graffiti on the wall and knew that he was finally in Sea point were a rebel group was in control. A little up the road Askari saw three road blocks which forced him to make a left turn to avoid it and come up the other way, but as he made the left turn his jeep was surrounded by ten Africans dressed in green and fatigue from head to toe pointing various AKS74s, M16, and AR15s shouting for him to turn off the engine in thick African accents which he did with no hesitation.

"American step out of your vehicle slowly are you will die." One of the Africans said with his rifle still aimed on Askari along with the others who were still staying in a military formation the entire time.

Askari took his time as he stepped out the jeep knowing what would happen if he made a sudden move, so he was especially cautious stepping out the jeep not to appear hostile without sacrificing his personal security. Once he was outside the jeep one of the Africans lowered his weapon and quickly tied Askari's hands behind his back with rope while another placed a burlaps sack over his head they were about to knock him unconscious when the lead

African told them to search him first; upon searching him they found a letter in his pocket addressed to *Jelani* written in their native language.

"Throw him in the van and take him to the base."

The Africans base was only a few miles from where they took Askari hostage, so it did not take long to get there and be transported from the vehicle to the holding corridors where they kept their hostages.

"We captured an American with this letter inside his pocket addressed to you Jelani."

"*Asante*, bring him in to me."

The smell of the room they had moved him to had a strong damp putrid smell as if blood had rotted on the walls and floor for months it instantly caused him to gauge a little as he entered the room. He could not see because of the sack over his head, yet he could hear a strange knowing sound as if a dog was chewing on a bone, but he knew that it couldn't have been a dog because the sound of the bones being broken would have been too big for a dog to break. When the African removed the sack from his head he saw that his assumptions were dead on for what laid before him was the biggest hyena he had ever saw chewing on a human skull with blood draped around its mouth around its neck was a huge brown leather collar that almost appeared black because of the constant blood that had soaked into it over the years and holding the chain which lead to the collar of the beast was Jelani a huge dark African dressed in black Kenta cloth with a matching head dress who was sitting in a large woven chair staring straight at Askari with an assault rifle not far from his left side.

"American what is your name?"

"Askari."

"An American with a Swahili name is your parents African?"

"No, they are from the states."

"Enough talk where did you meet my brother?"

"In prison, he was my Celly."

Escape from Failure

Jelani had yet to read the letter he just recognized the handwriting which was familiar to his little brother who he assumed was dead when he was smuggled into America. Not one to get his hopes up he wanted to question the American before actually reading the letter. After hearing that his brother was in prison, he decided to open the letter and read it.

Jelani

Brother, I send my soul to you in the form of these words to let you know that I am a live big brother. Apologizes are many for I have lost my way brother as well as my life of freedom for I am encaged for life within this American dungeon for taking a life. Within months of being in the system I was almost raped until Askari helped and saved my life from those savages. He also helped me educate myself and find a form of peace within these walls. I gave him this letter in case he would ever see the world again he could relieve any sorrow within your mind of your little brother Katlego.

Askari saved me brother so I am in his debt take care of him like one of our own. Kiss Amadi for me for I know she protects you. I realize now that poverty is not an absence of money, rather, it results from an absence of knowledge something I am now indulged in.

Imani...

After reading the letter he folded it back to its original shape not realizing that there was a picture inside of his brother and Askari until he tried to place the letter back in the envelope and it wouldn't go forcing him to look inside. The sight of his long-lost brother brought comfort to his heart.

"Release the Askari instantly. Jelani said walking from the back of the small room. Asante for what you did for Katlego without even knowing him we are in your debt forgive our treatment of you."

"I understand the circumstances behind your actions, but honestly I liked what I saw, and I would like for you and a few of your men to come back to the states with me. In my shoe I have a second letter from your brother that details how you and a few of your men can get to the states to meet up with me."

William V. Fields

"I am interested in hearing more about your plan of us coming to the states, but let's discuss it in different quarters."

With nothing blinding his sight Askari could see that he was in a small village about ten bungalows scattered throughout the one he was escorted to a building that lay at the end of the village. Inside the room within the bungalow sat a huge wooden table that stretched about forty feet long with chairs lined up all the way down. On the walls were maps of different parts of the city along with attack targets. Once inside the room seven armed men came in Jelani bringing up the rear closing the door behind him.

"I have read the second letter that *Katlego* sent with you and I understand that you are willing to help fund our cause if we help with yours, so my question to you is what will you need from us besides men?"

"I will need lots of guns, ammunition, and military training."

All the men in the room started to laugh at his request then Jelani got up from his seat and pushed on the wall behind him in a strange formation as if he was knocking for hollow points when suddenly the wall moved and automatically slid open revealing a secret room in which all the men begin to file into.

"When we fought for the British during the world wars we had to manufacture and export are own weapons due to embargoes so we have a surplus of weapons in that crate we have MAT-49, Israel Uzis, and DC9s. Over there in those crates Thompsons ranging from the M1921 to the M1A1. Against the wall in those crates we have AR-15 to the Imbel M964. Further down the hall we have Sig SG551-2. Of course, we have every type of AK from the 47 to the 74. We have TAR-21 which comes with grenade launchers; by the way that whole room to the side is grenades and explosives. The M134 is for when you are stuck in a corner as well as the Vector SS77 and M72 Kalashnikov. So which ones will you need?"

"All of them will suffice."

"Then all them you will get."

After getting the tour of the gun room Askari and the group headed towards the kitchen area of the village to eat.

"Askari let me introduces you to the men who will be coming with me to the states. Over to your left the first three men are *Abidemi and Akachi.* To your right is *Boi pelo, Chidubem, Ekwu eme, and Chike.* They have been with me over twenty years and they are all top-ranking soldiers in my army they will not disappoint."

Shortly after eating dinner Askari went over a few more things with the men before making his way back to his hotel room he had a couple more days in Cape Town in which he would go to Table Mountain to try the ostrich steaks then he would prepare to fly back home his goals for the trip were accomplished now he had to put in motion his other plans in Los Angeles which were directly connected to the results received on his current trip.

As he lay in his bed Askari thought about giving Carole a call once he got home to let her know he was back in town, but he knew that it would not play out the way they probably would want it to, honestly, he thought about not even calling her just to save confusion later yet the thought of her beautiful smile made him want to be home to have her near.

Chapter 8

Concrete La Jungla

Hello Stranger by Barbara Lewis was playing through the speakers set up in the back yard of the apartment building that sat nestled between 81st and Hoover as Shy Rock made his way to the bar-b-q grill to grab himself a couple of his home girls famous carne asada tacos which he had been craving for twelve years; no matter how good a spread he prepared or package canned item he received nothing came close to taste the seasoned beef packed. As he ate, he prepare his tacos his scanned the back yard through his sunglasses taking in the entire event as well as all the new little young homies who had plagued their allegiance to the big bad one eight gang. In their eyes he saw them sizing him up as if wondering if he would live up to the legend they had been hearing about all these years before most of them even wanted to claim the fame, in his younger years he would have looked at this behavior as a threat or challenge, but at 32 years old his mind was not far removed of how it was to be new and young homie on the *barrio* he knew their posturing was more out of reverence than anything else.

Shy Rock was grooving to the oldies when he saw Shy Girl coming from out the house with a foil pan about to put some more carne asada on the grill.

"Hey home girl you still have the best carne asada in South Central."

Shy Girl was caught a little off guard as she turned to Shy Rocks voice that she had not heard since their late teens. She was not expecting him to come through until later in the afternoon when all the older homies were at the functions.

"You've been saying that since we were kids Benito."

"That's because it is true, you need to open up a restaurant and hire all the homies to work for you."

"If I had the money I probably would you never know."

"That's right you never know how things will turn out in the La jungle."

Escape from Failure

"So how does it feel to be out Shy Rock?"

"Good I guess I really don't feel too much different than when I was locked down the only difference is, I have a bigger yard to roam and conquer."

"Hopefully, Shy Rock you get use to feeling free again and can relax."

"Hopes are for faggots I'll relax when I have my hand on every vine around here pulling in resources."

"Resources are few and in between Shy Rock my uncle Renee has a sound shop on Manchester across the street from the Bargain O if you need money in your pocket."

"So, Renee finally got his shop out the garage and into a store front, I might have to check him out some time."

"That would be good Shy he would like to see you."

With that Shy Rock made his way through the small back yard shaking hands and listening to the latest street news from old heads to young ones, but all that kept going through his mind was that he had to piss test tomorrow for his new parole officer all the way in Long Beach. He hoped that he wouldn't get some over the top new booty P.O. who was going to act like Robocop with him as if he had to show him who was boss he had road this road before and preferred a veteran mainly because they didn't sweat the small stuff as long as their parolee didn't come in contact with other law enforcement. Nighttime fell along with the number of individuals at the party all that were left were a few older drunk homeboys who didn't have anywhere else to go and Shy Rock who was talking to Shy Girl the majority of the evening.

"So, who are you staying with Shy Rock?"

"My parents for right now until I get on my feet."

"Give Renee a call tomorrow I'm sure he will have something for you to do around the shop."

"I'll check it out before the week is up definitely."

"Just make sure you do before you get caught up Shy it is too easy to end up right back."

"Thanks for the concern Shy Girl you have always been a solid home girl."

Shy Rock had never been on the street long enough to make it happen with Shy Girl if he wasn't in jail she was or either one would be in a relationship with another homie thus was the case again with Shy Girl talking to a young homie named Puppet.

"Shit I almost forgot me, and Puppet were supposed to be going out tonight." Shy Girl said seeing His White Escalade pull into the driveway.

Shy Rock had been hearing about the young homie Puppet and how he was getting money real strong in the barrio what he didn't know until that moment was that Puppet was with Shy Girl in that instant he thought to himself that them being together must not be meant because there seemed to something or someone standing in the way. That night on his way home he thought about how Puppet looked at him like he was a rival from another area when he climbed into his 87' black Regal and their eyes locked. Obviously Puppet didn't know that he was La Eme for his behavior would have been different yet it was possible that he did know, but just didn't care and if that was the case Shy Rock knew he would have to kill him despite his older brother being a *camarada* arrogance and lack of respect were the ingredients to murder in Shy Rocks gangland.

After folding up his Levi's and cleaning off his white Nike Cortez Shy Rock took off his white T-shirt folding it as well placing all his clothing at the foot of his bed which was located in the back room of his parent's home. He had been up since six that morning yet he couldn't find any sleep at one in the morning his mind was racing filled with a myriad of thoughts of how he had ended up 32 years old back at his parent's home with a bag of hygiene, letters, and photos to symbolize his existence when his initial goal was to break free of their rules and find his own way now he lay back at square one depending on them like a child. Morning came around as usual with Shy Rock only getting hours sleep in three to five minute fragments he had to see his parole officer at 10 a.m. which meant he had to be down in Long Beach in about four hours giving him plenty of time to do his *berpes* routine he had been doing for the last eleven years of his twelve-year sentence.

***

Another banged out *ese* Brown thought to himself after laying eyes on Shy Rock with his short sleeved white t-shirt, blue Levi's, and of course tatted from head down about 90 percent of his body from what he could see. It was his fifth add on this week a top of twenty caseloads he had already fifth teen being Hispanic from nineteen to forty.

"So, Mr. Hernandez have you got any ideas about what you are going to do?"

"Actually, I am scoping out some jobs in my area."

"Good as long as it is nowhere in your old neighborhood you have stipulations in your parole that prohibit you from hanging with other gang members or even being anywhere in the vicinity where you were arrested."

"I understand I can't hang with the homies, but what if I find a job in my old neighborhood?"

"Look Hernandez your old school and so am I you just stay away from the police and come in every month to give me a clean piss and we are straight. I'll be by your house tomorrow to do your house visit so make sure you are there between 5 a.m. and 5 p.m. this will happen about once a month or whenever I am available so be there or I will violate you. Honestly, I know you are probably going to do your thing just make sure I don't receive any phone calls are we clear?"

"Yeah."

Short and to the point the way Shy Rock wanted it now he had to make his way to the next destination on his agenda which was in Hawthorne at the Best Value Inn on Imperial highway. Pulling into the Best Value he instantly noticed that Sharky's 87 Red I-Roc Z was parked next to some Black SUVs. Shy Rock parked his car on the opposite side of the vehicles and proceed upstairs to room 211 were the rest of the Mexican mafia members were having their meeting. After giving his coded knock at the door it instantly was unlocked and he made his way into the smoked filled room which was occupied by four other individuals that he knew well.

There was Salvador "Sharky" Marquez from Pomona 12th Street a gang that was very violent and was known as the CHP killer gang for an officer that they had killed a few years back while he sat in his squad car they were also notorious for killing African Americans. Sharky was 35 years old the oldest out the group who had a huge P12 on the back of his head and 12th Street tatted underneath his left eye on his chest he made multiple pictures of naked women with La Eme collogued in between the women. He was about 5'6 with a medium build that reflected his time in and out of prison 8 years being his longest stretch at which point he put in work to be recruited into La Eme. His thick mustache gave him a slightly older look which made it easy for him to sneak up on his victims with his choice weapon which was a sawed off 12 gauge.

Miguel "Character" Sanchez was from F13 an eastside gang whose main enemy besides the 18th Street was the East coast Crips. At 30 years old he had seen a lot of deaths, wars, and prison bars. Before being recruited into La Eme he would have tried to kill Shy Rock and Speedy, but now he had to work with them as brothers something he had to come to terms with once he had become a *carnal*. At 5'2 he had always caught hell from individuals in his neighborhood about his stature, but it proved to be an advantage once he started gangbanging at the age of twelve his small size helped him avoid getting shot whenever he found himself in a shootout or sneaking up on an enemy to kill them. He was considered a *hood rat* because he was always hanging out in his neighborhood with his *Loks* on *hitting* anybody up who seemed like a threat even though he was small he loved to carry big guns underneath his big shirts or in arms reach of where ever he was. His short man complex made him ultra-violent and he was known for going overboard whenever he was called upon to perform. Character was also known for being very animated hence the name especially when he shot up heroin, he was known by most his rivals and law enforcement by the huge F13 tatted on his neck.

Rene "Camel" Moreno was the only member in attendance that was not from the L.A. county area he was representing East Side Rive 13 a gang that resided in the heart of Riverside for the last twenty years that originated from a gang called the Tiny Dukes who lost their title once they couldn't keep up with their kill quota on African Americans in their area now it laid on the shoulders of the ESR to run methamphetamine throughout Riverside county and commit hate crimes not only on the 12th Streets a Black Crip gang in the area, but also anyone who was Black. Not only was he not from L.A county, but he was the youngest out the group at 28 years old most of that 28 years being spent doing a life sentence for the murder of a young Black male who he had a shootout with; his case got over turned on technicalities in his if it had not been for his parents having a little influence in the area he was raised he would have still been rotting away up at Pelican Bay with his other *camaradas*. A lot of things separated him from the other members in the room including the fact that he was not looking to actual become a member it just sorts of happened that he was going wild throughout prison because of his life sentence which caught the attention of La Eme. Camel got his name because of his 6'2 height and long protruding face which wore the symbol of the Riverside bell along the left side of his neck, the only other tattoo he had was ESR spelled out in block letters going across his right forearm. Even though he went to prison for murder he was not a killer, but rather a fighter his father was boxer back in his youth so he taught him how to fight as he was growing up unfortunately he used his fighting abilities for the wrong reasons.

Jose "Speedy" Ruiz was also from 18th street, but from a different click called smiley drive which was located by the Jungles which housed the BPS a blood set that had been beefing with them for over ten years. Speedy had known Shy Rock since teen age years when they met at LP and eventually went to camp Gonzales together for different crimes. They were only a year apart Shy Rock being the oldest, so they had been through a lot of similar situations together which caused them to have a stronger vibe with each other than with the other La Eme members in the room.

After the handshakes were done and everyone that was supposed to be there was in attendance the men got to work on what they needed to do to put La Eme new mission into order.

"Starting tomorrow we have to start identifying all the young homies that have potential to make it in school, by now you should have an idea of who needs to be hitting the books over the pistols. It is very important that they know that we need them to push forward with the new order as if it were them putting in work the same energy needs to be used to ensure their progress in the new system. Sharky already has a younger brother enrolling into UCLA later this year while in Community college he pulled up all the school districts that we will need to concentrate on to bring test scores up. See to it each one of you make sure you pick up a packet read it, know it, and apply it. Camaradas this must be put into effect as soon as we step foot back in our barrios. There are thirteen meetings taking place right now as we speak with the same info, we have so the Black Hand will fall all at once."

It was the most any of the members ever heard Shy Rock speak outside of Speedy he was a man of few words so they listened intently to what he was saying eager to see how the new plan was going to come together. It was definitely a different spin on how they had done business in the past and quite honestly it was beyond the scope of most of them fortunately they were just followers one of the few situations where that was a positive.

 "We'll be meeting up at a different location in a few months to go over the numbers we discussed tonight so be ready to do so next time we meet up."

Once Shy Rock got up from the table and crushed his cigarette into the ash tray the other members knew that the meeting was over so they gathered their things and made their way to their vehicles with Speedy and Shy Rock staying behind.

"*Junta* went well ese, so do you think the little homies will be feeling the new program?"

Speedy asked pulling a camel out of his coat pocket.

"They'll have no choice either fall in line or get on the *lista*."

"All this time we've been telling the homies fuck school now we'll be telling them to go and get scholar ships too their going to flip their lids when they hear this new program."

Escape from Failure

"There will be some casualties in the beginning from a handful of assholes who don't want to fall in line, but after they get killed it will make the process so much easier for us to enforce."

"Right before I got here I got a kite in the mail on a *dropout* named Pee Wee from Little Watts not far from here who I have to *make bones with* you want in there might be a stash in the house."

"I could take some of that action."

"Cool we'll go in my ride my stash should fit you're Taurus and my 9 I can't believe you still got that big monster of a handgun after all these years."

"You know how hard it is to find a good gun that won't jam on you especially a revolver that has a chamber for ten rounds."

"Good guns are hard to find that why I always change my up every few months to keep it fresh I don't have time for cleaning guns I just pass them on to the little homies."

"So, is it still hot over there in your part of town?"

"A little they still got the gang injunction on us real tough and the *mayates* so it hard for us to go in on them without having to listen to scanners because Crash knows the hot spots that we hit."

"That's the beauty of what we are about to put in place it will give us another route of attaining power while the crash dummies sizzle out. We all always use and need our foot soldiers, but even they will have little use in the future besides showing society why don't need to be on the streets."

"In the meantime, we have to get rid of loose ends like Pee Wee who don't understand loyalty. That is his apartment complex right there we'll probably have to hope the back wall to get to his unit so I will leave the car here so that we can come out the front once we are done."

Doing hits for La Eme was nothing new for Shy Rock and Speedy although this was their first street hit for La Eme the others were prison hits that they both got away with. Most of their practices for hits came from their earlier years as foot soldiers when they would kill or have shoot outs with rival gangs in their thirties, they had the expertise of seasoned war veterans. There was a slight coolness to the night air that night as they made their way through the back streets of Hawthorne to get to the opposite side of the building. They had all black on including beanie and gloves. Once they found the back of the building they hoisted themselves up over the wall to the other side without much effort as soon as their feet hit the ground they heard voices coming from around the small alley they found themselves in yet they continued to move forward not wanting to have to shot it out from such a narrow position. Speedy stepped out the shadows first with a lit cigarette in his mouth to give the appearance he was on the side smoking giving Shy the opportunity to gathered himself Speedy quickly noticed that it was just a couple of Black teens talking and nothing else so they both proceed to the apartment building that seemed to be leading them to the far back of the unit a perfect location for a dope spot which Speedy heard was being ran by Pee Wee baby momma.

"Looks like their apartment is back there at the very end of the hall by the way the numbers growing so it might be possible to do a kick in and just go inside."

"Let's go." Shy Rock said pulling his revolver from his waist band placing it to his side.

Little to no noise could be heard from the outside of the door as both men stood silently listening waiting to kill. Simultaneously they both looked at each other as they heard Donnie Elbert Have I Sinned coming lightly from inside which became their invitation inside with Speedy kicking the door open while Shy Rock ran in grabbing the first person he encountered which was a male short in stature while Speedy chased down a woman who tried to run towards a back room pistol whipping her in the back of the head knocking her unconscious between the bathroom and the room she was running towards. Seeing she was unconscious he checked the room she was running toward as well as the bathroom once that was secured, he closed the front door which was still usable. Shy Rock kept the revolver trained on the male while Speedy tied up the woman with the telephone cord and then tied up Pee Wee with clothing, he found lying on the floor. Once ever thing was secured, they moved the male to the bedroom then the women throwing them both on the bed with their faces pointing towards the headboard. The woman started to come around after a while which they both were waiting for. She knew not to scream so she did not she just asked what they wanted, in which they replied Pee Wee is this him she shook her head yes.

"We are going to kill him tell us where everything else is and we will let you live we are only here for him." Shy Rock pointing his revolver in Pee Wee direction.

Without hesitation she told them where the fifth teen thousands were along with the weed and Methamphetamine stashed in various places around the one-bedroom apartment.

"Stupid bitch they're still going to kill you too you just paid them to do it now."

Speedy had gathered up all the items that Pee Wee baby momma had told him about in a pillowcase now all they had to do was decided how to do the killing.

"There are enough pillows in there to muffle the sounds, but I'll have to use the 9." Speedy said knowing Shy Rocks gun would be too loud even with a pillow especially the Wal-Mart cheap kind the couple had.

"Cool I'll wait in the front until you are finished."

Speedy had done a lot of home invasions throughout the years which made him an expert at tying people up with items in their own home as well as executions; Pee Wee lived up to his name so it wasn't hard for Speedy to straddle him from the back with his struggling do little to nothing although a man grew increasingly strong when he was near death from his past experiences he always took caution. The double down went easily On top of Pee Wee struggling neck and head it was going to be a little difficult getting a clean shot Speedy thought as he tried to place the barrel on his head against the pillow then impatient set in and instead of shooting him just once like he had planned he had to shoot him three times in the head which really pissed him off because he wanted his work to be clean like 007, but now it looked as if some junky had did the hit. Nevertheless, he moved right on over to the women once Pee Wee body stopped moving who wanted to scream all of sudden about she thought he wasn't going to kill her as he barely got the pillow over her head before he had to squeeze off two shots that went more into the side of her face then her skull, but the job was done she was dead.

"Thought I was going to have to come in there for a minute once you went over a minute."

"You know how it gets once they try to put up a fight, plus it has been a while since I had to do the pillow and pistol technique, I was kind of rusty."

"You'll get plenty of practice these next couple of months as some rebel against the plan."

"Probably so, but for now the only problem we have is counting this money and dividing these drugs."

"Yes, Camarada lets focus on the present as we walk through this la jungla of life."

Chapter 9

Friends Become Strangers

Four months had passed since the robbery in Red Lands at Chase bank and Toy Box was down to her last twenty thousand cash from the lick they had hit she had purchased herself a condo not far from her set at first she was going to get an apartment, but she had talked to a few people and they advised her to just buy into something that she could own in the future which made since to her; it was her first real place and it felt good coming home to something she could call her own. It was a nice two-bedroom condo that was in a nice area in her city she loved. Life had been good for her the last few months having money at her disposal was a new feeling that she had grown fond of. Of course, now that she had the money, she really did not know what to do with it outside of buying a place to live, clothing, cars, and jewelry. She did a lot of average things such as party and ate well, but there really was no fulfillment involved that felt good. She often thought about checking into El Comino or Trade Tech, but always found herself putting it off plus she was plagued by her past bad experiences with the school system simply put she was beginning to become burnt out living the life. For the time being she had stopped all personal relationships with her women to focus on her credit card scamming ring which was doing moderately to keep her bills paid. Looking over at the clock she knew it was time to get out of bed and get the hustle started so she made her way downstairs to make a pot of coffee when she noticed a standard yellow envelope laying on her floor as if it were slid underneath her door which was strange because only a few people knew where she laid her head. Turning the letter around she noticed that it did not have her address on it, but it did have her homie K9 handwriting on the front who she had not heard from in years since he got a life sentence. The thought of how the letter got there slipped her mind temporarily as she opened the letter to read its content. From how the letter begin she knew it was written by her home boy, but there was a different flow to the words in the letter that also caught her attention even more as she read three pages of an individual named Askari who she needed to contact if she needed any type of help to get on her feet. After reading the letter she folded it up the way it came then she walked up stairs with the letter to put it in her drawer, but she didn't make it far before she heard knocking at her door. Who the hell is this she thought to herself as walked to the door asking what she was thinking?

"It's Iceman blood open up the door."

"Blood its nine in the morning and you talking about open up the door."

"Blood you know it must be important if I am coming this early."

As soon as Toy Box opened the door Iceman tried to sock her in the face, but she ducked rather quickly avoiding the punch already cautious that he had come to her home at that time of morning; missing the punch made Iceman loose his balance giving Toy Box the opportunity to run upstairs to grab her gun which was sitting on her night stand with one in the chamber she quickly fired her weapon striking Iceman in the shoulder and chest sending him stumbling down the stairs with Toy Box right on him continuing to fire on his body as it stopped moving at the bottom of the stairs. Damn she thought to herself as she grabbed all her most important information which wasn't much and head out the door to her vehicle down stairs where she heard footsteps approaching and noticed that the steps were coming from Red Flag who started to fire on her with a Mac 10 which left seven bullet holes in her driver side door as she dived to the floor to return fire with her 40 Glock that didn't find its target she got to her feet to find a vantage point to shoot Red Flag who she heard reloading his gun."

"Like that blood, you trying to kill me."

"Fuck you bitch you should have thrown us some of that money when we took loses."

At that moment Toy Box was enraged that they were going to try to rob her because they felt she should have given them some money when they all started out with the same amount. She knew they were hating on her, but she did not think it would come to this. Each time she fired off a few shots she got closer to Red Flag who did not have that much control with his gun to fire off single shots. Once she heard him trying to reload again she ran around the car he was hiding around and shot him in his neck as well as other various places in his face and head as he tried to lift his gun to aim with the clip half way in. Toy Box blood was pumping as she jumped in her car not having any real destination except away from the scene of what was now a double murder. Her mind racing as fear set in of getting caught she knew she needed to ditch her Ford magnum which was bringing a lot of looks and stares because of all the bullet holes in the driver door the further she drove up Manchester the more panicked she got as to where to dump her car as well as a place to lay her head. Melody came to her thoughts as she made it closer to Vermont, she still had the keys to her place plus she lived by an alley with garages. From the looks of the area everyone was either at work or out trying to make a dollar before getting out the car she checked her clip to see how many bullets she had left; too few she thought only counting six or eight plus the one in the chamber. Being it was Friday she knew Melody was probably out with her daughter and wouldn't be home until later, luckily the keys still worked unfortunately so did Melodies bad habits of not cleaning up as well the house was a mess with dishes in the sink and clothes everywhere, but it would do for a place to gather a plan for her next steps. From the Texas Ranger hat she found in the bedroom it was obvious Melody was back messing with her baby daddy from 83 gangsters the local set in the area she was in it was one of the reason they had fell out because Melody couldn't figure out if she wanted men or women a dilemma Toy Box didn't want to have to deal with a woman and her confusion issue of rather she was gay or straight her lifestyle was not a fad neither where her emotions for someone who wanted to embrace the rainbow for shock value or curiosity. A few hours had gone by and there was still no trace of Melody or away to contact her being she didn't have her new cell number so Toy Box sat and turned on the T.V. dreading to flip through the channels and see her face with an award for her whereabouts, it was three minutes before the four o'clock news would be showing so she braced herself and watched as the top stories where glazed over for the four o'clock hour with the murder in Inglewood topping the list.

"Early this morning in a residential predominately professional community in Inglewood a double homicide took place claiming the lives of two known gang members in what authorities are calling a robbery gang feud. Authorities are hoping you can help identify this woman who was videotaped having a shootout in the parking garage before fleeing in a red Ford Magnum. She appears to be in her mid-twenties, African American, and about 5'6. If you have any information, please contact the Inglewood police department of course there is a 25,000 reward for the apprehension and conviction of this individual. This is Leo Stallworth reporting for eyewitness news back to you Dallas."

Toy Box new she had to act quickly and get out of town without the reward being on her head she probably had a few months to lay in the city before having someone tell on her, but with 25, 000 on her head she knew everybody and their momma who knew her or of her would turn her in without a second thought plus she would have to deal with the homies who were related to Iceman and Red Flag it was apparent she had to go fast, but she had nowhere to go then she thought about the letter she received early so she checked her pockets and didn't find much outside of lent which meant it could only be one place in the car. This was a chance she had to take she thought as she punched in the numbers off the letter two rings went by before an answer.

"Can speak to Askari?"

"This is him how can I help you?"

"Quickly if you can, this is Toy Box K9s home girl I need your help asap if possible, I need you to pick me up if you are near."

"Where are you?"

"On 88th street between Manchester and Normandie."

"I can get to you in about twenty minutes from where I am right now."

"Alright just give me a call on the number you see on your phone when you get close."

"Sounds like a plan."

While waiting Toy Box cleaned her car out taking whatever she felt she really needed as she killed time until Askari came to get her. From the sound of his name she wondered if he was an African or something of that nature. Within moments Askari was in the alley not far from Toy Box car he had had a GPS

Escape from Failure

system built into his phone while in Africa which allowed him to track any wire taps or incoming calls.

"I'm in the black Audi behind you when you are ready get inside."

The phone and appearance of this stranger she did not know had Toy Box on edge she was starting to wonder if she had made a wise decision in contacting him, but now it was too late to have second thoughts it was time to move she could sort the details out later.

"It looks like you have been through a lot today."

"You don't know the half."

"In fact, I do they have your face on all the local news stations including CNN, see look for yourself." With that said a T.V. screen flipped from the roof showing internet news top stories around the world.

"So, you know about the reward too."

"Sure, do and so does everyone else it is probably how they found out your government name so it looks like you will need a safe place to lay your head until the heat cools down."

"My only choice is to go out of town and start from scratch."

"There is never just one choice in life you always have options you just have to come outside yourself to see them."

"Sounds good on paper, but the reality is I am wanted for a double gang related murder and from where I sit there is one option and that is to keep moving and avoid contact with the one time."

"If I could give you a choice besides having to run the rest of your life would you takes it?"

"Askari, I appreciate you coming to pick me up, but I'm into vagina not men."

"This I know K9 told me awhile I go so let's clear something's up I don't want anything special from you or sexual all I want is for you to live out your potential."

William V. Fields

"So, what is the choice that you are offering?"

"I own a cleaning company that hires the unemployable and trains them how to survive in a world that they might find not understanding or difficult to adapt. I also provide housing for these individuals as well as food, schooling, and counseling is this something that you would be interested in being a part of?"

Opportunities were few and in between in the ghetto yet they did exist more so could be grasped if one put fourth an effort to want better for themselves too often individuals let opportunities pass like buses choosing instead to wait for another which often times didn't come or arrived too late ;then they found themselves veering off course taking another route that was not even in their initial intentions or meant for them to travel yet they go down it anyway getting lost in the process physically then mentally to the point where most forgot how they ended up on the road of destruction. Toy Box had traveled far enough down the road of pride she knew it was time to go back the way she came in hopes of finding herself.

"How soon do I start?"

"First we need to get you cleaned up and a new appearance so that you don't stick out then I will get you to work, but don't feel any pressure because there is none your recovery is what's most important."

"Recovery...recovery, what do you mean by that?"

"Recovery from all you have been through up to this point, living in these streets is not healthy or normal the fact that individuals such as yourself don't understand that is the main reason are communities remain in limbo because their hearts tell this is not the way to live, but media influence tells them that it is so we as a people adapt to the life convincing ourselves with each sip of the bottle or hit of the cigarette that nothing is wrong with us."

"That's *brazy* I was just having this conversation with myself a few minutes before I got into the shoot out."

"Everything happens for a reason Toy Box so find the reason in today's events and grow from them."

"So where are we going right now?"

"To Altadena where you will be housed and trained on what to do in the company, you'll have your own room so you won't have to worry about anyone evading your privacy or taking your gun."

"How did you know I had a gun?"

"I do my homework Toy Box I heard about your reputation on the streets, besides after what you've been through today who wouldn't want to have some warm steel close."

This is tight Toy Box thought to herself as they pulled into the curved driveway of an all-white Spanish rival looking home. It reminded her of a house that they would film a reality T.V. show

at or a millionaire would stay in.

"Your company must do well?"

"For a new company it is doing alright we are overly aggressive in are advertising as well as customer service you will learn a lot of useful things here. Are you ready to go inside?"

"Yeah, let's do this."

The house was just as nice inside as it was outside she thought to herself as she stepped inside the huge home taking in all the painting on the wall that depicted pivotal moments of the Black Panther movement as well as the Brown Beret in the late sixties and seventies they were beautiful black and white stills and color one's throughout the home a first for her to see. All the walls where gray and eggshell which gave the home a large look that was complimented by furniture of the same hue fresh laundry oil scents could be smelled throughout the home giving it a very relaxing feel as she ventured further through the house getting the tour from Askari.

"There are five bedrooms in the home and four bathrooms three down stairs and one upstairs the room you will be staying in is upstairs on the north side of the house along with the other room which is adjacent to yours the other two rooms are located in the back of the house near the back door which leads to of the back yard which we are approaching now. Back towards the wood shed is the exercise room in case you need exercise feel free to do so any time; as you can see the yard is huge plus there is a lodge area around the side of the house for other recreation you may want to do such as reading, cards, or dominoes. Is this a place where you would feel safe until you got yourself together?"

"Definitely, this is bool right here I can do this."

"Good, there are seven other individuals that live here as well they are from South Africa you will meet them tonight at dinner so if you want to rest or clean up before tonight do so at your leisure."

"Good looking out Askari I appreciate you coming through for me."

"No problem I live to serve."

It did not take long for Toy Box to find her room which was fully furnished with a bed and nightstand as well as clothing that appeared to be a beige uniform neatly folded at the foot of the bed. Despite feeling safe from her current situation, she still took her gun with her into the bathroom to shower her guard refused to come no matter what or nice the place she was at appeared. Waking out of her sleep she tilted her neck over a few degrees to take notice that night had fallen much like her tiredness, strangely enough she wished that her early experience was somehow not true, but that would mean she would have been waking in her bed instead of another. Gathering herself she made her way downstairs following the sound of voices to what she sensed was the kitchen. The kitchen had gotten quite quickly as Toy Box stepped in from behind the shadows of the living room.

"Glad you decided to come join us for a meal. Now you will get a chance to meet the other men, sit anywhere you like at the table Abidemi will get you a plate to eat."

"Good looking out I haven't had anything to eat all day Askari."

"Problem solved take whatever you like there is plenty. While you eat the men will introduce themselves."

"My name is Jelani which means mighty in your language I am a descendant of the Khoekhoe tribe as well as all the other men you see at the table it means men of men. We are from South Africa and we reside in Cape Town."

Jelani was huge compared to the average men she was use to seeing he wore a green rag tied around his head which was obviously bold due to how the rag fit snuggly against his scalp at 6'4 he was the tallest of all the men at the table as well as widest he wasn't necessarily cut, but just solid all the way around with a dark skin complexion. His voice was low to be such a big man and he spoke English rather robotically as if it took a lot of concentration to get the words out. From his look he seemed to be about mid thirty with the rest of the men looking to be early thirties.

"My name is Abidemi and my name means born during father's absence you can call me Bid for short."

Abidemi was a slender brown skinned curly haired South African who had served with Jelani since the age of five it would have been sooner, but he was unable to fire an assault rifle any earlier, Abidemi's dad served with Jelani in the military upon his death he made Jelani promise that he would take care of his son that he hardly got a chance to see do to his service in the military. Jelani had been like a father to Abidemi as well as Boi Pelo, Chidubem, Chike, Akachi, and Ekwu eme all young courageous soldiers unafraid of death or killing there was no hesitation in their kill reflex. The night went on with Toy Box being introduced to all the men at the table she learned that Akachi stood for the hand of God and that Boi Pelo meant proud she talked with each one briefly before moving on to the next. Chidubem was incredibly quiet and talked rather low so much so that Toy Box had to pull herself in close to hear him as he told her his name meant guided by God. Chike was the complete opposite in that he was filled with energy as he told her his name truly expressed how he felt daily like he was filled with Gods power. Dikeledi was darker than the others almost purple his eyes were red and watery as if he couldn't stop crying she soon learned that it was a medical condition that was treatable, but his family lacked the resources to cure it so it worsened over time which truly garnered him his name tears. For some reason Ekwu eme resembled more of an African American look then the others she thought to herself as she spoke to him; his face was much fuller then the others as well as his physique his name also hit home with her more so then the others because it was a motto she lived by he says he does. After dinner they all filed outside to relax in the lawn chairs underneath the cabanas that set in the middle of the large yard. Every now and then Toy Box would smell a strong stench that smelled like something rotten whenever the wind would kick up a bit. An hour went by and she could still smell the fetor, but it didn't bothered her as much when the stench first entered her nostrils then there was the unmistakable eerie laugh that sent a chill up her spine as she asked the others did they hear the sound?

"What sound are you referring to?" Jelani asked seeing the troubled look in Toy Boxes eyes.

"A laughing hissing sound as if it came from an animal or someone has their T.V. up loud watching lions."

"You have probably heard Amadi in the back we keep her in the basement."

"What type of dog makes that kind of noise?"

"None from my experience only hyenas make that type of noise."

"Hyena...is that what is making that sound I've been hearing?"

"I don't know we would have to go down there to see if she is making the sound that you heard."

"It's not necessary now that I know where the sound is coming from."

Hyena... Toy Box thought to herself as she made her way back towards the back of the house she couldn't understand why someone would have a hyena furthermore how they got it in the basement she now was starting to wonder what was going on with Askari and the Africans. Her intuitions were not sending off any danger signs, but she knew she would have to keep her eyes open around them at all times.

"You're retiring early?" Askari said peering over his newspaper while sitting at the kitchen table.

"Being in a zoo can be exhausting."

"Have you met Amadi?"

"No, but I have to ask why you have a hyena?"

"Jelani brought her back from Africa when he came over it is his pet; he's had her since she was small he found her near death by a bush when out on surveillance that is where she got her name Amadi which means destined to die at birth. I know it caught you off guard it also caught me off guard the first time her putrid smell was captured in my nostrils I'm still amazed whenever I see the creature it is a sight to see she is huge with red penetrating eyes that gaze on you like you are prey. You have had a long day and the news of Amadi probably added to the confusion you have been through today just go relax in your room we start your training tomorrow."

***

"Hurry up with the blunt; you've been hogging it all morning."

"You sound like my baby momma." Uzi said taking another hit of the weed.

"Did you hear about that bitch Toy Box from I.F. *murking* Iceman and Red Flag?"

"Yeah, it was all over the news yesterday and shit, it's a wrap for her if they catch her."

"Under those circumstances it doesn't matter if they catch her or not, she through with money it's too bad though because I wanted to knock that little cock down."

"Shit nigga don't you get tired of tossing hoes?"

"Hell *naw* my dick is like a predator taking on all competitors it needs a steady diet of new cheeks, why else would all these little hood rats be running around here they want to get tossed by a nigga like me."

"Nigga you crazy for that shit."

"Why, it is the truth want else would they be doing if they were not getting high, drunk, or tossed? That is what I thought nothing that's why soft ass niggas like you do not be having any cock around, but you always in one of my bitches faces. Speaking of bitches looks at that little bitch right there leaving Saint Michaels in the white genes."

"Uzi you still be hitting them high school girls?"

"They got pussy too, don't they nigga hell yeah I be knocking them down I'm about to push up on her right now."

Uzi frequented the Manchester car wash regularly not only could he get his car washed for free whenever the manager was there, but he could also scope out his next underage sex victim. He loved to sex high school girls because they were usually naive and not schooled by the streets that well although there were a few that he had ran across that had been laced onto the game he would run by an older aunt or cousin, but even they couldn't hold out for long and would eventually spread their legs and lips. Females his age wanted too much to hit they had bills as wells as mouths to feed plus an immunity to low grade weed and low budget liquor made a night out with them costly a young high school girl was happy just be in a car let alone a nice one so all her other friends could see.

"Slow down you to fine to stop for a nigga?" Uzi said trotting across the street behind the female in the white genes.

"I have to catch the bus home that's why I am walking so fast."

"Where do you stay?

"Why, you ask a lot of questions."

"Because I'll give you a ride if you are worried about being late to wherever you are headed."

"Are we going to ride on your shoulders, we both on foot?"

"Jokes my car is over there at the car wash in fact that is horn blowing for me right now."

Keisha looked towards the carwash to see a black on black Dodge Charger sitting on some chrome rims.

"I don't even know your name and you want me to hope in the car with you."

"Uzi."

"Uzi, I've heard that name before don't you have a little homie that goes to my school?"

"Yeah, you know him?"

"Not really he hardly comes to school and when he does, he is always trying to fight somebody."

"The little homie is active that's why he is underneath me, so what's up with that ride so that I can get to know you."

"I stay in the Swans you know where that is don't you."

"Come on now, are you from Swans?"

"No, but my family is. How old are you anyway?"

"How old do I look?"

"I don't know about twenty-five."

"Yeah I'm somewhere in there how old you are?"

"Seventeen next month so now that you know I will be expecting a gift."

"That's cool we can finish talking in the car let's get off this corner."

As they made their way to the cross walk to cross back over to the other side Uzi was contemplating how he could take down Keisha as soon as possible. She had a little spunk to her which turned him on he didn't care too much for straight push over he enjoyed breaking a wild spirit of an overly confident female it had been that way since he was a child and he would push girls in the mud after it had rained especially the little light skinned girls who thought they were all that because they grew up in a different neighborhood than his. Once they were in the car Uzi went into his general pussy probing questions that eventually lead to an episode.

"Spoke something nigga." Keisha said putting her folder on her lap in case he needed her to roll up the Kush.

"Here light it up." Uzi quickly realized that he would not have play any mind games with Keisha she seemed to already know the business. This had its pros and cons of course the pros were she wouldn't try to act like a virgin on him the con was that she would definitely try to milk him for all she could before the day was over everyone had a role to play in the ghetto game even the gangster there would always be some form of tricking in the form of drugs, rides, or alcohol if often times very redundant, but it was the way Uzi had gotten use to existing so he was game as long as she didn't try to do too much.

"So what house is yours?"

"The one on the right I'll run in and come right out."

"Cool." While she ran in the house Uzi's scanned her eastside frame Keisha was light skinned with big lips that his homies referred to as *d.s.l* her but was so big that it barely kept the brown belt she wore fastened he had token down cheeks like that in a while they were firm too because they didn't even move when she ran across the street this told him two things one she wasn't getting pounded on that much or two she just had good genes besides he knew major rats that had been super pounded, but still kept their little cheeks right. Normally he would have to be extremely careful when he came into the Swans neighborhood, but the street she stayed on wasn't that hot as the other streets yet he still had his pistol on his lap ready for action if it came his way. Keisha was running back across the street to his car when he noticed a familiar face coming out of the apartments right behind him in his rearview at first glance he thought to his self it couldn't be then he heard Keisha say hello to the female addressing her as Ivie. Once Keisha was in the car, he reversed to see what he come of his comrades almost wife who had two kids now living on the Eastside.

"When was last time you visited Gina?"

Ivie knew the voice instantly even though she had not heard it in years she hoped in those years that he was either locked up with a life sentence or more to her desires laying in dirt dead. She raised her head slowly as if in a trance to see Uzi unique smirk staring back at her sending a chill of hatred followed by fear up her spine.

"Don't speak to fast I see you got your hands full with your little nigga and daughter I'll make sure to tell K-Stone you said what's up." With that Uzi drove off leaving a tearful concerned Ivie who knew that Keisha was in the car with Satan himself everything Uzi touched was destroyed in some type of way and now he was infecting the generation under him with his sick behavior and thoughts.

"How do you know Ivie?"

"She used to date one of my homies back in the day, how long has she been living across the street from you?"

"About three years now she lives with her baby daddy he doesn't bang he's been living over here all his life he's a security guard down at Auto Zone on Hoover and Century."

"That's cool so what time do you need to be home?"

"Whenever I get there, I'm no little kid nigga."

"Right, right I should've recognized."

As the night progressed they relaxed watching old school DVDs on the couch while being sarcastic towards one another for younger female Keisha held herself well she had been having vaginal sex since the age of twelve and fellatio since the age of ten always with older males older then herself some by a couple of years and some by over ten years she had always had a well-developed body from early on which made her notice quickly how men treated her differently from not only the darker girls, but the less developed girls she seemed to always get her way growing up and that set well with her she was use to men thinking they were in control of her body thinking they were the man when most had little dicks and she knew she had seen plenty in her sixteen and a half years short and small long and skinny to nigga you not about to put that in me big, but one thing always stayed consistent she could never be satisfied no matter what for a length of time she always found herself moving on to the next once she was burnt out. She knew Uzi would be no different he would come with the same arrogance most came with acting as if they knew what she wanted when all they were doing was imitating the stroke used on the last female they had had sex with. Sex was something that came easy to her unlike other things in her life she knew what outfits made her body look tight she knew what attitude to have with certain type of dudes she had no preference unlike most if she was feeling them and was horny it would go down. By the way that Uzi was looking at her she knew he was ready to take her down and like most she knew he would want his dick sucked and for her to turn around spreading her ass so that he could hit it from the back she knew the routine and laughed to herself whenever males would go through their corny mating rituals to get the pussy when all they really had to do was just chill and it would come their way. An hour had went by an it happened just as she knew it would the invite to the bed room, the want you get a nigga right speech which basically meant bitch give me some head, the play with my the pussy with their fingers because they were no longer hard because they had come in her mouth, and the classic let me hit it from the back. No originality just a repetitious act that lasted too long.

***

Unease resided in him when joy should have been the outlining emotion yet it was near impossible for him to feel relief when he knew what lied before him it was a struggle after all to rather he would reveal the paper work to what was left of his set that had mostly died out or had life sentences much like he had just a few days ago; his release took a little longer than the others who were involved in the string of corruption steaming from the 77th C.R.A.S.H unit because he had actually taken a deal to avoid a jury trial so he had to spend extra time in the law library working on an appeal that pertained to his situation which wasn't an easy task nevertheless he prevailed. Andre "G-Liz" Harris knew that the information he had on his homie was not the type you showed around he would have to kill this individual and that didn't sit well with him because it put his freedom on the line again when he had barely tasted its flavor yet his deprivation from society made him uncommitted to the luxuries of life that had eluded him for so long if he was going to kill he needed to do it right away without hesitation yet part him needed someone to talk to, but he didn't know who he could trust anymore with what he knew for this individual was one of their most trusted members at one time and the only way he had found out was through reading through countless documents during his incarceration if he hadn't stumbled across it his self he probably wouldn't have believed it coming from the mouth of another. The only dilemma he had now was finding a gun discreetly without the streets talking he already knew it was too late to stop people from knowing he was out so he had to make his movements as less noticeable as possible.

"Andre, Kevin is here to see you." His father said passing by his room.

Much like his other homies he had not seen K-Stone in years even though he had heard how he had changed his life. He wondered how he knew to find him at his father's house.

"How did you know I was here?"

"That's how you greet me after all these years? I knew you wouldn't have too many places to hold up after being gone all these years."

"Oh, that makes since so how long you have known I've been out?"

"A few days, a couple homies hit me and let me know you were touching down this week I figured I come by before you got to running around full time."

"You don't have to worry about that I plan to take it real slow."

"Good that's the way to go, it's a little stuffy in this room you want to go in the back yard or for a ride."

"Not really I need to get some things together before I begin to start mingling again, I don't mean to be rude, but I need some time alone so I will catch up with you later."

"Alright, I'll catch up with you later then."

K-Stone couldn't understand why G-Liz was acting so strange they had been real cool before he took the deal for twenty years a few years back, but K-Stone knew that years in prison could change a person drastically in all types of ways good as well as bad so he wasn't taking it personal he just hoped that his comrade didn't lose his mind behind the walls because the last thing that the community needed was another mentally challenged individual roaming around waiting to cause some chaos directly or indirectly with their aloof behavior.

William V. Fields

A few weeks went by and G-Liz found his paranoia start to dissipate as he got used to being free again he managed to come across a 38 revolver from one of his cousins from ETG and was ready to rid the community of what he perceived to be a parasite that fed off the trust of those close to them just to have an escape goat later on down the line when they found themselves in a jam. Nighttime had fallen on what was a casual Friday night casual in the since that there was no gun fire or tires burning rubber all day. The Naked Booty was a club that set nestled between other business along the strip of Florence it was a place where the local gang members would go to drink, get high, and hangout while watching the local strippers which consisted of baby mommas, smokers, and prostitutes it was also the place where G-Liz knew he would catch his target. Being a local club he didn't have to worry about being patted down at the door so he just passed on by the security that had been working there since he was a teenager into the club where he was greeted by cigarette smoke, laughter, and eyes scanning him over to see who was entering the club. It was 10p.m. and the club was filled with about ten strippers of various shapes and sizes with collages of tattoos old and new covering their bodies most looked tired and warn as if they wished someone or thing would put them out of their misery, but until that happened they were ready and willing to make that dollar the best way they could to provide for their children or drug habit. Hey baby you want a dance was a theme that he knew he would be hearing all through the night and he was prepared with a solid no for each one that asked. Most of the customers were around the small stage that set in the middle of the room right next to the juke box that the strippers would pass to get on the stage before selecting their song for their dance routine the rest were spread throughout the club sitting at tables or shooting pool at the table that set in the right hand corner of the club that was only about the size of a small Burger King. G-Liz found a booth not far from the stage that gave him a view of everybody that left and came into the club he ordered a Hennessey with rocks shortly after getting settled into the booth relaxing waiting on his moment which came not soon after he had put down his drink.

Uzi had stumbled into his favorite after hour spot since he was young with Baby Uzi in tow; he had heard that there were some new strippers that had started to work at the club so he wanted to come check them out. As he mingled through the club, he spotted a face that he had not seen in years which made him proceed in the direction of the stranger that he thought was gone for twenty years.

"G-Liz you really got out that's crazy." Uzi said sliding into the other booth seat to sit down.

"Yeah it is crazy, that's what I thought too."

"So, have you got any pussy yet nigga?"

"No, I'm just taking it easy for right now."

"You aren't on dick, are you? You didn't get turned out in there I hope."

"Nothing like that a brother just got to be careful nowadays."

"That's what condoms are for nigga. So, what you got going, did they break you off some bread?"

"A couple of thousand, but comparable to the other people involved on the case."

"Sounds like you might need to flip that little bread then to get on your feet I could help you invest that bread so that it can double for you. Plus, you have been away for a while and shit is different so I can get you back on deck."

"Sounds like a plan lets go out in the back so that we can talk some more the smoke in here is choking me out."

"Cool let's push, but before the night is up, we going to toss one of these strippers in here."

Outside in the back Uzi lit up a camel cigarette and continued to small talk with G-Liz.

"So which homies were you up there with?"

"A few older homies, but mostly a bunch of little homies who had just turned the set I have a few flicks let me show you."

Instead of pulling out pictures G-Liz pulled out the 38 revolver he had stashed in his waist band and by the time Uzi saw the gun G-Liz had him by the collar of his T-shirt and was in the process of firing all six shots into his chest and stomach before releasing his limb body which collapsed to the floor as he made his way to the back fence which set adjacent to the alley it all happened so fast that G-Liz didn't take into consideration that to shoot someone that close there should have been blood splatter on him; before that epiphany settled in bullets from Uzi's 45 automatic did leaving him clinching the gate fingers paralyzed as the first bullet entered the back of his neck exiting through his Adams apple the rest of the twenty shots found their way into various parts of his body as he hung there on the fence as if he were climbing it G-Liz was dead while Uzi was half way over the other fence into the alley on his way back around to the front to get into his car not knowing why G-Liz tried to kill him more so why he would shot him in the body knowing that he stayed with the vest he must have forgot he thought to his self as he got into his car tearing away what was left of his burnt up T-shirt.

The people in the Naked Booty heard the first six shots from G-Liz's revolver, but did not pay too much attention to it thinking it was just the normal shooting that went on in the neighborhood. After hearing Uzi's gun fire they knew that the gun shots were much closer causing his homies to run to the back to find G-Liz stuck to the gate with blood drenching his shirt the few stripper that ran behind the gang members to be nosy ran away screaming once they laid eyes on G-Liz's dead body. Most of the new homies who had ran to the back didn't even know who he was while a few older homies recognized him and walked back to the front knowing that the police would have to be called so they made their way out of the club with only a few strippers left remaining and the club owners.

Chapter 10

Gang Life

When the C.R.A.S.H unit arrived detectives had already been at the scene of the murder an hour taking statements, photographs, and gathering evidence from off the body.

"Apparently the neighbors heard multiple shots being fired from the direction of the club when they stopped so did our victim who was a Linebacker at USC visiting his mother for the holiday. We have another dead body that we need you guys to identify across the alley." The detective said motioning for Vasquez and Rodriguez to go across the alley.

Coming through the front of the Naked Booty the C.R.A.S.H unit made their way to the back of the back of the club where they were met by more detectives who were working the case.

"Hey fellows we need you to I.D our D.O.A on the fence before we take him down."

Rodriguez walked to the gate and knew he was looking at before he got up close.

"Your victims name is Andre Harris *b.k.a* G-Liz he just got out of prison on a technicality a few weeks ago he runs with the 83 Hoovers."

"From all the shell casing we have found someone wasn't too happy about him being out, but the odd thing is we found roughly about twenty-five shell casings twenty coming from a forty five automatic and six slugs coming from a thirty eight revolver the slugs from the revolver were found all in one location so whoever fired them hit their target not knowing they had on a bullet proof vest."

"Detective it seems that Harris shot the other person first not realizing they had a vest on until it was too late stupid fuck thought he had got away with murder and tried to make a run for it." Rodriguez said spitting on the ground.

"Well yes, but the good news is we found possible DNA evidence on a cigarette that might belong to the person he tried to kill."

William V. Fields

"Great now you have to do is catch him so that we can charge him with murder."

"Actually double murder because the bullet that entered the head of the young man across the alley apparently came from a forty-five too we just need to find the slug during the autopsy and our perpetrator will have two murders to fight along with other charges."

"From the number of rounds fired and the accuracy I have a feeling of who could have done or had something to do with the murder."

"Well I hope your hunch is dead on because we don't need killers like him running around on the streets it's not only a danger to the community, but to us as well."

Rodriguez knew that only a few of the Hoovers could have that type of fire power and one of them was Uzi. Two weeks had gone by and Uzi was nowhere to be found they comb the streets and found nothing, but a bunch of dry leads yet they were not worried because they knew he would pop up eventually. Besides, they had the funeral of Andre Harris to watch the next day which was on the same day as Shawn Davis who had also died on the same day across the alley. Andre's funeral was held at City of Refuge in Gardena with a guest preacher doing the service there were about two hundred people in attendance fifty or so were the victim's family the rest were his homies from his turf who had come to pay their respects the rest were just there because they had nothing else to do.

The attendance of Shawn Davis was much greater in that over five hundred people came out to pay their respect to a life cut short too soon.

"Come with me in prayer as I open up this service with Ecclesiastes 3. Thank you all for attending this farewell to Andre Harris loving son to Timothy and Gertrude Harris. I've known Andre since he was a child growing up I went to school with both his father and mother he was a good child who had a lot of dreams, but I must be frank and say that when you live by the sword you die by it and I truly hope that you young people will wake up and stop killing one another God did not intend for us to be killing each other in the streets we are supposed to be loving each other like sisters and brothers in Christ our

Lord. This is the twenty fifth Blackman that I have buried this year due to gang violence."

As the preacher preached an all too familiar sermon K-Stone looked around the church observing all that were in attendance at the service most were off in their own worlds not really taking in what pastor Blakely was saying because they had heard it all before and would hear it again sometime down the line maybe at their own funeral. K-Stone was sickened that as a thirty year old man he was at the funeral of another young Blackman that had died prematurely the magnitude of it all really resonated with him as reflected on how unnatural in the scheme of things it was when compared to other racial groups he rarely read about young White, Asian, or even Hispanic children being gunned down in their front yards as they played or watched T.V. in their homes it was acceptable to kill Black youth he conclude to his self because it was still taking place in the Black community with no real outrage expect for a few days after it took place then it was back to business as usual until another Black child or person was murdered in the streets. Black people don't value Black life for if they did they wouldn't allow for these types of behaviors to continue he knew that as long as they viewed themselves as niggas that they would continue down the trail of death and despair; so in many ways he was numb to funerals attending more so out of habit then remorse hoping one day that the only funerals he would attend would be those of natural cause or age with a few crime related sprinkled into the equation because he was not aloof to the fact that crime was going to happen, but gang murders didn't need to those types of killing were deliberate acts that were encouraged by the gangs and gang members that do them. It was painful listening to the preacher and the other speakers try to find something good to say about G-Liz what could they say, but he accepted God before he was killed or he was a good athlete at one time in his life it was really pathetic when in death you realize how much of life you have wasted run around in the streets there was never any legacies left behind just fatherless and motherless children who would have to become the burden on one parent or more likely than not the grandparents the cycles was both preventable as well as predictable yet no one seemed to know how to make it stop or wanted it to for once one walked through the doors flagging it was known were they stood and would stand until it was their time for words to be spoken.

"We will now have words from friends and family, please keep your statement to under five minutes." Pastor Blakely said passing the microphone off to the first person in line.

"For ya'll that don't know me I'm Big Limp I'm a little bit older than G-Liz, but I remember him growing up in the hood because he was always trust worthy whenever we shot dice I never had to watch him because he was straight up. That's what made him a good nigga to me and I'm sad to see him gone."

After about four of those types of statements G-Liz father made it to the podium.

"I heard a lot about respect from the people who spoke about my son so my question to you all is when is the person who killed him going to be brought to justice it's only obvious that it was one of you that did it being where it took place so I just ask that if you really loved him like you say give his family justice so that another family want have to suffer like mine."

There were a lot of gasp and sighs at G-Liz's fathers request because everyone knew who did it, but they were not going to turn him in it just was not the way things were done. K-Stone still couldn't understand why G-Liz would try to kill Uzi the only thing that he could think of was that he was still mad about Uzi giving him a hard time when he was sentenced years ago, but that was more than seven years ago along time to hold a grudge K-Stone thought to his self he knew Uzi well enough to know that he wouldn't have killed G-Liz out in the open like that if it was an absolute must something wasn't right and like most things it would all play out to a conclusion.

***

"Rodriguez just got word from one of my informants that Mr. Lamont Jackson has been right here under our noises the entire time we have been looking for him." Cham said climbing into the squad car.

"Whereabouts is he staying?"

"On 83rd and Hoover right when you enter the alley the first apartment building on the right on the first floor, we could get a marked car and do surveillance on him."

"Sounds copasetic let's go ahead and get the Charger right now and see what turns up."

Two hours later Rodriguez, Cham, Vasquez, and Pikes were riding through the 80's hoping they would apprehend Uzi.

"You got to be kidding me their goes that asshole right there smoking a cigarette on the porch." Rodriguez said in disbelief.

"So how do you want to go about apprehending him you know he is probably armed and if we shoot him that's our ass because we are still under investigation so we have to make sure we do this strictly by the book." Vasquez said unbuttoning his button on his holster.

"You're right if we bring him in without incident it will look really good on us all, but I know this asshole is going to try something."

"Not if we corner him off Rodriguez, we will wait across the street and call for back up that way we can catch him when he leaves and corner him in traffic."

"Vasquez you are on the money today let's do it, we can park across the street."

Within thirty minute the C.R.A.S.H unit had three marked cars positioned around the apartment with a helicopter on standby they had wanted to catch Uzi for years with a crime that would stick and now they had their opportunity with DNA evidence at the crime scene linking him to the murder of both men this time he didn't just kill another gang member, but a model recognizable athlete he would definitely go down for this crime.

"The suspect is driving up Hoover approaching Manchester in a Black Chrysler 3000 take extreme caution when approaching the vehicle, he is extremely armed and dangerous." Pikes said to the rest of the unit over the radio while they formed behind Uzi's car. The only way we can do this clean is to side swipe him when he makes the turn at Jack N Box.

On a count of three the officers side swiped Uzi vehicle sending it spinning into the middle of the street facing the opposite side of traffic at the point of impact Uzi assumed that someone had ran into his car sending him into his normal reflex of reaching for his gun, his hand had barely grabbed the handle before he realized that he was surrounded by C.R.A.S.H who had had the car completely surrounded with guns drawn ready to fire if he so much as flinched. Uzi was not stupid he knew it would be asinine to try to shoot it out when he had no way of escape at least in custody he could post bail and prolong whatever charges they were arresting him for.

"Please try something muthafucker, please!" Rodriguez said with sweat streaming down the tip of his nose. He wanted to kill Uzi so bad it was hard to resist the urge to just shoot him in the face.

"Open the door slowly and place both of your hands outside the window, now step out of the vehicle with your hands in the air and walk backwards towards my voice." As Pikes gave Uzi the directions of exiting the vehicle Vasquez along with the other officers at the scene rushed in on a now prone positioned Uzi handcuffing him. Once he was secured and they checked the vehicle for weapons and other people they secured the scene placing Uzi in the back of a squad car while they cleared his vehicle from the middle of traffic which had created a traffic jam that carried all the way up to the 110 freeway.

"Good work fellas we have finally taken into custody one of the leading gang members of this area." Lee said shaking the hands of his fellow officers it was a proud moment for them all it felt like they had really made a difference by taking Uzi off the street, but the reality was that the only ripple effect it was going to have on the community was less murders for that night or the next few days, arresting Uzi the person was no occasion for celebration because the mentality that he possessed was still running rampant through the streets it was a mentality that needed to be arrested and given a life sentence not the person; there were thousands of Uzi's running around all over the place throughout the world various age ranges and colors all bent on doing behavior that they deemed to be correct under their own understanding. Nevertheless, Uzi was in custody and the L.A.P.D would be holding a press conference announcing the capture of him in a few days along with the new District Attorney of Los Angeles Stephanie Merge.

Stephanie Merge was originally from Charlotte North Carolina she had come to California to finish up her law degree. During her last few years of law school she interned at the Downtown court build which was referred to as

CCB by those who worked in the system, shortly after graduation she actively pursued the position public defender with the purpose of learning the mentality of the criminals that she planned to prosecute in the near future as a district attorney. At 40 years old she finally achieved the dream that was hers since a small child locking up bad people. While in the pursuit of her dream she had little time for anything else love, family, and friendships were of little importance to her for she had a driving force in her that did everything possible not to end up like her mother who was killed by her alcoholic father who later hung his self with jumper cables from his car in front of their home that sequence of events lead to her being raised by her grandmother who could barely take care of herself let alone a little girl poverty, ignorance, and lack of education is what she felt created the situations of her family and she would be damned if she ended up that way. No matter how many times her mom called the police to report her father for abuse they would always lock him up for a few days and he would be right back beating her mother again if only the prosecutors would have done their jobs she knew her life growing up would have been better most importantly she would still have her mother.

Chapter 11
Gang Land

2010 ended hastily setting in motion new changes for the new year as the Senate was taken over by the Republicans in what many were calling an embarrassing loss for the Democratic party who had the majority of the house and popularity not too long ago too most it was a sign that Americans were not pleased with how the country was being run under the current administration they wanted the change that President Obama had promised them and anything outside of that was unacceptable the American people had put all their hopes and dreams into this man much like the Hebrews in Egypt did when Moses was leading them to the promised land and much like Moses President Obama was beginning to realize that no matter what one did people were going to be unsatisfied as if they could do better which was unlikely because if they had it in them to do better they would be in the positions that they had such critical opinions about thus was the nature of men to criticize while loathing to be criticized by others always looking to explain away their faults while crucifying the next individual or individuals that they have their sights on. Askari knew that with the shift in parties there would also be new cuts to programs that affected those in lower income communities as well new laws; with his business up and thriving faster than he expected he was elated that he was able to provide jobs to felons and the functioning illiterate the training program that he put into place taught his employees how to conduct themselves in different types of environments by working on reading, writing, and speaking skills the men and women were developing well under his program which made him able to bid on various contracts and secure them because people felt comfortable with his employees who were always professional in their dealings on and off the job. January 11, 2011 Askari was up a little earlier than usual preparing to meet up with his comrade K-Stone for a morning run up the mountains at Kenneth Hahn Park.

"Nice run, that felt really good I was kind of surprise that I went the whole five miles without stopping." K-Stone said taking a seat at a table that set atop the hill they were running up overlooking the city.

"I not surprised you were always a good runner K-Stone."

"It's been a while since I got a chance to hang with your comrade, but it's good to see you are still focused I have been hearing about your company throughout the community you are reaching a lot of people and giving them employment when they would have been off doing who knows what."

"I'm only glad that I can provide the service. Did you catch wind of the new RICO Act?"

"Yes, I read that they were about to start targeting OG's from different sets charging them with crimes that their young homies do."

"So, what's your take on that?"

"I think it's about time that the individuals with say so start to be held responsible for the pollution that they put into these young people's head a lot of the killing and nonsense that is still present in our communities comes from the OG homies not saying enough is enough with the killing one another. I'm tired of not being able to go in certain areas without my strap on me or chill without wondering if I am going to have go all out on another Blackman because he is in fear of his life just because I am Black and he doesn't know what page I am on."

"I coincide with you a hundred percent so let me tell you what your comrade has been putting into play since we last spoke. Throughout my incarceration I met a plethora of gang members and shot callers from various sets throughout California with two significant characteristics, either they were so gone into their gangs that they were nihilistic or they saw the destruction the gang mentality was having on the ones they loved and the communities they were raised in that they wanted it to stop before it ruined another generation. In accordance with the one is that wanted change I formed alliances with them that they would kill their own if they killed another Black person banger or non-affiliate once peace was declared in the streets this year. The days of taking Black life for granted is coming to an end this year. It is time comrade to take that stance and empower or people by getting rid of the nihilistic who want nothing else, but to destroy the little we have left. Unfortunately, there will be more casualties then rescued because the negative mentality has been spreading rampant through the minds of our community for so long that what I have to do could be compared to Chemo Therapy in that I will take lives to save lives."

"I hear where you are coming from, but what are you going to do about people who have family members that don't want to change are they supposed to waste their own blood."

"At this point its ride or die there will not be any straddling the fence all those recruited into my army know what will be asked of them and are willing to execute at a moment's notice for the greater good of our people."

"So where did you find your soldiers Askari?"

"I found them through referrals I received from the individuals I mentioned who were incarcerated with me, they all knew a few of their homies that wanted what we all wanted so through correspondence throughout the years we have been putting this movement into motion."

"So how many did you end up recruiting and how do you know you can trust them?"

"I received the last of the recruits in December putting the total number at 303 strong men and women ages ranging from eighteen to fifty. Each member was made aware that they had to supply information detailing their families whereabouts for the purpose of taking care of them in case of their death more so if they violate the codes of the movement their family members would be subject to death with extreme prejudice in any case we couldn't get a hold of them regarding an act of betrayal."

"I see you have your bases covered; how can I help?"

"Comrade I just need you to keep your ear to the street and scoop up the residue that's left after this cleanup is done. I want you to meet the troops today to see how they are coming along."

As Askari and K-Stone made their way to their vehicles K-Stone knew that he wouldn't be seeing much of his comrade after this meeting Askari was focused ready to go to war with whoever crossed his path there would be no stopping him once he started he would see it out until the end. K-Stone dropped his car off and jumped in the car with Askari not knowing what to expect.

"K-Stone your most important duty in all of this is to provide programs, guidance, and alternatives for the young people who will eventually be free from having to gangbang or worry about getting killed in the streets just because. Where I see most programs go wrong is they provide no out let's for when a person walks away from their old lifestyle in that envelope besides you is a check for two hundred and fifty thousand I want you to put that towards your nonprofit to help fund some learning workshops, job etiquette workshops, and future planning workshops so that we can identify the wants and needs of these individuals. I also want you to hire a few counselors so that your program can counsel these individual to see if they have any issues that need addressing while they work through the programs."

"Good looking out Askari I will be able to fund a lot of programs with this donation once the smoke has cleared. I see you moved way out here to Altadena."

"I found the home at a good deal plus the community is established which means I maintain my privacy."

Walking into the house K-Stone was taking in the décor of the house which was just as beautiful inside as it was outside it looked nothing like a training ground for war, but more so like a paradise in the middle of the city. As they made their way to the back of the house leading towards the back yard K-Stone was taken aback by another structure that set nestled against a huge oak tree it was the size of a single bedroom house from the wood finish he knew it served as a storage unit are garage. Once inside the structure he could hear muffled thumping as if someone were pounding lightly against a wall.

"Tell me what you see inside this garage K-Stone?"

"Tools, equipment, and old newspapers mostly; where did all the newspapers come from?"

"They were here when I bought the place; I thought it gave the garage a fuller more used look. So, your first impression of the garage was just that a garage?"

"Basically, it doesn't seem to be much of a training ground to me there's barely room to do a push up let alone train with all this dust everywhere."

"The reason I brought you out here is because I wanted the training area to pass your approval before I made it complete official. You have always been a very sharp individual K-Stone and I knew if you saw something out of sorts you would have mentioned it immediately the fact that you saw what I desired for you to see lets me know that this training area is copacetic."

K-Stone was still unsure about what Askari was eluding to until he noticed that Askari was tapping his foot against the floor in an obvious code which followed by three opening surfacing around them big enough for two men to fit inside.

"I'll meet you down at the bottom K-Stone." Askari said positioning his self to slide down a fifth teen foot slide which lead to the underground training center.

At the exit of the slide K-Stone found his self on a cushioned mat being helped up by a young Black man wearing all black military attire with a 45 caliber automatic handgun on the right side of his hip from the tattoo on his neck he knew he was from Rollin 60's, the man next to him had ETG tatted underneath his right eye and was helping Askari up off the mat. Once they were up off the mats Askari lead K-Stone down a long hallway towards the sounds that K-Stone was hearing upstairs, the hallway leads to a huge room that was occupied by at least seventy-five people men and women doing a burpee routine simultaneously lead by an individual who was in the front of them. The room also consisted of tread mills, weights, and various exercise apparatuses. By the sweating dripping off the individuals he could tell they had been at the routine for a while.

"They have very good form their also in sync with each other Askari."

"Yes, they are we have three, three-hour classes three times a week that consist of strength training, MMA, and various burpee routines. When they

Escape from Failure

are not doing their physical training, they are working on target practice in the gun range.

"Askari, was this underground lair already apart of the house and you happened to stumble across it?"

"I wish then it would have saved us a ton of work. No comrade we built it from the top down with all the former inmates that I hired into the company there was an immeasurable amount of resources at my fingertips. Most of these brothers who joined had certificates in electrical, plumbing, carpentry, and drywall so there was no hurdle in putting together this underground facility once we had all the material. It took us about a year to complete it working nonstop."

"So how big is it down here?"

"Big enough to hold a kitchen, training area, sleeping corridors, shooting range, weapons room, bath rooms, and a surveillance room that monitors the entire property through hidden cameras we can even monitor what's going on in every major city are video cameras are connected wirelessly."

"Very impressive you have created a military matrix underneath your home in which you will be able to invoke change. It is good to see brothers coming together for a greater good."

"Malcolm X said it best comrade, we don't need to exist the times of sitting around ignoring the plight of our people must stop now the only option is to embrace. There are no sets in this movement only people trying to create a better life for not only their selves, but the future of all people living in systematic poverty."

Askari gave K-Stone an entire tour of the underground facility it was set up like a spider in a sense that it had eight hallways leading to different wards steaming from the body which acted as the entrance to the facility. The kitchen was huge resembling a typical military style kitchen fitted to feed numerous people they kept enough food to sustain five hundred people for ten years if they ever had to go underground. The shooting range was typical with moving targets of all designs mostly human forms. Overall, the facility was airtight the soldiers logged in and out and had their specific duties every day there was always about a hundred soldiers on standby for whatever situation needed their assistance. After the tour Askari took an elevator back to the top with K-Stone.

"Well comrade I have dropped a lot on you visually and I know you need to preserve your energy for your other endeavors you have lined up for the day, I will be in touch with you periodically as we move forward with what we must and will do."

"Definitely, I will have my eyes open for the signs in this gang land."

Chapter 12

Harsh Realities

James had just picked Jaenay up from cheer practices and was taking her to his aunt's house he was still riding on the high of getting an acceptance letter to UCLA in the mail a few days ago once he dropped off his niece he was going to go to the library to research the history of the University on the internet since he didn't have a connection at his home. He was finally going to get a fresh start just like his parents had promised him all his child hood and to think all he had to do was study and keep his grades up to achieve his dream of being a doctor one day. Now he was one step closer to achieving his goal.

***

"We have a possible robbery suspect heading eastbound on Crenshaw in a stolen gray Chevy Caprice; we need all available units to pursue the vehicle."

"Looks like we have a Friday evening chase partner, and their go are suspects right there." Lisa said holding on to the side roof of the police cruiser as her partner simultaneously punched the gas and hit the sirens.

"Jaenay, don't be scared I get pulled over all the time because the police think I'm a gang member because of the car being an older model; this shouldn't take long." James pulled over as instructed by the officers even though he didn't understand why they were pulling him over for no reason besides him being Black as he put the car into park he remembered that he had put his registration in his trunk earlier that day when he was cleaning his car without much thought he opened his car door to retrieve his registration out the trunk.

"He's got a gu……n! Cham yelled firing seven rounds from his Glock 40 into James upper chest while Lisa fired into the vehicle immediately after seeing movement from Jaenay who was trying to get to the bottom of the car once she heard the gun shots, but it was too late Lisa 9mm rounds had found he head and neck killing her instantly when the gunfire stopped thirty shell casings lay on the ground and two Black youth dead.

"Shots fired suspects are down officers are approaching vehicle." Cham said into his walkie-talkie hanging from his shoulder. Oh, fuck he had keys in his hand, not a gun... check the other suspect.

"Cham, it's a little girl what was she doing in the car with this gang member?" Lisa asked checking the vehicle for any other passengers. All clear on this end Lee we are going to catch serious back lash for this.

"It was an accident we'll be alright they'll just put us on leave for a few weeks until it all blows over then we'll be right back patrolling just look at it as a paid vacation."

Waters had been prepped on the situation before he arrived at the crime scene, he knew it was serious by the fleet of news media flocking his vehicle making it hard for him to get out.

"Word is you can't keep your officers from murdering civilians in the street." One of the reporters shouted towards him as he approached the dead bodies. Of course, he did not respond he just made a b-line towards the two officers involved in the shooting.

"Lee, Clarks, are you two alright?"

"Yes." Both officers answered simultaneously.

"So, you got a call of a possible stolen vehicle that matched the description of the two suspects and a chase pursued that lead to both suspects being killed in short."

"Yes, we hit the sirens for the suspects to pull over the male suspects exited the vehicle with an object in his hand that I perceived to be a gun in which I opened fire officer Lindsey saw movement from the second suspect and opened fire as well." Cham said irritated by all the commotion being generated by the incident.

"Okay, let me talk to the detectives to see what directions this is pointing to."

While approaching the bodies Waters noticed that one of the yellow cones that marked the bullets was numbered twenty-five which let him know that too many shots were fired which meant a media storm was to follow.

Escape from Failure

"Detectives what do we have?"

"Sergeant the male suspect was James Taylor an honor student at Crenshaw High school has no criminal record or any gang affiliations. The female suspect was his niece Jaenay Brown she is ten years old, there weren't any weapons found and it appears that he exited the vehicle to retrieve his registration out the trunk since that is where we found it; the object in his hands were his car keys we'll be finished with the crime scene in a few Sergeant Waters."

"Thank you, detective." Damn Waters thought to his self his officers had shot too many bullets on this one, but he wasn't worried he had seen countless situations like this one before he knew the words to use to make the shooting seem justified.

***

"This is Leo Stallworth with the Channel Seven news reporting on shootings that took place in Los Angeles earlier this month that left two Young people dead at the hands of L.A.P.D officers earlier this afternoon. The victims were eighteen-year-old James Taylor a stand out student at Crenshaw High and his ten-year-old niece Jaenay Brown; from our reports James was picking his niece up from Cheer practice when he was pulled over by officers in which he and his niece were shot and later pronounced dead at the scene. Official are saying that it was an accident and that James vehicle had fit the description of a vehicle that had been involved in a robbery earlier that day. We will be talking with the parents of the victims on the ten o'clock news."

A press conference was held a few days after the shooting with the new D.A. and the Chief of the L.A.P.D. the Black community was outraged once again about another Black life being shot down in the streets with little regard. The officers involved in the shooting were there as well trying to keep looks of despair as much as possible as if they were in deep anguish behind the parent's loss.

"Ladies and gentlemen, we meet here under dire circumstance that can't be changed, but through your assistance can possibly be avoided soon. From what I hear the two victims were incredible young people making it more difficult for their sudden loss. The officers involved are extremely remorseful about what happen even though the shooting was deemed justified."

The crowd filled with family and prevention groups gasped as they took in the Chief's words that flowed so emotional less as he mentioned the killing.

"My officers are under extreme pressure every day to perform in highly stressful situations unfortunately they shot the wrong individuals this time we as a department are also in mourning with the parents of these kids; I will now take questions."

"So, you are telling us that the shooting was justified, and the officers are going back to duty." James dad asked through tear-soaked eyes.

"James had an item in his hand that Officer Lee could not distinguish right off, plus James exited the vehicle without being commanded which put my officer's lives in danger. Truthfully if your son did not exit the vehicle without permission, we wouldn't be holding this press conference."

"My name is Ruben and I'm with A.P.U.U. and it sounds like you are saying that this deceased young man death is his fault."

"No one is at fault in an accident our officers will receive even more extensive training to prevent situations like this in the future with the help of people in the community we can stop this from turning into another violent situation my doors are always open to any concerns you may have."

"Listen Chief, we've heard this song and dance before when Devin Brown was killed, you remember that thirteen-year-old child don't you or have there been so many deaths at the hands of your officers that you have forgotten? What happened to the extensive training from that murder that didn't prevent this murder from happening?"

"May I ask your name?"

"My name is Michelle a member of A.P.U.U. as well as a concerned parent."

"Your concern is warranted of course, and to answer your question yes there has been training put into action regarding the death of Devin Brown, but each officer's response to that training is different when confronted with a real situation in the field were the officer must protect not only their lives, but those of their partners."

"It's interesting that you didn't mention the protection of the residents within the community at all just your officers and their Chief Williams lies the problem that we are trying to convey to you and your officers tonight; we are people just like you and the people you go home to at night yet your department continues to gun us down in the street with little regard or penalties for the actions of the officers which sends a message not only to your officers, but us that inner city life is worth nothing. Then you waltz in here with TV camera and a panel of officers like we are supposed to be appeased by you coming to talk to us for an hour which sadly some of us are, but a lot of us are not fooled by the appeasement meetings to ensure that another riot doesn't take place and effect your standing abroad."

"Unfortunately, I have to attend another meeting, but I feel that we have discussed some solid issue that my officers and I will express to the entire department so we can implement a plan that will make a better Los Angeles for us all. Thank you for coming out to express your concerns."

Chief Williams was use to the mundane of these types of public meeting as well as the well-spoken community activist that had too much to say they were the most dangerous because they got people to thinking and asking questions which was always a nuisance. Now that the meeting was over he could head back to his offices to go over a contract that he had been offered a few days ago to work for a security firm he was strongly considering going for it which meant he wouldn't have to deal with cleaning up Los Angeles a task that was becoming impossible to do when there was some type of controversy every other month.

"So, what did you learn from the public sit-down sergeant Waters?" Williams asked cracking the passenger window of the Crown Victoria to smoke a cigar.

"Not a damn thing, I'm tired of having to come down to churches, school gyms, and crime scenes to have to talk about prevention that should start at home there's never any responsibility placed on the parents its always he was a good kid spiel coming out of their mouths when they get killed. The truth of the matter is if James were not driving a known gangbanger vehicle, we would have not been having that meeting tonight. Honestly, they should be glad it was us and not some gang members that killed him purposely, motherfucker jumps out a vehicle without being ordered and wonders why he got shot. If these people spent more time being parents, then organizing meetings we would all be better off. So, to answer your question I thought it was bullshit like all the rest they have had and are going to have when we must kill another dumb motherfucker for doing criminal activity. Seriously these people dress the part of gangster then complain when we jam them up or they get approached by gangbangers who react to their dress which leads to them getting killed one way or other personal choices put them in dire situations."

"So, I see we came away with similar thoughts; so, I assume that you are wondering what this new group A.P.U.U. is all about?"

"Not really because I already know who they are. There a group that's assimilated of one member from each Hoover set that prides itself on being advocates for peace and urban unity thus where their acronym comes from, they've been focusing on providing tutoring and safe passage for children going to and from school once a year they through a community event at Manchester park where they give away free school supplies, medical screening, and toys. Deputy chief Clifford's has been working close with them to develop some new program where they will start to prep kids in the community to join law enforcement."

"Why is that I'm just hearing about all of this now and why is Clifford always working so close in the community like he is still part of it doesn't he realize that he is an officer now?"

"I imagine so, but you know that he is a Black man who grew up in the same community so he feels he is obligated to help out as much as he can. It's no big deal in a lot of ways it makes it better for us because we can use him to calm certain situations down before we go into them."

"Are thoughts coincide in one area and that is we can continue to use Clifford as our liaison, but I must admit if he could be trusted to do his duty when put in a touchy situation. Think about it he is one of us who to say he doesn't turn coat on us if something arises more so when I leave, he will be chief; could you really imagine a community sympathizer being chief?"

"We'll cross that bridge when it comes for now, I have my guys watching."

"So, what was your perspective on the meeting K-Stone?"

"If you want to pacify the Black community wear a suit and talk it pacifies all the time. If you didn't call me I wouldn't have even came down here I know the routine I've heard it for years offer fake promises and smiles no remorse for the victims just lies and we'll be more careful, but I can't be mad at them.

"Why is that they need to stop killing our babies."

"Until we start to take Black life serious how can we expect for them to. These police and politicians don't respect us they just tolerate us that's all and tell us just enough to make us feel like we are important for the moment."

"That's real, but you can't get bitter K-Stone let their behavior continue to fuel you we have to save the ones that want to be saved that's all."

"True that, well I'm about to head to the house my head is hurting from listening to all this non-sense it's a harsh reality, but it really is upon us as a people to change the conditions we live in and no one else."

Chapter 13
Unacceptable

There were five snipers positioned with M-68 Sniper rifles equipped with suppressor spread around the pool hall with one target in mind Cham Lee. The five snipers were specifically chosen for the mission because they were the type out of their classes that varied in different weaponry the success of the movement from this point laid on their shoulders so they were fully aware that the assassination had to set the standard for what was to come in the future. Sniper one and two were positioned 2,000 yards out on two separate buildings that set adjacent to each other. Sniper three and four were positioned about 1,000 yards away nestled in debris that had been discard for years in the area. The fifth sniper was 500 yards away from the target and acted as a backup in case any of the other snipers rifles didn't discharge; he was positioned in a dumpster that set counter corner to the target allowing him to discharge rapid fire into the target if need be.

Cham Lee had been in Mr. Lucky's Middle ground the majority of the night relaxing shooting pool with the regulars as he normally did on a Tuesday night, he was in his last game before he was set to head out all he needed to do was sink the eight ball in the corner pocket.

"Good shot Lee, I'll get you next week. What are we now anyway?" Henry asked racking up the balls.

"Eight and twelve from my recollection, you eight loses and me twelve w's."

"Sounds a little lop sided, but we'll settle the score next Tuesday."

"Tuesday it'll be then Henry."

The night time air was cold and bitter much like most Tuesday nights in February, but it didn't bother Lee much cold weather hardly did he had gotten used to it the few times he had to sleep outside because his pride wouldn't allow him to just go home when he had chosen to stay out all night violating the curfew his parents had set for him. Damn, he thought to his self as he noticed that his Black Charger was leaning towards the street on his front driver side.

"Pick up the phone... Rodriguez, are you busy?"

"No, just laying here with a naked woman I met tonight."

"Look, on the way over to Middle ground my acceleration on my car was slipping so I thought maybe my battery needed charging, but when I was leaving I came out to find my front left tire on flat, now I have to sit out here and wait for AAA to come which want be here for an hour."

"So, if you called triple A why are you calling me?"

"To see if you want to shoot a couple of games to pass the time, I'm tired of beating Henry."

"I'll be there in thirty minutes, make sure you check to see if your car starts just in case it's more than the tire because a deflating tire shouldn't have that much effect on the acceleration of your car.

"Good point, check you when you get here."

The first two shots from sniper one and two found their targets which were Lee's elbow joints nearly tearing his arms off which served the purpose of immobilizing him from reaching for his service pistol which he kept on him; sniper three and four bullets found his knee caps less than a second later shattering both knee caps instantly preventing Lee from running for help sniper five waited a few seconds as Lee used his shoulders to crawl forward around to the front of the car before he could fully make it sniper five sent a bullet through his neck with the intention not instantly killing him because he wanted him to bleed out on the streets slowly with nothing on his mind besides who had done this to him. Askari had been keeping tabs on Cham and Lisa ever since the shooting watching and studying their behaviors and routines down to the people they had as friends he knew everything about them he needed to know in order to assassinate them correctly. Every Tuesday from 5 p.m. until 10 p.m. Cham would frequent Middle ground faithfully and for good reason if he left slightly intoxicated he wouldn't have to worry about traffic because from Middle ground to his house all traffic in the area came to a standstill for some reason in the area Askari attributed it to fact that there was nothing on the street that anyone needed at that time of night. It took about three long minutes for Lee to die from his wounds.

When Rodriguez arrived at Middle ground he was curious to see the damage done to his partner's vehicle before he made it half way around the vehicle his attention was pulled astray by a substance that appeared to be blood going towards the sewage drain past his feet coming from the direction of a body that resembled Lee's form after moving in closer he confirmed that it was his partners body triggering him to instantly grab for his service pistol securing the area before calling for help from the amount of blood on the streets he didn't bother checking to see if Lee was alive years on the force told him that when there is that much blood loss the victim was dead.

"We have a plain clothes officer down immediate unit are needed on the scene for what it appears to be a homicide."

Middle ground was completely sectioned off as well as the entire block of Hawthorne Boulevard by cops from L.A.P.D. and Torrance Police department since the killing took place in their backyard they would be controlling the case, but do to the nature of the crime they were more than willing for a joint investigation with the L.A.P.D. to figure who had killed one of theirs. Investigators were stumped when they first arrived on the scene because there was no shell casing at all just Lee's contorted body against his car.

"So, did you hear any shots, screams, or car accelerating at high speeds Henry?"

"No detective Cham had left as he usually did; I didn't hear any type of shots or anything out of the ordinary."

"Lee was shot multiple times by what appears to be a high caliber weapon and no one in here heard a sound on an empty sound less night?"

"Detective if we heard anything, we would be more than willing to fork over that information if it would help in the apprehension of whoever did this to our friend."

"Thank you if we have any other questions, we will contact you, until then we need you to maintain inside the billiards while we continue inspecting our crime scene."

"So, did they give you any reliable Intel?"

"No, unless you can solve a case with, we heard absolutely nothing when he left from our establishment Rodriguez. So how long after you talked to him do you think this happened?"

"Had to be immediately, because it didn't take me long to get down here from my house."

"Detectives we have found some slugs ingrained in the asphalt." An Officer said moving Lee's body out of its original position."

"From the damage of the slug it appears that we are looking for a sniper because a bullet with that type of damage is usually fired from a distance."

"So, you are saying that this was possibly a hit of some kind?"

"Rodriguez, you know I never speculate I'll have some cement answers for you in a couple of days after we have sifted through the evidence."

After two hours of investigation Lee's body was finally taken away to the morgue for further investigation which would come out during the autopsy. The dilemma the officers had at the scene was determining rather this was an isolated incident or was there someone out killing cops they shuddered slightly at the second thought there had been a few situations in the past few years where individuals pacifically targeted cops, but the individuals was always caught or killed mostly the latter; what made this situation different from the others was that there were no leads or physical evidence from the killer and that didn't sit well with the officers because it seemed professional.

Set afar on a roof top was Askari watching the entire investigation on an iPad touch which was linked to mini cameras that surrounded the crime scene from the officer's behavior he knew they were perplexed by what exactly happened to Lee which left them oblivious to what was going to happened next their ignorance was the sign that Askari was looking for before he put the second part of his plan into action. Tracking Lisa Fain had proved slightly more difficult for Askari then Lee because she rarely went out in the day time except to the gym by her home which made her always in the sight of others which would involve other in the hit something he didn't want; the only other place she went routinely was to Peanuts in Hollywood on Tuesday for lesbian night so it only made sense for Toy box to be assigned to establishing more Intel on Lisa and if possible kill her.

Peanuts was in full swing by the time Toy Box arrived at the club's peak hour which allowed her to slide into the club and blend with the crowd of straight and lesbian women that were either intoxicated or high off of ecstasy. Spotting Lisa wasn't difficult she looked the part of an officer with her short burnt coal colored spiked hair she still had her stocky build from the academy training received years ago which often made her look like a man from the back. Her eyes instantly caught sight of Toy box's sensual shape passing by in her black leather pants attire that had caught an eyebrow raise from half the club. Lisa liked Black women especially those with large breast and butts she could grab and squeeze onto during sexual positions. Toy box saw Lisa checking her out through the corners of her eyes and knew that lust had taken over all other sense which would make her objective easy.

"Cop is military?" Toy box asked looking over her shoulder from the bar edge.

"Cop, is there a problem?"

"No, just wanted to see if my assumptions were correct."

"Assumptions can get you into trouble."

"Only if the assumption is wrong and the costs are high."

"Even then uncertain inquiries can be detrimental; by the way, my name is Lisa."

"Nice to meet you my name is Toy."

"It fits you. You seem like someone that is fun to play with."

"There you go assuming."

"Well you could prove me wrong Toy."

Escape from Failure

After a few more sexual innuendos Toy Box was on her way to Lisa's place in Carson. Lisa lived in a town house that had surveillance cameras so Toy Box knew that she could not go up to her place without being seen by the cameras then it occurred to her that they could go somewhere else. Before Lisa could get out of her vehicle Toy Box was at her car door slightly shivering from the early morning air.

"Let's go to the park before we go up to play."

"Don't you think it's rather late for all of that?"

"Not if I'm suggesting it. Don't be afraid to try new things with new people."

"Alright there's a park not too far from here let's go there."

"I'll follow behind you."

Toy Box was ready to kill Lisa in her car as they spoke, but she didn't want to run the risk of her driving off once she was shot besides she knew the park would be wide up to do her mission. When arrived at the park Toy Box had made a quick run over of the park for any stranglers she knew there wouldn't be any because she had cased all the parks in the area previously, but she knew conditions could always change. The park was clear, and Lisa was out of her car walking towards Toy Box.

"When is the last time you were pushed on some swings?" Toy Box asked as they neared the apparatus bars.

"Ten or eleven years old it's been quite a while are you volunteering?"

"Yes. Why not, everyone should be entitled to fun in their life."

Toy Box was working up a mild sweat that caused goose bumped to spread across her entire body as she pushed Lisa on the swing. Toy Box had pushed Lisa approximately nine times before she pulled out her 40 Glock while going into her firing stance taking direct aim at Lisa's head as she swung back on the swing towards her. Just as Toy Box was pulling back the trigger Lisa was turning her head towards her to ask her to push her harder the shots came in three sets of three rapid fire shots the first volley struck Lisa right below her left ear drum exiting through her bottom lip knocking her entire row of lower teeth out the force of the bullets along with graviton from the swing coming down caused her to dangle and dragged through the dirt before she was spun loose, once on the ground Lisa attempted to run, but was cut down by the second volley that tore through her right thigh instantly grounding her. By this time Lisa was going into shock as the cold air mixed with blood loss was taking effect causing her to shake violently as Toy Box stood over her with the pistol's silencer hovering over her head as Lisa gave a look of why while holding on to the last bits of her life before the flash entered her right eye ending her life.

Phillip had just finished his Colt 45 for breakfast before heading to the park to collect cans this had been his routine for years a beer before work and a beer after work he enjoyed getting out before the sun had risen and the children were standing on the corners waiting on the school bus besides they were often disrespectful to him when he walked by them to pick up a can or plastic bottle off the ground. The morning dew was still sliding the blades of grass as Phillip made his way up the park's mini mesa towards the garbage cans that were always filled with Gatorade bottles from the basketball players at night. Before he loads his bags with the nights treasures he was petrified by the dead body of a white woman that laid only feet away from him it was the first time that he had seen a dead body and it had frightened him to the core of his soul it was one thing to see dead bodies on television, but in real life was another beast all together to totality of it all frightened him most. Upon leaving the park he told the gas station attendant what he found at the park and the attendant put a call in to the sheriff department.

Chapter 14

No Lesson

"Recently, the Los Angeles Police Commission made a radical change in policy, now with holding the names of officers involved in shootings, as well as incidents in which cops use fists, flashlights, batons or other objects to subdue suspects. By most accounts, these changes stem from the still unsolved murders of Officers Cham Lee and Lisa Fain who murdered a month ago. Most residents are in an uproar because they feel this policy is a severe threat to police accountability in an environment where the police are a major threat to the citizens who pay cops salaries through taxes. This is Leo Stallworth with Channel 7 news at four we will keep you up to date as more information comes in regarding this story."

A month had went by with no leads on the murders of the L.A.P.D Officers all that the police had were hunches about what had happened to their comrades the majority of the officers believed that it was retaliation for the deaths of the Black teenagers that had been killed when pulled over by the officers the only clause in that theory was that the killings had been done by a professional not some street punk with a grudge to settle as far as their leads went there was no group in Los Angeles that was capable of doing such an act. Since the murders the police had been on high alert with a sense of vengeance in their hearts to avenge the deaths of their fallen which they did in small incremental ways that only the impoverished could feel which only set into motion another act to have to take place against them by Askari's group until they got the picture that they would indeed have to protect and serve the communities they patrolled not violate it.

"As we stand here today, I am proud of the accomplishments that we have all accomplished academically, financially, and strategically as a group. Academically you have all completed your associate degrees and are moving forward to complete your bachelor's degrees in your chosen fields. Financially you all have invested your earnings through the company thus providing for your selves and families more so your incredible hard professional work at Clean Corp has gotten us numerous contracts with companies that would have normally denied a minority business access our company growth is amazing and will continually grow thus creating even more career opportunity for the disadvantaged. Lastly, I read an article a few days ago concerning leadership were it defined good leadership as an infusion of vision, direction, and purpose into a campaign that mobilizes both people and resources to undertake and achieve objectives; after reading the article I truly felt in my heart that the words epitomized us as a whole we are truly the vanguard for the change that must take place in our community. Fortunately, we have yet to experience any setbacks in our movement, but they are bound to happen there is little we can do about that fact, but our response is under our control. Well as you all have read in our agenda this morning we have some rogue officers who have taken it upon themselves to exact revenge on the community for the deaths of two officers this of course is unacceptable and must be dealt with; three different teams have been assigned that will be led by Chi, Bid, and Jelani most of our training has been military, but the next objectives will be more geared towards guerilla style warfare reason being we need to know how to counter military advancement in case they employ military forces which they have done in the past for less resistance. If you were given a red card meet up with Chi, if you received a blue card meet up with Bid, and if you received an orange card meet up with Jelani; it is imperative that the missions go well and that all the members are proficient in using their environment to launch attacks as need on those we pose as threats meeting adjourned."

 After the meeting Askari made his way to the front of the house towards his car he had a newspaper interview with an old friend that wanted to do a story on his company at twelve p.m. in downtown L.A. at C.P.K. February still sheltered the cold air of December yet it was hard to tell how cold it actually was by just looking at the sky from behind a car window which gave the appearance of summer although the shivering people on the streets going to work in the tall downtown buildings told the true story of the weather with their shivering bodies and big coats normally downtown L.A. was congested, but today traffic foot and cars was light he attributed it to the weather keeping people in doors weather conditions often played a significant part to the plans people made it didn't matter much to him how the weather was he was comfortable in all types. He always made it a point to go to yard when he was incarcerated no matter the temperature or condition for the purpose of adapting in all conditions he felt it was important not to have weakness that could be overcome. The aroma of the pizza being cooked tantalized his nostrils as he stood still riding up the escalator to the restaurant he rarely ate out anymore so it was definitely out of the ordinary for him to come out of his strict diet of lean proteins and vegetables. He took notice of Carole sitting a few tables away from the entrance looking over a menu as he entered the restaurant he also took notice of the slight rhythm change in his heart as he got closer to the table she was occupying and before he could say a word she looked up from her menu to see him looking over her.

"Askari...what are you doing here?"

"I have an interview with this very talented journalist at twelve."

"Well, that's quite odd because I am doing an interview with a gentleman as well in this same place."

"May I ask who this gentleman is you are supposed to interview?"

"Sure, his name is Mr. Franks and he owns a company called Clean Corp."

"Askari is what my friends know me by, and Franks is what my business associates address me as."

"So, you are the man behind this phenomenal business that helps inmates after they get out of prison get jobs?"

"Yes, it was the reason I was flying out to Cape Town when we met to get supplies."

"It's all coming back to me as we speak, I'm surprised that I didn't put the puzzle together maybe because we never spoke after the trip."

"That is entirely all my fault to perfectly honest I was so determined to make my business work because so many lives depended on it that I completely forgot about myself."

"I understand for I am guilty of the same I could have picked up the phone or texted you."

"Enough of the explanations we are in each other's presences now so let's be in the moment what's new in your life?"

"New, let's see I've been back in the states about a month now I just came back from Jamaica doing a story on the drug lords out there who have ties to the U.S. it was very interesting working out there I had been on vacation before years ago to Montego Bay the individuals that I interview stayed in Kingston which a lot more lively to me than the other parts of Jamaica I'm assuming because it is the Capital I can't lie I am glad to be back in the states I have been doing nonstop traveling for the last two years."

"So, when is the next time you are leaving the states?"

"Probably a year I'm going to work out of my home for the next year and do local jobs so that I can refresh my skills a bit it's too easy to get burnt out."

"Good news that means I can see you again sooner than later."

"True, now that you are not so busy anymore."

"Still busy, but now I'll be busy making sure we spend some time together."

"All that attention for little ol' me now I feel all special."

"You should you're a special person who shouldn't be treated any less."

"Thank you Askari, you sure know how to make a woman feel appreciated."

"Every woman should be appreciated by the man in their life a man's sole purpose in a relationship should be to build his woman up not tear her down."

"Amen to that fortunately the men I have ran into have subscribed to that doctrine to the tenth degree believing in having more than one woman to appreciate."

"Huh, I believe in building a family not a stable I leave that to pimps and brothers that don't want to grow up."

"Seriously, I've gotten so caught up with us talking that I almost forgot I need to interview you."

"I'm ready when you are."

"Are you aware of James Butts?"

"If I'm not mistaken, he uses to be police chief of Santa Monica."

"Correct, but now he is mayor of Inglewood a position that he failed to get twice; the reason I asked if you are familiar with him is because some say the only reason he won the race is because he ousted his running mate Daniel Tabor for hiring a felon something your company proudly stands behind. What is your opinion on this matter?"

"Personally, I am saddened by the fact that voters would vote a candidate to reside over their city that stands against giving a human being a second chance that has paid their debt to society in the form of incarceration. I mean really what type of message this guy is trying to send."

"My exact sentiments; I feel everyone is entitled to a second chance if they have reconciled their error. When I hear about situations like this it makes me scratch my head because I wonder what they want these people with records to do once they are release and have to put yes I was a felon and then explain what they did."

"To a certain degree I understand the psychology behind employers asking about what type of crime an applicant has committed because it is important to know if a person is applying for a job at a school where kids will be and they are a sex offender or even a bank job and they have multiple charges of theft on their record these type of offense are definitely red flags to an employer to be cautious of. I've just had an epiphany; what employers should do is ask if a person has a particular felony that would conflict with the position they are applying for example if an individual is applying for any position entailing contact with children there should be a box asking are you a sex offender etc. Let us say a person is applying for a bank there should be a box asking to have you ever been convicted of robbery, theft, or identity theft and if so, how many times? When an employer is asking straight forward question that pertain to effective job performance, I can sympathize with them."

"So, let me get this straight Askari, if a person was convicted for robbery they shouldn't apply for a job at the bank?"

"I'm not saying they shouldn't apply, but they need to be realistic with themselves about if that would be a wise decision working around money better yet would they hire someone if the shoe was on the other foot. It all boils down to be honest with one's self on the direction they are trying to take their lives then they can map it out accordingly instead of making irrational decisions like applying for a job that you know will conflict with your past. My grandmother uses to tell me as a child that God forgives your sins, but that doesn't stop you from having to pay the consequence for the sins."

"Interesting so how do you motivate the individuals in your company to strive for betterment when the majority of them do have criminal backgrounds?"

"I start by getting them to acknowledge that they have made mistakes in their past most out of ignorance that they will have to be accountable for weather it was their fault or not; once they understand that they most build their lives from the now instead of trying to reconstruct some warped illusion of a distant memory to build on, we, me and them, can start to better their situation by implementing tangible goals that they are capable of reaching from their current mental launching ground."

"Do you ever get individual that you cannot help or don't want to acknowledge that they do need help."

"Yes, we do, but it is rare most individuals that come to our program already have some understanding that they lack understanding of how the world actually works because their blue print was warped from the beginning which put them in need of our program. You always have a know it all that comes through the program, but they don't last long because our program is extremely strict and disciplined to producing success that there is no room for anything else."

"This is a little off the subject, but I also read that you are partnered with a non-profit A.P.U.U. which provides after school programs for youth in the community as well as safe passage for youth going to schools in gang neighbor hoods; so the question I want to know is why did you pick this non-profit to work with out of all the others?"

"That's a rather easy question, I have a friend named Kevin Pink who works for the organization and once I was made aware of the work that he was doing in the community through the group it only made sense to help out financially to fuel his efforts through the group furthermore a lot of or employees have children, nieces, and nephew that benefit from the services that the program provides."

"Last question what is the vision of Clean Corp?"

"Our Primary objective is to create a rebirth of hope, community, education, and greatness that has been dormant for far too long in urban communities across the world; through enlightenment, understanding, and solid solutions that have proven success."

"Impressive, I have no doubt you will accomplish your goal by the strides you are already making. Thanks a lot for a great interview Askari you gave me a lot to write about as well as valuable insight to what Clean Corp is about."

"The real thanks should being going to you for doing your research on my company hopefully your article will get our message to even more people who either want to help or need the help themselves from our services. So, what is your next story going to be about?"

"Glad you asked I have an interview with Deputy Chief Clifford of the 77th St division about the recent deaths of the two officers who were killed a month ago in separate incidents and how the Black community is feeling the strain of overly aggressive officers with something to prove."

"Sounds intriguing I can't wait to read the article. What information have you gathered so far?"

"Not much the L.A.P.D. has been extremely shrouded when it comes to the recent murders because they have no clue to who actually did the killings."

"So why are you talking with Clifford?"

"He is one of the few that officers I feel actually cares about the Black community because he is naturally concerned; I feel if I interview him I can let the community know that there is someone on their side that wears a uniform."

"Sounds concrete I think people will appreciate that in the community because it only takes one officers to spoil the reputation for the good ones, unfortunately there was no lesson learned from the deaths of the two officers last month by the L.A.P.D. to help them build better communication with the locals."

"The death of those officers did more harm than good for the community it made them more trigger happy than before."

"Yes, I agree, but how did we allow ourselves to drift to such a negative topic."

"It's hard to stay positive when discussing those types of issues."

"I remember you telling me that you lived in the area when we were on the plane; I just purchased a Barker's Loft a few weeks back you should come by so that I can fix you dinner."

"Just tell me the date and time."

"Next Thursday 7pm."

"Great."

Chapter 15

Lesson learned

Death of a relative, friend, or co-worker caused different emotions to stir in certain individuals depending on how close one was to the person and especially how they passed away. Certain people like Hector Rodriguez became bitter and spiteful wanting revenge for the loss of a loved one while others like Luis Vasquez got a new appreciation of life from a sudden death. The investigation into the deaths of Lee and Fain had come to a standstill the only evidence investigators were able to gather from the scene were bullets from the scenes of the two murders which gave them no tangible direction to go into except hand the case over to the F.B.I. for further assistance in hopes they got some shred of a lead to solving the cases.

"So how does it feel to be back on the clock V?"

"Good I missed the patrol, but it gave me a chance to spend time with Maria and Anna."

"That's always a good thing me and my wife just found out that we are expecting."

"Boy or a girl?"

"Too soon to know, but it doesn't matter to me I just want a healthy child."

"So, who's warring on the streets this week?"

"The DLB's and the Hoovers have been at each other lately their youngsters have been doing a lot of wall banging."

"Up and down Figueroa as usual, these assholes just need to kill themselves and get it over with."

"I agree me, and a few brothers have been helping them along in that aspect."

"Yeah, Rodriguez mentioned it to me you think we'll get some action tonight."

"Lucky for you you're out on the day these assholes hang out the most. We did a raid a week ago on the Main Street Crips and came across a nice arsenal check underneath the arm rest."

When V lifted the armrest, he found a black handkerchief covering some type mini submachine gun with a laser pointer attached to the top.

"It's a PM-84P the bastards had three of them I turned in two and kept this one."

"Lethal, how is the recoil?"

"There is none, it just goes, but it sounds nasty when it does. I've laid one DL down with it so far let us see if we can catch a Hoover slipping tonight."

"We have an apparent Burning vehicle on the corner of 85th and Hoover will all available officers please respond paramedics are also on their way." The police radio blared interrupting the officer's plans.

"What the hell do think that is about V?"

"Let us go find out, it probably is just some drunk who got into an accident. Those assholes over there are always driving drunk."

When the officers arrived at the scene of the car crash they found an upside down Dodge Charger with smoke coming out of the engine with two silhouettes that appeared to be human in the driver and passenger seats which prompted them to get out of their patrol car to see if they needed to pull out any victims. Their departure from the patrol car helped to confirm their identity to Toy Box who was on a roof top across the street with binoculars; she quickly gave the signal to her comrades across the street that the officers were there intended targets. They had been telling Vasquez's partner for months and knew that his partner was involved in the death of a Denver Lane member a few weeks ago.

"What the hell is this, these aren't real bodies V their manikins." This could not be Vasquez partner thought to his self as he reached for his service pistol realizing that they had been set up. Vasquez, I think this is a……….

Escape from Failure

Rapid gun fire rang out from Akachi's AKS74 tearing through the vest of Vasquez's partner dropping him to the ground, but not before his arm beat him there which was instantly torn off by the rate of fire that came from the assault rifle. By this time Vasquez was behind the door of his patrol car firing shots at the gunman who were taking positions behind the Charger while tearing the patrol car to pieces within seconds Vasquez was out of bullets and behind the back of the patrol car thinking of what his next move should be while his partner laying bleeding to death in the street.

"I am Akachi, the hand of God your sins have brought you death." Those were the last words the officer heard before Akachi held the trigger tightly while the nozzle was over the officer's face.

Vasquez could hear the boots from the gunman moving around once the firing had stopped he thought that they had probably assumed him dead and left, but he knew he was wrong when the butt of the rifle hit him across his face knocking him unconscious. All that was left at the scene when the other officers had arrived at the scene were two deserted cars, a dead officer, and unanswered question.

"Okay tape this entire block down there will be no traffic coming down any of these streets for the next few hours we will find out who is responsible for the death of our brother!" Sergeant Waters said through gritting teeth.

"Sergeant, Vasquez was patrolling with Vasquez today, but there is no sign of him here."

"Immediately put out a missing alert for officer Vasquez, I don't believe this shit we have an officer dead and one missing and no one heard a thing around here this is the third officer we have loss in less than two months all from our division it is becoming apparent that something is going on dam it!"

The officers at the scene did the typical investigation of the scene, but it was extremely difficult for them to stay professional when they were dusting for prints, but couldn't find any or the fact that they knew assault rifles were used, but the only shell casings that could be found came from Vasquez's weapon which they knew didn't eat up a patrol vehicle that way.

"Lee, Fain, and now Phillips we just took the black tape off of our badges now it is going back on it's starting to become a part of our uniform."

"I definitely feel where you are coming from Rodriguez, but instead of focusing on the departed let's focus on finding Vasquez."

"It's hard to focus Pikes when I keep wondering who is behind the deaths of not only Lee, but now Phillips. This is the second crime scene where there are no shell casings, no witnesses, and no suspects; even the F.B.I is stumped."

"I agree it is frustrating, but you have to remember that we are the law and must stand up for what is right even when it is extremely difficult; we cannot allow ourselves to be of criminal mind Rodriguez."

"You tell that Boy Scout shit to Lupe when she has to explain to Maria and Anna that their father is missing and probably dead."

"Hopefully, I want have to if we start to look for him instead of sitting around here upset with each other over a situation that we have no control over."

"Obviously, we have someone targeting officers from the looks of the crime scene someone set a dummy car up to bring a unit out in which they ambushed killing Phillips and kidnapping Vasquez or top priority is to find out who did this crime and get them off the street. I want you to shake down every informant that you know to find some inkling to what the hell happened out here every dope spot, hangout, and after hour needs to be tossed up around the city to find this cop killer and most importantly find Vasquez. We will be working in conjunction with the sheriff department on this case so hit the streets hard and find those responsible."

When Vasquez gained consciousness, he realized that a black sack was covering his head preventing him from knowing where he was; when he tried to move his arms he was unable as well because they were handcuffed behind his back. He was about to scream for help, but then rejected that thought he didn't want to feed into his captures authority by showing the fear that spread through his body he knew if they removed the masked and showed their faces that they would definitely kill him so his heart sank when the mask was removed revealing a familiar face from his past standing before him.

"Franks.......?" In an instant it all made sense to Vasquez why Lee had been killed and he was kidnapped instead of killed during the ambush.

"I was a different man back then I have children now and a wife."

"I know. Opportunities that you had stolen from me years ago by placing evidence on me, you of course remember that. So, my question to you is if you were such a changed man why didn't you right your wrongs years ago when you had the opportunity?"

"If I did that then they would have taken my career from me and possibly sent me to prison."

"Of course, they would have, but you wouldn't be sitting here right now tied to a chair."

"I have money; I can pay you. You don't have to do this Franks."

"Yes, I do have to do this and no I don't need your money your family will find more use for it after your death then I will."

"Fuck you!"

"Thanks." Askari said before shooting Vasquez in the forehead six times with a 357 snub nose revolver that left is face completely unrecognizable.

"Throw his body in front of the gas station on Manchester and Vermont tonight the police patrol the area frequently so the they will find it and seal the area off which will draw out Rodriguez making it easy to track him. Jelani you know what to do after we put a tail on Rodriguez."

Askari helped with the removal of the body which was a bloody mess as well as the cleaning of Vasquez brain fragments on the floor and ceiling it was the first time he had taken a man's life which left him feeling numb, but not sorrowful in the least bit in that he knew he was in a war that would involve much death; Vasquez death had little to do with revenge for his self for he had already forgiven the man years ago it was more for the inmates he had served time with who were still incarcerated because of evidence tampering done by Vasquez. Yes, his death was a form of exoneration to those who would never get the chance to raise a family or walk along a beach again.

Vasquez had ruined too many lives for Askari to let him sail into the sunset so it was imperative for him to deliver the message to him personally that his dirt had caught up with him by one he had wronged and not some harden criminal with no agenda.

***

"Hurry up over there and put a sheet over Vasquez before the media shows up." Sergeant Waters ordered the officers securing the scene.

"So, let me guess the gas station attendant didn't see someone drop a dead body in front of his service pumps?"

"Correct he didn't even call it in."

"Well who called it in?"

"They just called and hung up according to dispatch, so we don't know."

"Alright finish up your investigation officer."

Sergeant Waters was highly frustrated as he paced the crime scene trying to figure out who was killing his officers which came to no avail; he had a meeting with the chief that night and knew he needed answers to why there were no suspects dead in the street or in custody by now. A thought came to his mind to what was going on, but it soon drifted when he saw Rodriguez approaching Vasquez's fast as if he was going to go underneath the yellow tape and remove the sheet from his body.

"What the hell are you doing here Rodriguez; this is an ongoing crime scene?"

"The same thing you are doing here, trying to figure out why another one of my partners is lying under a white sheet with looks of bewilderment to how he got that way on everyone face."

"Rodriguez I'm going to have you escorted home by one of the officers on hand to make sure you make it home safely; I don't want to take any more chances."

"I can protect my damn self-Sergeant; I don't need a chaperone."

"I'm sure Lee and Rodriguez thought the same thing before there dicks were knocked in the dirt I said you will get escorted to your house where you will stay for the night until I get word to you on the next move."

Rodriguez stormed off to his car with a plain clothes officer trailing behind him. The drive down Manchester to his home felt surreal as he neared his home the thought came to him to weather Pike knew about the death of their partner, he would have to give him a call once he was in the house. Rodriguez movements in his home were near robotic in that he kept the same routine which included hanging his jacket on the coat hanger by the door and his keys on the kitchen cabinet. A bizarre smell caused him to gage slightly as he took in a rather poignant smell that made him think he was having a problem with the pipes again which made him make a mental note to get them checked this week. Another part of his routine was not turning on the lights until he made it to his bedroom something he had been doing for years it was something about the dark that made him feel like he was in his element a habit that would cost him his life tonight. The smell that caused him to gage got stronger as he approached his room instinctively his nose drew him to the scent which brought him to yellow glowing eyes at the foot of his bed. Terror griped him as he patted his sides to holster his weapon, but fumbled to get it out before Amadi bit his wrist breaking it instantly as she clamped down making Rodriguez's right hand incapable of defense the pain of his hand sent him reeling to the floor with Amadi in close pursuit biting at his boots which he used to keep her at bay to no avail as she tore into his right ankle as well crushing it in the process; not wasting any time Amadi bit in between his thigh while locking and shaking him to tear the meat away from his bones. Rodriguez tried to scream, but his energy would not allow for him to fight and scream so he tried his best to struggle while wondering how the hell a hyena got into his home. His last attempt at defense fell short when Amadi ripped the fingers off his left hand he was using to hit her snout. The pain was intense as he lay helplessly watching the hyena maul his now numb lower body; just as he was slipping into unconsciousness he heard a whisper which made the hyena stop tearing at him he could make out the silhouette of a huge man before he lost consciousness. When Rodriguez awoke all his eyes could see were white walls and breathing machines out the corner of his eyes and for a slight minute he thought it had all been some bad dream caused by alcohol until he tried to move his legs to get up from the bed and nothing happened which immediately triggered him to reach for the sheet to see if he still had his legs, but there was no movement from his arms as well, his brain was sending the signals to move, but no response was happening causing him to look over at his arms that were both gone. Tears started to flow down his face as the reality of his situation settled in. In all his confusion he did not notice that there was a guard sitting parallel to his hospital bed.

"Over here." Rodriguez said with a hardly audible voice it had been a few weeks since he had used his voice and his throat hurt as he tried to speak.

"Save your energy, you barely survived."

"How long have I been here?"

"Three weeks today."

"How did I get here?"

"I don't know, but when I saw you moving around, I alerted Sergeant Waters that you were responsive as well as the doctors they will explain everything to you shortly."

Dr. Kim was still perplexed to how Rodriguez sustained wounds that appeared to have come from a wild animal wounds which lead to both his legs and arms having to be decapitated to stop blood lose.

"Officer Rodriguez do you remember anything before you went unconscious?"

"Are you responsible for saving my life?"

"Well yes, but..."

"Why the hell didn't you just let me die? I can't live my entire life being a cripple."

"Once you heal up completely, we can start therapy that is often times successful in giving people their independence."

"If I had my hand, I would slap you right now my life and career is over, and you are telling me about independence. No matter what type of procedures they try on me I will never be the same again."

Waters had seen a lot of tragedies over the years, but the sight of Rodriguez still sent shivers up his spine whenever he came to visit him since the attack.

"Doctor Kim do you mind giving us some time alone."

"No problem, but I and my staff need to know what type of animal the attack did so that we know what type of diseases to check him for."

"Rodriguez, what the hell happened in your apartment?"

"I came home and did my usual routine of walking through the house, but I kept smelling this strange smell that I thought was a bad pipe in the house so I didn't pay it much mind, so when I walked into my room the smell got stronger quickly causing my nose to follow the scent which lead me to two big red eyes that belonged to some type of dog I thought at first until I got to struggling with the animal and realized that no dog was could be that strong; this is going to sound crazy, but it was a hyena..."

"Wait Rodriguez, a hyena was in your home waiting on you?"

"No, someone else I don't know was waiting for me they just happened to have a damn hyena with them instead of a gun."

"Do you have any ideas who could have done this to you?"

"I'm assuming the same people who killed Lee, Vasquez, and Fain, but I just can't figure out why they didn't kill me too. Who called the ambulance?"

"We don't know we just received a call saying that an officer was down and when the team arrived they found you unresponsive mangled on the floor they thought you were dead at first, but they were able to revive you in the ambulance on the way to the hospital."

"Where is Pikes?"

"On protective leave, he'll be back on duty in a week we were concerned that he would be targeted next once the investigators linked the fact that all officers attacked up until now worked together at one point in time so we are now coming through all of your arrest to see if we can pull out any suspects who could have pulled something like this off."

"Honestly, you think any of the dumb motherfuckers that I have arrested over the years could have done all of this damage. I highly doubt it; they can barely take care of themselves let alone orchestrate the killing of two police officers and attempted murder of another."

"Then who do you think is behind it all Rodriguez?"

"The hell if I know if I did, I wouldn't be laying in this bed missing limbs."

", you will get the best medical attention; I will keep you informed on the investigation."

Rodriguez watched as Sergeant Waters walked out the door a rage filling his body as he contemplated ways of killing his self.

"So, Sergeant Waters' do you have any information regarding the attack that we can use to further the treatment of our patient?"

"Well he said he was attacked by a hyena."

"I see that would explain the deep puncture wounds that he had received, they were too large to be from any dog breed we have on U.S. soil."

"Doctor, you're telling me that it is possible that my officer was actual attacked by a hyena, how would that even be possible?"

"That's a great question with few answers, but if you contact an animal specialist, I am certain they can point you in the correct direction."

"Thanks for your time and information doctor I am certain that there is a lesson to be learned from all of this."

Chapter 16

Hot Tea

"This is view is beautiful how did you find this place." Carole asked sitting underneath a cabana that overlooked the downtown area.

"A client I had needed their business and home serviced and so happened to live here; it was the first time that I had heard about the condos, but I can say that I was instantly impressed so I checked if there were any vacancies available and brought down a deposit the same day when I heard yes."

"I don't blame you this was definitely a great location to nab."

"Thank you; I have been enjoying the decision."

Askari had been seeing Carole since their interview at CPK between their busy schedules they had been able to see each other at least once a week for a few hours at a time. This was the first time that he had her over to his home and was glad she was there she had proven to be an intelligent and interesting woman with her plethora of stories about people and places she had been over the years. Normally she kept her hair in a ponytail when they would meet, but this evening she had her hair down in a wrap which slightly passed her shoulders as it caressed the straps of her black dress; she wore her hair natural which he admired he felt that every woman should be proud of the style she was born with before finding pride in another's style. Since either of them drank alcohol they sipped on cold Perrier as they talked and watched the downtown horizon turn from gold orange to purple blue. Stepping away from the cabana Carole made her way to the corner of the roof top to capture the last glance of the sun setting behind the sky scrapers as Askari wrapped his arms around her from behind meeting her hands with his in the front causing her to release her already relaxed body even more into his embrace. Askari felt Carole's body give in to his as her firm butt pressed against his groin which was now beginning to rise from the heat generating from the close proximities of their pulsing bodies. It had been so long since he had held a woman in his arms and felt the intimacy it produced the scent of her hair and body enticed his nostrils as he greedily took in each breathe of her now quivering body. After the sun shed its last light for the day Carole and Askari made their way back into his condo where Lonnie Liston Smith & the Cosmic Echoes was serenading the end of a relaxing day as well as setting the mood for the evitable.

"How long has it been since you have been with a woman?" Carole asked sitting on the couch with her legs crossed as her dress slid up slowly.

"Have my actions shown absence of affection?"

"No, just wanted to know for my own files."

"It has been years since I have been with a woman intimately."

"Is that by choice?"

"For the present I have made the choice to stay as I am until the right woman comes along; in my past I was given little decision-making power in the process."

"The redundancy of rushed sex with no real connection has made me celibate for years as well most men only see my brown skin and gorgeous body, but you on the other hand looked passed all of that and at me you have always treated me like a person something I truly appreciate."

"Carole, you've always made being kind easy since we first met in the airport and you blessed me with your infectious smile."

"My only question is why you are so far away from me?"

"I just enjoy standing by the window talking, I didn't mean to offend."

Shortly after Askari walked over to the couch to sit next to Carole who moved from the edge to his arms.

"So Askari after all this time you have never thought about sleeping with me?"

"No, but I have thoughts about making love to you."

Instantaneously Carole raised her head up from Askari's chest to meet his lips which were approaching hers passionately she could taste the sweetness from his orange chew stick on his tongue as she took it in her mouth sucking it as if his penis was in her mouth a thought she had played with many times in her loneliness the thought of having him in her made her vagina walls throb like never before causing her to pull at his V-neck shirt in a way that signaled to him to take it off which he did in one swooping motion that revealed a body that looked like it had been carved out of stone Carole never realized how muscular Askari was until her tongue was running down his nipples to his six pack she kissed every part of his upper body before straddling him on the couch returning back to kissing him all in one motion; in the midst of catching a breathe he removed her dress revealing an athletic body that he was equally impressed with. They remained downstairs for a while enjoying the exploration of each other's bodies until they were both completely naked in the middle of the living room. Askari stood naked with the light of the moon casting a slight light across his body while he admired Carole's beautiful body that was flawless. With her nipples erect as well as his penis Askari took her large breast in his mouth sucking on them hungrily as the juice from her vagina trickled down her leg causing her to moan as her hands caressed his massive erection that throbbed in her hand then she palmed his chest slightly pushing him back as she dropped to her knees to take his massive erection into her mouth as he ran his hands through her hair moving rhythmically with the flow of her fellatio that had him nearly wanting to release in her mouth, but he refrained not wanting to waste his seed. Carole had never in her life felt a penis so hard before she could feel every pulse and vain on her tongue and lips as she took more of him in her mouth. Feeling his self about to cum again Askari pulled back and proceeded to pick Carole up taking her to his upstairs bedroom once upstairs he laid her on the bed spreading her legs apart while placing his hands beneath her butt pulling her vagina to his mouth while she rotated her pelvis muscle while his tongue satisfied her deepest desires the pleasure was intense as he pulled her back in every time she came and would falter back in pleasure giving her even more to the point it was unbearable then right before she came again he pulled up and penetrated her with both hands still underneath her butt holding on firmly Askari thrust into her vigorously going deeper with each struck as Carole moaned holding on to his huge back as he moved in her like he was making love to her very soul they were both on one accord in their movement with Carole begging for Askari to cum in her which he did with the force of a volcano erupting while his man juice came pouring out of her vagina like lava all over his sheets as he held her tightly as years of frustration seemed to seep out of his penis. Carole was spent as she lay sprawled across the bed entwisted in his sheets as Askari went to the rest room when he returned he had two dry towels in his hand that he placed on the bed and beckoned for her to join him in the shower. As Carole walked in the bathroom she was greeted by an array of black candles that gave the room a beautiful back drop as they moved through the steam into the shower where Askari began to lather her body with Neutrogena body wash that infused the room with a fragment wood type smell that suddenly awakened Carole out of her or maybe it was Askari penis entering her again this time from the back as her hands had nowhere to go but the wall as if she was getting frisked her strong calves kept her positioned tightly as Askari's hands held her waist securely as he stroked away as suds streamed down her wet butt that pounded against his pelvis as he reached completely into her stomach with each stroke. Back in the bedroom Askari oiled Carole down while massaging her before they climbed into bed the rest of the night was spent talking until, they both fell asleep in each other's arms.

In the morning Carole awoke to an empty bed, but a nose crowded with an array of flavors coming from the downstairs kitchen she looked around for something to slip on and found brown rob lying at the foot of the bed.

"Good morning chef Askari!"

"Top of the morning to you, how did you sleep?"

"Very well plus I get awaken to breakfast a girl couldn't ask for more."

"I am glad you have an appetite I've prepared a couple of dishes that I hope you will enjoy."

While eating breakfast Askari could hear the news caster from CNN reporting on an officer related shooting happening in the city of Inglewood last night which caused both to pay attention.

"These police shootings and killing are starting to get out of hand I have to do a story next week on the current rise of violence against officers in Los Angeles for the L.A. Times."

Escape from Failure

"So, what is your take on the police deaths over the last few months?"

"Mixed, I've been doing my research on some of the killings that have taken place and all of them steam from some type of negative run in with the communities they serve. None of the killing seems to be random, but this recent one seems a little different from what CNN is reporting I will have to investigate that one as well. The main baffling factor is that the police department has yet to catch the individual or individuals responsible for the killing I've talked to my sources and they have absolutely no leads to who is responsible for the deaths."

"What other type of information do your leads give you regarding cases?"

"Absolutely nothing that would jeopardize a case, but anything that will come out eventually I tend to get a heads up on that's it."

"Sounds like a reliable method of gathering Intel it's good that you have connections that can give you a head up so that you can stay on top of your game in your field."

"There's no other way to survive in this line of business without some type of advantage; especially with this type of case everything on this matter is completely hush-hush even for my inside connection. On another note last night was amazing so where do we go from here?"

"Hopefully into forever, I've gathered enough on you in our time spent together to know that I want you in my life long term it doesn't take me long to notice that I have someone special."

"You're never reserved on expressing how you feel."

"Life's is too short to be reserved especially when love is involved."

"Thank you for that."

"Why are you thanking me?"

"Just for being a decent man, there are so few nowadays I appreciate your sincerity, kindness, and love that you bring to the table."

"Now I must thank you for receiving all that I have to offer without doubt, remorse, or confrontation to why you deserve the best."

"Unfortunately, I have to be going in a few hours there are a few errands I have to do around town, how about we hook up tonight for dinner."

"It all depends on how much work I have to catch up on myself, so I don't want to make a commitment I cannot keep I will definitely keep you posted as things open up for me."

"Sounds good let's see how everything turns out."

When arrived home after leaving Askari's place she found a bouquet of flowers sitting at her door which instantly brought a smile to her already pleasant face. Once inside the house she reached for a flower vase that was in her kitchen cabinet and ran some water into it in preparation to place the flowers inside as she was unwrapping the flower something bounced off the kitchen counter and hit the flower when she went to retrieve what had fell she started to scream in joy as she placed a diamond ring on her finger.

Askari set in his kitchen taking time for meditation after just asking Carole to be his wife she had been pleasantly surprised by the ring which made him glad he planned for them to have a great life. Hearing his tea kettle scream Askari got out of his chair and poured the hot water into a cup so that his green tea could brew; between sips he put together areas he wanted to discuss with his team later on that day. He was not too surprised about the officer related shooting in Inglewood he heard about at breakfast even though he knew it did not involve his comrades he needed to know what had happened and who was involved. As he set in his kitchen drinking his hot tea, he knew it was time to put his next plan into action now that his comrades were aware of their strengths.

Chapter 17
Last Breathing

Stephanie Merge had been under tremendous press lately from the mayor to move forward with the prosecution of Lamont Jackson in the murder of a rising USC football star who had been gunned down months ago in a gang related shooting; tensions were high throughout the city with all the police shake downs and beefed up patrols of the community then to make matters worse non-profit groups were breathing down the mayors necks through public protests for him to bring justice to innocent who had been being gunned down in the streets with little regard of solving the cases causing the mayor to lean on the D.A. to produce so that he could focus his energy on getting the cop killers off the street in his district which was frightening off outside entertainment from coming to Los Angeles to spend money which was hurting every bodies pockets in some type of way he couldn't allow this to go on any longer which also made him apply pressure to the police chief to get the cases solved of his fallen before another killing took place in the city further adding to the stigma.

Uzi was in his cell making beats with his fist against the desktop when some familiar faces from his past came to his cell door to speak with him.

"I'm surprised it took you muthafuckas so long to come holla at me, a nigga about to start trail any day I guess this is your way of showing me I really need you guys."

"Uzi, you really fucked up this time you are involved in a killing that the public actually wants justice for."

"I don't know why it's just another nigga that got killed it's not like I *murked* a white boy or some shit like that besides this cases ain't got nothing to do with the feds so why you down here?"

"You know we only come when we need something, besides the person you allegedly killed has a huge family that has strong ties throughout the community which means that you are going to possibly go down for this one."

"Bullshit they ain't got nuthin, but some circumstantial evidence on a nigga like me no witnesses and no weapon."

"Lamont are you aware that they do have a shell casing with your fingerprint on it?"

"So, what they found a shell in an alley with my fingerprints on it that could have been there a long time ago you know how many times I have shoot at niggas in that alley."

"You are going to lose this case if it goes all the way and we already spoke with the D.A. there will not be a deal we need your assistance on solving a case, but we need you to agree that you will help us entirely without falter."

"What's in it for me this time besides a free ticket out?"

"You'll find out. Crack the gate bailiff."

Pikes had been following Uzi's case for the past few months even as his fellow officers died around him he felt like it was his duty to see his conviction through to the end being it was their last major arrest together more so he wanted him to go down because of the influence he had in the community so when he saw Uzi being lead out his cell by F.B.I officers anger went through his veins like never before as he practically ran in their direction as they walked towards the garage exit.

"Where the hell are you taking this inmate and why his hands are cuffed to the front he is on trial for murder."

"Officer Pikes this issue doesn't concern you it is highly confidential matter that involves the F.B.I you can voice your concerns to your commanding officer."

The two agents continued down the hall towards the parking garage where they placed Uzi inside the back seat of a marked car once they were all in the vehicle the agents made their way towards their downtown office. Once they arrived at the office they placed Uzi in a room with a recorder in it and a two way mirror he had been through this before when he informed on a few murders that the feds were interested in years ago which allowed him to slide on a few murders of his own. The two agents Stacy and Klein had worked with

Escape from Failure

Uzi before when they were new to the field and had been promoted to a lot more assignments because of the success they had garnered working with Uzi before.

"It's been a while Lamont almost ten years since we last spoke with you; despite your current incarceration I know you are aware of the officers who have been murdered in the past few months."

"Yeah I've heard about it I know you ain't try'n to put that shit on me."

"Of course, not we know you are not capable of doing this type of crime or have the resources, but we feel you know of individuals who are capable of doing so and have the desire."

"There are a lot of nigga's that want to kill cops that I know and don't know; you got Mexican nigga's and White nigga's that also want to kill cops so I guess you expect me to infiltrate them too. What makes you think that it is nigga's doing the killing anyway?"

"The demographics of the area leads us to think that some type of new age Black vanguard is responsible for the deaths it is highly unlikely that an outside group would come into a predominately Black community and start trying to liberate it through tactical assaults on police officers."

"So, if you are so certain that nigga's are doing the killing or some type of neo Black panther party why do you need me why don't you send one of your undercover agents?"

"Lamont, we believe that the group is recruiting reputable gang members from different gangs throughout Los Angeles so an agent who has been around since birth to say in a neighborhood wouldn't stand a chance of being recruited by the group."

"Let me get this shit straight you want a nigga to be the nigga version of 007 in the streets. So, I would basically do what I've been doing in attempted to get recruited by this mysterious group then once inside I would report back to you guys so that you can do your superman shit."

"Yes."

"Alright what's in it for me it's going to be a hard to get scooped by a group when my pockets are hurting in case you forgot I've been locked down unable to get my bread."

"We understand that and we have envelopes that you will be able to pick up at a P.O. Box we will assign to you down stairs in the parking lot we have a gray Dodge charger waiting on you once you take the keys be aware that you are committed to accomplishing the task until we tell you otherwise any violation of our terms you will be left to your own demise and the F.B.I will cease in any further contact with you."

"So, in the midst of a nigga doing his thang to get recruited the police swoop on me what will ya'll do?"

"We'll let the hire ups know that we have a mole working the case and your information will pop up informing any arresting officer to let you go in as subtle away as possible."

"Sounds like a plan. I just got one question when am I going to get the first envelope?"

"It's in the glove compartment of the Charger. Work quickly Lamont we are trying to prevent the next death."

After the interview Uzi was led to the parking garage by the agents and given the keys to the Charger as he walked to the car he kept thinking to his self that this was some bullshit, but it sure beat sitting in a cell counting calendars for the rest of his life now he just had to figure out a way to infusion his self-back into the community without raising any suspicions about how he got out on the murder charger all of a sudden he would think of something like he always did one thing he knew about nigga's was that they would believe anything especially from a nigga they respected. Once inside the car he found the envelope which contained thirty-one hundred dollar bills enough he thought to get him back on his feet with a gun within reach. He knew many would consider him a snitch for what he had done and was currently doing, but he realized a long time ago that he was out for self and was willing to do whatever it took to be the last one breathing.

Chapter 18

Let Down

"Merge have a seat, I know you normally like to stand because you are always on the go, but what I am about to lay on you would've made you want a seat anyway so let's get to the point."

"Waters what is going on I received word today that the feds picked up Jackson early today."

"Yes, they did and that is why I have called you into my office the feds took Lamont for a special investigation regarding the murders of officers Vasquez, Fain, Lee and the attempted murder of officer Rodriguez. Through their investigation they have determined that the deaths were the result of kinetic activity...

"Excuse me Waters kinetic activity, what is that?"

"Terminology for combat, during their investigation they kept coming across shell casing that shared a relationship with weapons used in war another red flag was the way in which the acts were done they seemed to be very well planned out and executed military style which leads the F.B.I to believe that they have a group of neo BPP on their hands."

"So, do they believe that Lamont Jackson is somehow connected to this group?"

"Not necessarily, but they feel he meets all the qualifications of what the group is currently recruiting."

"Of course my next question with all due respect to the officers that have lost their lives is what about my murder case; please tell me that I have to postpone it at the worse until this is solved."

"This is the part where you would have wanted a seat; because Jackson agreed to help in their investigation the feds have offered to clear him of all charges concerning Shawn Davis."

"So, what am I supposed to tell the family of the victim? Sorry we can't proceed with the trail against the person who killed your son because something more important came up and by the way the killer is out and about on the streets as we speak."

"No, you tell them that the evidence that you currently had is not sufficient enough to proceed with a trail at the current time and to save them from a lengthy trail that you could possibly lose your office is choosing to drop the charges against the suspect due to lack of evidence."

"For the record we had Jackson a criminal your officers have been trying to put away for a long time and now where just going to let him go so that he can murder again where is the justice in that?"

"Individuals like Lamont Jackson come and go, but the individuals behind these killing don't it is way more important that we catch the people responsible for these killing before this type of out lash spreads through the street and if that takes letting go some gangbanger to get that accomplished the means definitely justify the results. Rather the family understands that or not it is of little concern to me just notify them because the case is over having a decent day."

Merge set there in the Sergeants office for a while after he had dismissed her angry about her helplessness at the moment she had educated herself to escape feelings of hopelessness that she hadn't felt since a child all the months of planning were for nothing she thought to herself and for a brief minute she wanted to through in the towel, but thought that there were countless Lamont Jacksons that she could lock up all she had to do was stay the course she would get him on the next go round.

***

"Jelani, how has Amadi been adapting to being in America?"

"Just fine she seems to like her new sleeping corridors and the run of the yard at night. Speaking of Amadi I have a question regarding my last mission."

"I'm all ears."

"With all due respect why did you have me call the paramedics to save the cop when he was a breath away from death?"

"Often times death is too easy especially for people like Rodriguez who have ruined so many lives with their abuse of authority to kill him would have been doing him a favor on the other hand to cripple and watch himself destruct by taking away what matter most to him his authority and strength why should he be able to walk around an enjoy life when those he helped incarcerate illegally can't he needed to be taught a lesson that is why I didn't have you kill him out right."

"I see this man has caused a lot of pain in so many lives it is only fitting that he experiences some his self."

"Know that you can always come to me brother with what's ever on your mind I will never make decisions based on my emotions for they would be detrimental to the cause as well as the group, but I adhere to giving people what they have coming such as corrupt police and individuals who help in the destruction of our community."

"In correlation to the destruction of the community our next meeting will be focusing on getting rid of those certain individuals who are not incompliance with our movement."

"I am aware that it will be a touchy subject for most to address being they have ties to certain individuals who may fall by the hand of the group, but this has been spoken on before they even decided to join it was made very clear that as a group we may have to move against those in our past to achieve our goal. I am very confident that all will go well at the next meeting.

***

Rodriguez was having a difficult time adjusting to his new life as a quadriplegic he could barely look at his self in the mirror let alone function day to day leaving him to ponder aimlessly to why the group behind the deaths didn't kill him. Even though his body was recovering at a healthy speed the doctors kept him in the hospital for an extra couple of weeks to monitor his mental progression as he adapted to his current physical conditions.

William V. Fields

"Rodriguez, I haven't seen you smiling this much since you've been here let me in on your happiness." Steve his physical trainer said as he helped him on to his exercise mat.

"The bad dreams I've been having have subsided for the last few days plus I am coming to grips with my new life."

"That's great that will make your recovery all the better today we will work on your core we really want to make sure we build that up before you leave the hospital even though you will still be coming to physical therapy."

"Sounds good to me, I don't see the foam rollers we used a few weeks ago do you mind going to get some that's when I really feel a burn."

"Sure, I'll be right back."

The rehabilitation room was always empty whenever Rodriguez was having his session, he assumed it was because of security purposes whatever the reason he was glad no one was around to see him struggle in the ground like a huge caterpillar looking for a hole. The first time he did training he broke out in tears at what he had become and had to tell his trainer to stay away as he let it all out on the mat every day was a struggle for him not to break down and he had been given over to killing his self he just needed an opportunity that now lay before his face in the form of the pool; while Steve was looking for the supplies Rodriguez squirmed across the mat to the pool where others did there rehabilitation once he was at the rim of the pool he placed his head over the edge to take in the chlorine smell that tinged his nose before he rolled his body into the water the in flush of water into his lungs burned as his body contorted back in fourth trying not to drown it was taking longer than he thought as he tried to speed the process before Steve came to get him out and then it happened he blanked out similar to when he first got attacked. Steve was returning with the blue foam rings when he noticed that Rodriguez was nowhere in sight which sent him scrambling over the center looking for him not wanting to follow his first mind by looking in the pool, but had no choice once he spotted the body floating he jumped in the water immediately swimming underneath his body while pushing it to the side surface of the pool since Rodriguez was already on his back Steve began to administer CPR after the first initial pumps with no response Steve feared for the worse, but on his third time going to give air Rodriguez spit up water while trying to bite Steve's cheek, but missed by a few inches.

"You stupid… mother fucker you should have let me die!"

Steve was stunned by Rodriguez's behavior leaving him no choice, but to call security which came ran in taking him away to his room.

"So, what happened in here Steve?" A security guard asked pulling out a note pad and pen.

"Rodriguez requested that I bring him some foam rollers before we started his exercise, but it took me a while to find them because they were stacked behind a lot of other equipment when I returned he was nowhere in sight so I looked around for him thinking he wiggled to another part of the room, but I found him face down in the pool so I jumped in without much thought to get him out of the water and then performed CPR on him."

"So, do you think it was an accident?"

"At first I didn't know what to think, but then I when he came to, he asked me why I did let him die and tried to bite my face while I was bent over him."

"So, you're telling me he tried to attack you after you had saved him because he was upset that you prevented him from suicide."

"Yes, that is just how it happened."

"I've seen it plenty around here with veterans coming back from the war torn to pieces and their minds gone I don't blame them I would probably kill myself too we'll take him to suicide watch later on and the doctors will evaluate him for placement."

"It's rather sad kind of a letdown he was coming along rather well with the treatment hate to see a strong individual end up that way."

"Hey, it happens to the best of them."

Chapter 19
Churches

That God is a good God could be heard every third Sunday up and down Figueroa by residents and strangers passing by in their cars from the 54th street church that was a staple in the community for years.

Reverend Hayes had been the pastor for years at the church, but as of recently had faded to the back ground as his young son Robert took the reins thus reviving a church that was losing its young congregation to nearby by churches that catered to the youth of the day more than the church did before Robert stepped into the pulpit igniting the fellowship tenfold with his high energy preaching and God loves you for whatever you do as long as you pay your ties on time style of preaching that filled the collection plate up generously every Saturday and Sunday the congregation grew so rapidly that the church had to get construction done to extend the space within to accommodate the swelling services that brought in a variety of individuals from ex-cons to homosexuals, but mostly single mothers looking for God to send them a man to make their life better if not Robert himself who had been single the entire four years he had been preaching. This Sunday morning had a few new members who came to hear more than a word from the lord they wanted to have a few words with Pastor Hayes and his son in regards to why they were not spending church funds on those prostitutes, gang members, and dope fiends that riddled the track directly in front of their church. Askari had assigned a special task force from within his organization to monitor all the churches in the community to see where their resources were going in regards to the communities they were serving and the results were shaming which came of little surprise to Askari who held churches and their congregations to a certain standard since they had been the corner stone of survival for African Americans once they were placed into slavery so it baffled Askari that the churches had back slid so drastically in their purpose which was helping sick people who needed a hospital to get well the chief physician being God. There were millions pouring into churches yet known of it seemed to find those most in need until now.

Escape from Failure

"You see God has a blessing for you and it is upon you to retrieve, receive, and to cling to whatever it takes to get your blessing! Ya'll do not hear me up in here. Some of ya'll do not want to pay your ties but let me tell you this ya'll going to be tied to whatever is plaguing you if you do not give God his! Ya'll don't hear me up in here!" The preacher said as he made his way down the aisle sweat pouring down his face eyes bulging as he stared down every pew. In the scripture it says plant a seed reaps a harvest! Ya'll do not hear me. Pastor, pastor the economy is bad, I can't pay my ties or give an offering that's what people say to me, but let me tell you if you don't have faith you don't have nothing! The pastor said stomping his feet as he made his towards the podium as the choir went into song. Ushers stand to your feet and get ready to receive the offering. Don't forget that we will be having the miracle offering in two weeks."

After the service Askari waited patiently in his row as people made their way to the parking lot to gossip while others were in a rush to go to Sunday breakfast at the local restaurants. Once the crowd inside slimmed down to just the elders of the church Askari signaled for one of his men to approach Robert to get a vibe on him.

"Awesome message in today's sermon pastor, I'm looking forward to come back next Sunday."

"Glad you enjoyed the sermon and God spoke to you. How did you hear about the church?"

"I saw a billboard on the 10 freeway, so I decided to come check you out."

"Great, God does work in mysterious ways hope you come back again."

"Pastor I have a question?"

"I'm in a bit of a hurry, but I'm sure I can answer a question."

"I've just paroled from prison a few months ago and it is hard for me out here does the church offer any programs for felons?"

"Not currently, but we do have a men's prayer group every Wednesday that you can attend, and I am sure there is someone in the group that can give your assistance."

William V. Fields

"Thanks pastor."

"No problem God blesses you."

"So, what did you think of him Rico?"

"Very stand offish as if I was bothering him by asking questions plus, he wouldn't look me directly in the eye his eyes kept shifting looking around the room at I presume the women."

"Did you find out what the miracle offering was all about?"

"Askari he was acting so rushed I didn't get the opportunity to do so."

"It's alright I'll find out through Toy box."

"I see why he was in a rush, that's him over there talking to the lady who was in the front row."

"At least we can confirm that the emerald Jaguar is his vehicle the Intel was on point as always." Askari said pulling out of the church parking lot on his way to Altadena for a meeting he had schedule with the rest of the group to discuss their next plan of action in the coming months.

"As always it is a complete honor to be surrounded by so many beautiful strong brother and sister working in synergy to accomplish a better place for us to exist. Before I lay out what are goals are for the next few months let me congratulate all of you who are near completion of your degrees it gives me great joy to be apart and witness your continued success I know I say it a lot maybe too much, but you don't know how humbled I am by you all daily we as a people have been down this road countless times before, but never to this extent and that's not to take credit from our brothers and sister who have walked the pay before us setting in motion the blue print in which we are able to grasp our current path to victory. In correlation to that the C.R.A.S.H unit that was a part of a lot of corruption in our community is now disbursed do to the deaths of the officers in the unit this of course has caused the police to crack down a little more than usual in an effort to weed out the individuals responsible for the deaths these shake downs don't sit well with the local gang members of course because it is interfering with their currency flow causing them to revert back to senseless gang violence that we must address. This is an issue that is highly delicate in that most of you have family members and homies still heavily involved in the gang culture so I bring this issue before you because there are no big I's or little U's just equality."

"Askari my brother is still heavily involved with the 60's are you suggesting that I knowingly allow for the group to kill my brother?"

"Boo Rock I understand your concerns and I would never ask you to take the life of your brother, but I must remind you that we all came in this group knowing that there would be hard decisions to make to make this movement work. So, to answer your question we will allow you as well as any other member to reach out to their family member before any lethal action is taken."

"Too keep it real I know brother is not going to stop."

"Then you most ask yourself why you joined this group if you know that he wants stop then it is quite clear that he is against all that we stand for as well as yourself. To put it into context he is against a peaceful environment for our kids to grow up in where men and women feel safe and the thought of being killed is absent when they want to walk to the store to get some milk. Boo Rock when is the last time you felt safe walking to the store to get anything or better yet when was the last time you walked through your community without having to have a gun or worry about some Hoovers jumping out trying to kill you?"

"So long I can't remember."

"Our purpose in case anybody has forgotten is to restore normalcy back in our community real normalcy where are seeds can grow without having their childhoods raped away from them by niggas who don't give a damn about nobody, but themselves. So, I ask you brother is one life worth many and I do not need your answer because that is a question you must ask and answer yourself. As some of you know we have purchased some new property not far from here that was just on the market the reason this property was purchased is because I knew these issues would arise so we are building another underground facility that will double as a holding and rehabilitation center for those of you who have family members who are intent on nihilism we will also start circulating literature throughout the community circa BPP to grasp the attention of those inquisitive to the transformation that will begin to take place around them as you can see it is time and quite honestly it is going to get brutal very soon as we attempt to cleanse the streets of a plague that has been here too long. I don't mean to jump around, but like I mentioned earlier we will have the new facility up and running by next week as well as crews assembled who will go on non-lethal excursions to gather our groups relatives once they are in custody we will brief those effected on our next course of action in regards to their relatives. Now on to the second goal it has been increasable apparent that prostitution is growing amongst our young women especially in the South Central area again we find ourselves in a delicate situation in that most pips have been replace with gang members who have dominated this hustle rapidly although these gang members don't gangbang so to say anymore they still bring in an influx of drugs and pedophiles into our community with the allure of sex. Lastly, we want to press on the local churches to start to do more which we have been already doing because when we take the gangs off the street the few members remaining will need a place to go as well as the prostitutes so it is imperative that we have programs available for the transition that will take place."

"Askari are we still recruiting?"

"Not currently, but we always have our eyes open for new prospects. Are there any other questions?"

"Yes, I speak for the group when I say we all came into this program not knowing what to expect, but we all wanted a better situation then what we were currently apart of thanks to you we have that now most importantly we have pride in ourselves and what we are a part of we are ready to die for our belief."

"So am I, the missions have been colored coded as usual so find your mission folder and prepare to take part in a history defining moment that will impact the future of our community forever."

For weeks the group staked out different neighborhoods to gather Intel to how they operated and which members posed the most threat normally there were only five to seven true gunners from each set depending on how deep there were on the street once the individuals were labeled they were targeted by the groups some time they caught them in the midst of their crime on another or on their way to commit a crime whatever the case they took them effectively and precisely without much resistance all that was left most times was a corpse on the floor near a vehicle that was riddled with bullets; investigators went on with business as usual thinking they were just gang related killing, but not Pikes who had been promoted to detective he knew something was a fray gang members were popping up dead all over the city including surrounding cities at an alarming rate and all of them were prominent members being killed the ones that called the shots which rarely happened at the rate it was happening something was amidst he could feel it.

"Detective Pikes do you know this kid?"

"This is one of the 107 Hoovers top members Selo Steve or should I say was."

"Looks like one of the Denver Lanes got lucky."

"No, they don't have assault rifles that make holes this big. Pikes said pointing to the wounds on the victim chest. Plus, they would have left the shells whoever did this had a rifle with a shell catcher attached."

"This is the ninth killing in this area this week and it's only Tuesday we haven't arrested anyone and where is the graffiti they usually write all over the damn walls when they are at war giving us some type of hint."

"Your right there hasn't been any Black wall banging in a while... I am surprised that I did not notice that earlier. Pike said scratching his head with his ink pen as he jotted down notes on a small yellow writing tablet. Only these killing have similarities one there all done with high power weapons two there' hardly any physical evidence at the scene expect bullets from the victims gun and third we have no suspects whatsoever, but the one thing all this evidence has in common is it was the same scenario with the cop killing we experienced a few months back which leads me to believe that whoever is responsible has an agenda that is definitely targeted at the Black community."

"So, let me make sure I'm hearing you correctly you think some Black group is behind all of these killing including our fellow officers?"

"Yes, there is no other explanation the only question I haven't figured out is why they are doing it and how can we stop them."

"Outside of killing our officers why would you want to stop them their getting ready of these thugs for us."

"Because what need will there be for us if they can police themselves one way or another there'll be a bumping of the heads which will mean an all-out war in the middle of the streets eventually."

"You're over thinking it Pike just stick to the evidence you have before you."

"I am and it is pointing in one direction I need to get back to the office so that I can sift through some old files to figure out who is pulling the strings."

"I admit your theory is the best I've heard so far, but how do you expect to get anywhere sifting through old files when the files are these streets we work every day not pieces of paper in an old cabinet ask yourself who do you know past or present that would benefit from killing cops and gang members? When you get that answered than you'll have your guy."

"Looking at it from that perspective it would have to be someone with a grudge and a ton of resources to carry all these murders out as well as military training; so I would first start by looking at all ex-military that have gang ties and then narrow my search down from there."

"See how the streets talk now you're making sense now you have the direction you were talking about."

"Alright I'm heading back to the station."

"One more thing Pike if I'm not mistaken isn't the F.B.I in charge of the investigation right now."

"Yes, so does that mean I am not supposed investigate because they are in control now?"

"It's your career do what you like Colombo."

Blue Rag had felt like he was being watched as he stepped out of his Tahoe truck in the city of Gardena to go up to his house, but he knew no one had followed him because he always took different routes home plus he always kept his hammer cocked on his desert eagle in case somebody managed to follow him which happen once before with the results being death for the potential robber after scanning the dark for a few he determined he was tripping until he felt an object slam into the fat of his neck with the force of a bullet, but he had been shot before so he instantly knew it wasn't a bullet when it didn't penetrate all the way through so he grabbed at the object which was long and sticking out his neck and pulled it out realizing it was a dart that he was struck with he wanted to start shooting, but really didn't know how to react nor had a target so he ran behind his truck to seek cover and gathered his thoughts on his next move, but before he could make a move to the door he was hit with another dart in his neck.

"What the fuck!" Blue Rag said pulling the second dart out his neck he about to make a run for his door when his knees went numb sending him crashing to the ground when he awoke he was still sort of out of it as he tried to adjust his vision then it dawned on him that he was laying on a cot inside some type of holding facility similar to a holding cell in the county, but cleaner.

"Hey, what the fuck is this shit police hitting niggas with darts now? I didn't even do shit!" Blue Rag said pacing the floor.

"Be easy brother you are safe." Askari said grabbing a chair to place next to the holding cell where Blue Rag was held.

"Who the fuck is you?"

"My name is Askari; I came to speak with you concerning your stay here."

"Nigga I don't want to talk to the police call me a lawyer."

"I'm not an officer brother and I prefer that we respect one another when we talk like I mentioned earlier my name is Askari and I am here to help."

"The only help I need is getting out of here and if you are not the police who are you?"

"I am a man who is intent on stopping the fratricide that is happening amongst our people."

"What the hell is that and why do you need me here to stop it?"

"To answer your first question do you remember Deshawn Winston?"

Blue Rag looked at Askari strangely before speaking he had not heard that name in years it had been so long ago that he hardly thought about it, but here this stranger was asking him about a dead man.

"I'll take your silence as a yes, you should remember the man you took his life an innocent man that you had mistaken for a Kitchen Crip. You seemed puzzled to how I know, but you should not almost everybody in the community knows you did they were just too afraid of your influence to do anything about it. Fratricide is the killing of one's brothers, sisters, or countrymen and you Blue have been doing this for years and it is time for it to end. Do you that Black murder victims are killed by other Blacks ninety-four percent of the time?"

"So, niggas killing niggas all day wherever you go why am I the only one here?"

"You're not an isolated individual you are here is purely because someone within or group wanted your life spared if not for them you would have been in front of your Tahoe dead."

"Bull shit ain't any of my folks involved in some borderline police shit..."

Just as Blue Rag was about to go on a verbal rant 1 Punch grabbed a chair and set down next to Askari.

"Cuzz, tell these niggas to let me out of here!"

"That want be happening for a while Blue we need you to get better first."

"Better...better what type of shit is you on Cuzz ain't nuthin wrong with me!"

"The fact that you kill your own people with little regard is a problem."

"Then you have a problem too because you use to do the same thang."

"You're absolutely right I use to participate, but after I left Corcoran, I stopped looking at my people as the enemy because I no longer saw myself as an enemy."

"I knew you went soft, but I didn't think you would go to this extreme, so now that you fags have had your scared straight moment when you going to let me out?"

"It all depends on your actions from this point forward and how soon you progress." Askari said standing up from his chair.

"What if I don't want to progress nigga?"

Askari had a saddened look in his eye as he glanced at 1 Punch and up at the control tower signaling for them to open the cell he knew what had to come next yet took no pleasure in it in his eyes it was one less brother in the struggle as well as one more enemy as Blue Rag made his way towards the exit door he was pushed back by the blow of the hollow tips coming from Askari's 40 Glock which penetrated his deltoids striking his spine as the bullets ascended downwards causing him to stumble to the ground as Askari moved in closer looking for a head shot before firing again once his eyes locked with Blue Rag he gave him three shoots to the head while 1 Punch stood by watching from afar.

"It's never a comfort to kill another human being or wise to let a male with hatred in his heart run amok amongst an already deteriorating community. I'll make sure he gets a proper burial."

1 Punch stood by the wall as Askari made his way to out of the holding facility past him his thoughts were ever where at the moment as he watched the blood of his cousin spew from his body into the hallway into to a collective pool that was coming from different exit wounds of his body. It hurt him inside slightly that he wasn't angry at what he had just witnessed for he was weak when it was time to do what he knew needed to be done for the streets to be safe from parasites like his cousin.

***

K-Stone was leaving his ninth church down Figueroa with seven more to go he was picking up actions plans from each Pastor concerning their plan to help the individuals within ten blocks of them going east to west and north to south Askari special units had paid each pastor a personal visit at their residence to fully convey how serious they were about their cooperation in helping to rebuild the spiritual relationship of the community through active work of the church and its members. Most of the action plans consisted of providing weekly food boxes, medical supplies, shelter, and mental health screening which would come from a percentage of the tithes and offering every week they would also provide weekly logs of how the programs were working as well as the names of all the new individuals they were coming in contact with the objective was to show their beliefs through actions in an active unified front that would blanket the community as a whole there would be no more separation amongst the congregations communication wise they were all in accordance with what needed to be done. The first few weeks were more difficult for some churches then others as membership dwindled as members were made to walk the streets and witness to their neighbors, local gang members, prostitutes, and dope fiends. The morale of these lost souls who normally took a false sense of pride in their ignorance slowly started to feel shame as these flocks of believers took to the streets in larger numbers taking back their communities one day at a time which became easier as the gang members who normally would have been resistant to talking to a church member became more reachable as the hard core members started to disappear from the streets thus allowing church members to find out the back grounds of the inflicted souls that considered the streets their solace and show them their possibilities outside of a corner with a street number assigned to it. Two months into the program the church members had become regular fixtures in the communities they worshipped in as those lost souls they sought to capture slowly started to attend services gaining their attention of the spiritual food more than the services the churches provided in correlation the crime rate started to come down and little children started to feel safe again playing in the streets as jobs were provide for those who chose to leave the street life alone the irony was they were paid to help refurbish small sections of their community which built the pride up in each member as they could say I painted that fence or repaired that building, but of course their always has to be one thorn in the bush. Pastor Robert wasn't particularly fond of his church funds being tampered with every week one bit he went with it because he thought by a month's time that multiple programs would have fallen off and whoever was behind the programs would have taken their money by now and went their way, but that wasn't the case because the programs were starting to get more in depth which meant more money coming out his collection plate every week furthermore he took notice that the congregation had started to take less in less to his sermons as the new crowd of people integrated into the church with ears wide open wanting to hear a solid message that could be applied to their mundane new lives they were not hyped by the normal prosperity preaching that normally got amen's from the crowd or people standing to their feet taking off their shoes waving them in the air for they were hungry for more than whooping and hollering about nothing they wanted empowerment from a righteous word that could only come from a righteous preacher who was in tune with his followers aspirations instead his own. The thing was energy could be felt without actually touching it similar to how a fire could be felt from a distance Pastor Robert was feeling the heat of the crowd dissipate every Sunday and no amount of I'm gone tell you about yourself preaching was going to get him out of his current slump. These were people's lives that he held and it was time to let them go if he wasn't serious about addressing the deep rooted issues that brought them into his church for betterment in the first place Askari watched from the back pews as the once flamboyant Pastor became more off course in his preaching as the months went by along with his congregation that was finding refuge in more seasoned pastors who believed in applying the word to daily life in a practical way.

The normal stench of despair that engulfed the city streets was drifting away as it was systematically replaced with caring and love from the local churches that had been present yet absent in action in the community for years they had lost their purpose along the way becoming complacent like most structures did with time when new life was not around to create purpose forgetting that their purpose was to create new life amongst deprived brittle seeds that only needed a daily dose of Gods light that came in the form of a sincere smile with a caring heart to love one as one would love themselves while providing instructions in the form of the word for daily tips that would help nurture their development.

Chapter 20

El Pecho

Zapp and Rogers's So Ruff so Tuff was playing loudly in the back ground from an old school stereo as Shy Rock stepped up for his fifth set on the pull up bar he had ad hoc in his garage for exercise when he couldn't make it to the gym. After two hours of burpies and other various bar exercises Shy Rock was ready to hit the shower he had to meet up with his Carnals concerning the recent Black on Black killings that had been dominating the news in a few hours at a hole in the wall bar in east L.A.

"Who the hell pick this spot out homie? It smells like cats have been pissing in here for weeks." Speedy asked taking a seat at a booth in the back of the bar.

"I see the platitude is true people change when they get money all of a sudden their too good for the ghetto." Shy Rock responded greeting Speedy with a handshake.

"Never I'm a ghetto baby, but I could do without the urine smells I guess Vato's taking piss's right on the walls down here that's why I don't like east L.A. homes mother fuckers are grimy."

"So how was your vacation?"

"It was nothing just a few months for a punk violation it didn't stop nothing."

"Cool, here comes the rest of the carnals we shouldn't be here long homie."

Mexican gang murders had dropped significantly over the last eight months since they stopped gangs from initiating new members they were hell bent on strengthening the members they had while redirecting the Hispanic youth in a different direction at first it was strange to the youngsters who grew up around the bangers all their lives to be rejected, some of the rejected even went as far to try to join other gangs thinking that their local gangbangers didn't think they had what it took to be a part of their gang, but instead of open arms they were met with those gang members telling them to go to school or get a job which left many young Hispanics confused being there were few lifestyle choices to choose from in the ghetto and of the few one was being taking away that provide some type of hope of being a man through drug dealing or other various crimes so with their choice being shrunk the majority went back to school in hopes of finding some type of direction.

"Each member needs to report on the progress taking place in their barrio." Shy Rock said lighting his fourth cigarette.

"Education wise I think it is going smooth, but military wise I think we need more troops on the front line without new blood who will carry on our traditions?"

"Character the intention is for us to be the last so that the majority can survive and re scope our future, if in ten years were still running amok we'll all be in prison unable to do much of anything as it stands now our young people are losing more and more of their Mexican heritage as they become Americanized immersed in a culture that is starting to have our own call themselves niggas.I don't have a problem with the Blacks, but I am not their nigga even though some consider me so it is the equivalent of us referring to each other as wet's in short for wetbacks and being proud of it. We cannot allow this type of ignorance to seep into the minds of our youth for it will be the death of us as a race."

"The youngsters in my barrio are not feeling having to go to school because the majority of them cannot read or write what am I supposed to do about that?"

"Sharky you need to find out what after school programs are available in your area so that they can take advantage of them."

"Okay, homie, but I have one other issue. The few that are going to school are telling the homies that the teachers are not teaching them a thing and when they ask for help they refuse to help them am I supposed to push up on the teachers?"

"Home boy you do whatever it takes to get the job done period. If you must sit in the classroom with them you do that this needs to be set into motion so that we can see results this is not optional. Camel what is your report?"

"Similar to the others their going to school, but they don't really understand why. Most of them go to continuation because they were kicked out of regular high schools so there just getting by plus a lot of them ditch."

"Like I told Sharky do whatever it takes in a few more years the local politicians are going to do a 360 and we need to get as many of ours in seats of power when that happens so that we can yield real power in this country not just street power which is fleeting the more we send to college the better chance that a few will get in key positions so it is imperative that we get as many through as possible. Now on to the other business I don't know whets going on in the streets between the blacks, but they are killing each other off more so then usual so keep your eyes open for that it seems as if someone is trying to come to power which means that eventually we'll bump heads with them if their goal is accomplished what concerns me is that I've been hearing that the streets deaths could be linked to the cop deaths that have been taking place so you see why this group is of some concern to the Carnals. So, you all are responsible for the success of your respective barrios."

After the meeting Speedy and Shy Rock headed back towards Shy Rock's place to talk about personal business they had been doing since they committed the home invasion together months ago the cash and drugs from the robbery enabled Shy Rock to get on his feet and out of his parents' home into a beat up one bedroom house that looked abandoned from the outside with its chipped paint, unkempt die grass, an old crooked screen door, but when the rent was six fifty a month cosmetics didn't matter much the water worked and lights came on that's all that really mattered to him.

"You seemed to be really hard on the camaradas Rock, what type of obstacles have you been running into with the young homies in your area?"

"Nada now that I found a program to put them in after school that's why I suggested that the homies find local programs around them."

"What type of programs do they have near you? I didn't know any existed around you."

"Neither did I. I stumbled across through this brother I know name K-Stone he works with this non-profit called A.P.U.U they have all type of mentors and programs that help the kids out. So, when we got to talking one day, he told me to bring the ones that needed help through and since then it's been all good."

"He doesn't mind teaching our people?"

"Not at all he even provides los l`apices for them to write with and libros for them to read he really takes his time with them and it's genuine. The only issue that I have now is helping the ones that want to go to school, but their parents are illegally so they can't fill out the necessary paper work to get them enrolled I might have to go to the schools and pose as big uncle so that the paper work can get pushed through."

"Make sure you have your hall pass when you go you don't want to get written up by one of those fine ass maestros." Speedy said laughing.

"That's the least of my concerns I have to drive to Boyle Heights to console a mother who just lost her child a few weeks back to one of the local gang bangers who was shooting at a rival passing by."

"It seems like you are becoming more of a counselor then a Mafioso why do you need to go talk to some grieving mother homes?"

"You know it's all politics there's been word that she is going to start a march soon to protest gang violence which will counteract what we are trying to do the last thing we need right now is a march and for the *hooters* to start focusing in on us giving us a bad light which will cause distrust amongst the community."

"So, what if she goes through with the march do, we kill her?"

"Nada that will really bring the heat down on us in a major way plus the high ups want like that. I'll just talk to her that's all-in hopes that it eases her over."

"Good luck doing that shit. When my brother got killed by the BPS a few years back my mother would not speak for a month and every time she saw his picture, she would break down crying uncontrollably falling to the ground in a ball. Mothers take it hard when they lose a child, but they all act different so be prepared loco."

"Sounds like you have a lot of experience you should come with me."

"If that's what you need, I can do that, but it will probably be better to speak one on one so that she doesn't feel intimidated by two tatted vatos paying her a visit."

Later that evening Shy Rock found parked outside the residence of the Romero's home contemplating how to go about talk to the single mother it surprised him that it was so hard for him to go talk to a person's mom when he killed with no hesitation at all. Closing his door, he made his way to the front door which was surrounded by volatile candles of various colors with pictures of Mother Mary's face slightly melted away it a second to maneuver pass the portraits of the deceased boy to get to the door bell, but he did it. After a minute of waiting a young teenage girl came to the door asking who it was so he identified his self and was invited into the home which had even more candles lit all over the place making the home exude heat from each corner of the room making him sweat slightly as he was escorted to a back room where a woman he presumed was Mrs. Romero was on her knees in a prayer position next to her bed. The woman spoke in a soft whisper as he approached her.

"Han capturado a los asesinos ya?"

"No. Es pore so que estoy aqui para asegurar que se, pero el espanol no es tan beena como la suya puede hablar Ingles?"

"Si, why do you come here to my home?"

"To make sure you know that the killers will be taking care of as well as the gang problem."

"You look like one of them are you here to quite me from talking to the la policia?"

"No, but I prefer that you let my group take care of the problem instead of involving la policia."

"Your group is the problem. You are La Eme."

"Si, but not the one of old we are about unity for our people we don't condone senseless violence let us help you."

"Leave my home reaper."

It just so happens that Dolores mission posada was taking place when Shy Rock was coming out the door of the house with a cigarette already in his mouth ready to be lit as he took a pull he walked down the steps and positioned his self behind one of the few trees that was left in the area do to them cutting them down or back to prevent gang members from doing what he was doing now lurking in the shadows. He watched as the crowd Mexicans walked by slowly holding candles that barely held there light against the night wind that was cold against his face some of the crowd was dressed in biblical garb for the occasion while others were in regular street clothes he knew all about the posada supposedly representing the plight of immigrants in America by comparing their sorrows to Joseph and Mary. His grandparents were immigrants as well and would participate in the march every year when they were alive. The words from Romero were still stinging him as he finished his cigarette his life was a spiral that seemed to never be stabled mostly from his own doing he had come prepared to kill the entire family if needed forcing him to digest her words maybe he was only death in the flesh coming to take as many souls as possible before his was taken by another. There was, but one joy in his life and she was on the other side of town waiting on him he thought it smart to find his way to her before it got too late.

***

Shy girl had had enough of coming over to the life less domain that Shy Rock called home while he was away, she told him she would come over to straighten his house out. She just couldn't take it anymore he lived like he was still in prison all he had in the kitchen cabinets were can goods and top ramen noodles by the cases with only three utensils in the entire kitchen to eat with. His room did not have furniture except for a nightstand and a piece of plywood that held up an old hard mattress. When she was finished, he had a refrigerator with actual food in it, more than three pieces of silver ware, and dishes for his bare cabinets. She had an uncle that owned a furniture shop so she was also able to get him a new bed with a box spring and matching night stands outside of a few pictures on the wall she did a nice touch up to his cell looking house.

Before stepping into his house Shy Rock finished smoking his cigarette he knew Shy girl was going to be pissed with him for taking so long, but he had a lot on his mind he was still thinking about what the old lady had said to him at the house the reason it bothered him so much was because his grandparents use to talk about certain Mexican gangs back in Mexico that same way they referred to them as reapers too.

When Shy Rock opened the door he instantly grabbed his 357 revolver out his waist band when he saw that the kitchen that he normally left on was off as well as all the lights in his house he thought Shy Girl was waiting for him, but she was nowhere in sight so he dropped to a crouched positioned with his revolver extended out a few inches from his face ready to put a hole in the first thing that moved as he moved at a turtle pace across the floor fully knelt he heard some movement in his back room and thought their making this too easy once he figured out where the noise was coming from he assumed that someone had broken into his house and was still their so he stood up and moved into the kitchen to secure it before heading into his room to meet the stranger. The kitchen was clear so he placed his back against the hall way wall a pacing his self as he made his way to his room door which was slightly cracked with a little light exuding from it; from the light he could see the silhouette of a figure tip toeing around unaware of his presence prompting him to place his barrel through the crack of the door opening while training his aim on the individual. When Shy Girl saw the huge black revolver pointed at her she quickly dove to the floor behind the bed as Shy Rock realizing it was her moved his revolver to the air and placed the hammer back on the cylinder.

"What the hell is wrong with you Rock? You fucking point a gun at me!"

"All the lights were off I thought someone had broken into the house."

"I'm just glad you didn't start shooting."

"Of course, I wouldn't have just started shooting then I would have had to clean blood off the carpet. Why are all the lights turned off any way?"

"I called myself trying to surprise you, but I don't know what I was thinking trying to surprise a Mafioso. I should have seen that coming."

"Well at least we know for the future that there should be no surprises at least any with the lights off. So, I'm ready to see the surprise."

"Amongst the confusion you didn't notice the new bed and nightstand, did you?"

"No, I didn't it is nice thank you so much."

"Thank me after you see the rest."

As they toured the small house Shy Rock had a smirk on his face that wouldn't go away he didn't know what to say because no one had ever been this nice to him not even his own parents he just kept thanking her for what she had done and asked what he owed her, but she told him he owed nothing.

"I would have never done this for myself nor for anyone else to think about it why did you do this?"

"Everybody should be entitled to some type of kindness even a Mafioso."

"Really, my life has been the opposite of kindness all I know is pain and disappointments. The only kindness I know about is the one found in romance novels which equals fantasy to me. Kindness is foreign to me, so I've chosen not to get accustomed to it for it is fleeting much like freedom in this gangsta lifestyle I live."

"Are you saying that you want take a chance on us because you are afraid of changes in a relationship."

"Shy Girl my path is set for La Eme I have done too much to turn back now. I've been to prison four times as an adult and I have no qualifying job skills more so the good jobs don't hire felons or I don't possess the required experience needed to get through the door because all my experience is in criminal activity. Please don't be mistaken in thinking I haven't been down that road working odd jobs trying to do right catching the bus from interview to interview to only be told we'll give you a call that I know I want get or we don't hire felons. I have a penitentiary disposition that I can't shake; it exudes off me in all my mannerism I just don't fit in plain society anymore I am no longer a citizen just a Mafioso adhering to a hierarchy whose constitution is written in blood an enforced with violence."

"You forget that we grew up in the same barrio together I know what you've been through, but don't let it taint your spirit homeboy I see you working with the little homies Monday through Friday making them go to school so why don't you go back to school so that so that they can see your words in action?"

"Don't think I haven't thought about it Shy, but I can barely read myself how am I supposed to get into college?"

"How is that you graduated with me?"

"Come on you really thought I earned enough credits to pass when I hardly came to school. The teachers just got me out of there because they got tired of seeing me coming in class high not listening. It is sad now that I think about it; I thought I was really getting over when they passed me through years ago when really all they did was help prepare me for failure. One thing is certain in this life all wrong will be righted eventually there is no such thing as getting over only bad habits that set fourth ruin of life."

"No one's God Shy Rock we all have disabilities and the worst are the ones that can't be seen such as learning disabilities. I can tell that you want to at least educate yourself want you talk to the guy that teaches the young homies to see if he will help you out when he is not working with them."

Shy Rock had thought about asking Askari for help many a times, but his pride kept holding him back he saw his inability to read well as a weakness that he didn't want expose to anyone let alone another man yet he knew that Shy Girl was right he needed to conquer his disability if not for his self at least for the agenda of La Eme.

"Your words have neutralized the excuses that I have been giving myself not to learn how to read I will consider talking with K-Stone about helping me out."

"Within your pecho is a strong heart use it."

Chapter 21
Silence is betrayal
Rise Up

What about us? The ignorant lot, the ones who are first to be forgot societies socially declined rot.

Young and old wasting away in a constant state of mental and physical decay because of the choices made day to day. In communities where the children cannot safely play without liquor bottles, shell casings, or graffiti invading their way causing dreams to stray.

Why is everyday a survival test for their young lives? In a world that seems to eat them purposely alive. Be they appetizers for the court or an angry gang bangers magazine. Both are truly saddening things that eventually numb the ability to dream.

Leaving one to ask what about us? The color rag wearer, ominous finger twister, and war story braggers. Black and Brown peoples self-imposed spiritual dagger. Most recognizable as a pants sagger, young woman booty grabber, and quick to pull a pistol rather than to knuckle up to squash an unnecessary beef more influenced to promote savagery through music and DVDs. Yet go to prison and become tolerant as can be once controlled more thoroughly by those that were once others. Decorum becomes the norm with a pinch of hey brother, but eventually those that have the experience return to the streets to murder one another.

Genocide concludes but is rarely important enough to be shown on morning or evening news. Which is crazy because it is not happening on the moon, but in plain view? In the streets of South Central, Compton, and Watts it is time for the gang violence to stop. Putting an end to representing unpaid for blocks instead investing time in educational stock.

But what about them, the tormented ones the queens who raise our daughters and sons often without physical or emotional support. To these women we call sluts. Ranging their importance by the size of their butts; quick to say a bitch ain't shit it is imperative that we quit this for it puts in motion a *future filled with misfits. Birthed off the tits of angered bitter battered held to a double standard being who we have all treated mean. Tactics created from a low self-esteem.*

What is a male who tramples on women and children's dreams?

It seems we have forgotten our reflections and what they truly mean. More of a reason for new life lesson and direction mixed with genuine affection. For those only capable of birthing new life aspiring to stop treating them with strife for they are neither hoes nor ½ clothed low lives. How can this be fitting for the future mothers and wives of the next generation?

What about those who chose another route, but forget those in their communities still in directional doubt? Responsibility is held by those who know history has shown it is the only way a race can grow so in responsible hands the ignorant can be shown not just the new way, but the reason it must unfold. These tangible goals will then be incased in their heart for through the young new trends, but most importantly revolution starts. No longer will there be interest in tearing our communities and people apart. For the knowledge will have created a spark.

So never should they abandon or think their absence doesn't play a significant part.

But then what? We will rise up no longer being the world's trainable pups, no longer will our women be called or carry themselves as sluts and brothers will pull their pants up because they will be priced up. Being the epitome of men, our women will liken us knowing that those who strive leave impossibility in the dust.

And our children, sisters, brothers, grandparents, mothers, fathers, ancestors, and others will admire us for finally wising up, but more importantly for finding the courage to RISE UP!

"I'm still confused to what this is supposed to mean Pikes." Sergeant Waters said placing the paper he had just read on his desk.

"Are you serious? You do see what this piece of paper along with the armed images is suggesting to the people in the community we patrol."

"Seems like a bunch of rambling to me. I don't see any evidence from this paper that suggests killing the police."

"Of course, but there is a clear message to start some type of revolution in the streets by whoever wrote this I have a strong feeling that the individuals behind this are behind the deaths of our officers as well as the recent slaying of gang members in the streets."

"So, run some prints and find out where the paper came from. I'm certain that I want find fingerprints obviously if this group is smart enough to avoid our capture, they have covered their steps."

"Of course, my next question is going to be why did you bring this to my attention if you had no plans of pursuing it?"

"To make sure I wasn't the only one seeing the connection between these words and the chaos happening in the streets. I've been seeing these papers floating through the streets since all these killing have been happening and like you never paid that much attention to them assuming they were just litter in the street until I read the words and through the words I now have an understanding of what this group may be intending to do with these killing."

"And what exactly are they setting out to do Pike?"

"Liberate the Black community by eliminating all perceived threats to the rise they are putting together."

"You sound like a pundit from the Nixon administration with this Black power movement theory that movement died with the BPP, Malcolm X, and Garvey. Black people look up to rappers and entertainers now not political figures your theory is absurd; do you really think in 2011 that blacks want to unite after they have been killing each other for centuries around the globe as if they had impunity. These are the same individuals who have engage in what some have called a civil war on each other and haven't gained anything, but death and prison sentences. You should ask yourself why now some group would choose to start a revolution now or period when all other attempts have failed?"

"Hope, there is always hope brewing in the hearts of those who want better."

Escape from Failure

"Great response you should quit this job and start ghost writing for Obama. Hope...hopes of what?"

"Read the paper again." Pikes said walking towards the door frustrated at the sergeant's response to the evidence he presented. His gut was telling him that the words on the paper were a warning to what was to come and if he didn't act soon, he knew there would be plenty of blood spilled in the street."

***

Character was still slightly irritated that he had to break into a school as if he were a teenager again, but he knew he couldn't just send his little homies to do the assignment that was passed down to him from the up top because if something went wrong his head would be on the chopping block besides he needed to make sure the files they needed from the computer were taken and he wasn't the type to put his life in others hands. Fremont High school was located on the east side South Central Los angles and was the home school of the MSB so Character was that uptight about going into their turf even though he knew the East Coast Crips often came through trying to catch a Swan or F13 slipping so he made sure he and his four young homies were strapped in case they ran into any resistance coming out of the school. By the time they arrived at the school the sun was going down providing them enough light to hop the fence break into classrooms and offices without having to use flashlights. The purpose of the mission was to get addresses on the teachers that were not teaching and have a talk with them on their performance.

"I'll hit the office while you guys hit the classrooms, we'll meet back here in the middle of campus in thirty minutes." Character said heading towards the office as his young homies scattered through the school breaking in classrooms with crowbars.

"All available units please respond to an alarm at Fremont High school that went off ten minutes ago."

"Do you want to respond Pike's; it could just be a window that was left open like before?"

"Where not that far from the school we'll check it out and call it in."

William V. Fields

When Pikes arrived at the school there were two other units there as well about to walk the perimeter of the school. After acknowledging each other they huddled as Pikes gave orders on how to proceed. Not far away from the police officers across the street was a pair of Askari's men who had taken to following the police for the last five months whenever they got a call so that they could monitor their behavior.

"Looks like your theory of an open window were wrong look at the gate's lock it's been snapped open. Let us split into groups of two so that we can corner in any one we come across." Pikes said leading the way into the school. Hearing movement coming from a classroom Pikes signaled for his partner to get behind him as he made his way around the building to see what was making the noise. With his gun drawn he came across Character who had a blue and green poncho on with his hands tightly gripping the handle of the Tommy gun that the officers were unaware of.

"Put your hands behind your head and drop to the floor." Pikes said with his 45 pointed at Character. Upon hearing his command Pikes partner came from the back of him with his pistol out as well prepared to back Pikes play as he moved in on Character who laughed at Pikes order before dashing back into the classroom backwards. When Pike pursued he was met with multiple gun fire the like he had never seen before from Characters Tommy Gun as he caught two bullets in his right arm and three in his right side right underneath his vest causing him to instantly drop his weapon as Character trained his Tommy on Pikes partner who managed to squeeze off one shot before falling victim to numerous rounds coming from the gun that ripped through his vest as Character stepped over Pikes body in proceeding to grind his partner down with rapid gun fire before fleeing though the cafeteria. Hearing the gun fire echo through the school the other officers as well as Characters little homies ran towards the sound and into each other presences where more gunfire erupted between the gang members and police officers who had managed to gun down the younger gang members who had less experience. Once the suspects were down they called for backup, but were unable to complete their call as Character came from the back of them with a reloaded drum that was half empty when he finished mowing the last remaining officers down who were helpless under the fire of the Tommy gun that left them twisted and bloody. Askari's men had watched the whole massacre and were retracing their steps to see if Pikes was still alive. When they found his body, he was barely alive from the amount of blood he had lost which also caused him to lose consciousness.

"Pikes is down and is near death, give command on next step."

"Bring him in." Askari said while giving orders for his medical team to get into position. Since they had never had any causality or injuries his medical team had never been used before accept in drills so now would be the perfect time for them to have a real patient.

Askari's men were in the process of securing Pikes when Character bent the corner firing on them causing them to drop Pikes body and roll into defensive position returning fire with their AKS-74S equally matching the fire power of the Tommy gun catching Character in the body with a couple of bullets that didn't seem to faze him which let the men know that he had on body armor as well. Seeing what they were up against one of Askari's men through a flash grenade towards Character feet who was so busy firing that he did not notice until the light went off causing him to shoot aimlessly in their direction. While blind one of the men came around from the back shooting Character in the head two times then proceeded to tend to Pikes body as the other man retrieved the vehicle meeting the other man in the front of the school who had Pikes hunched over his shoulders throwing him gently into the back seat as he climbed in the back with him to continue treating his wounds. It took about thirty minutes to get to Altadena with the night traffic, but they made it with pikes still alive barely. When they arrived they were met at the front door as if it was an actual ER unit there was a gurney as well as an IV that the team placed in his arm as they rushed into the medical wing of the underground facility.

"Brief me on what happened." Askari said from behind a desk to the two men involved in the shooting.

"It was a routine call about an alarm going off at a school, so we followed to make sure it was a clean arrest, but it turned violently kinetic within minutes with three Hispanic males killing six officers. We found three USBs near the bodies of the slain Hispanic that were killed by the police officers so it might give some insight to why they were so heavily armed to break into a schoolhouse."

"Good work we'll have some of the men check the content to see what was going on."

"We also snapped pictures of the deceased gang members in case we need to identify them later. The one with the poncho must have been the ringleader because he was more seasoned then the two younger ones."

"You're correct his name is Character he's from F13 we did time together in Pelican Bay he is definitely connected. Take the USBs you found to the lab so that we can process the items you found at the scene. I'll debrief with you later."

***

Vibrations from the L.A.P.D helicopter brought a stream of local's curbside of their homes to see what all the shooting was about as the copter flashed a beam of light into the campus where the police found the bodies of the slain bunched together with a mountain of bullets and debris from the buildings that were hit by the bullets that didn't find their targets.

"All the bullets and guns that were involved in this shooting are in our custody except the guns that belong to these bullets right here." The detective said holding a bag of bullets he had found at the crime scene.

"So, there were more shooters involved that are running loose. Do we have a K-9 unit available to catch a scent?" Sergeant Waters asked clearly irritated that he had lost five officers as well as had one missing again.

"K-9 units will be here shortly I radioed in a few minutes ago. We have searched the entire campus and there is no sign of Pikes. He must have been taken by the same group that took Vasquez which could possible mean we want find him alive."

"Unlike the other crime scenes there are three dead Hispanics which adds a bit of a discrepancy. The individuals behind the last killing were more methodical these murders appear to be on a whim wrong place wrong time type of situation although I do not understand why the one the Hispanics were so heavily armed to break into a school. Make sure you get identification on all of them so that we can figure out what took place here."

"Absolutely I'll make it a priority to get those files over to you before the autopsy is done."

"Please see to it that I get them right away we can't let this case proceed without some type of information to give to the media this time around we are starting to look like some keystone cops who are being picked off with no recourse."

"Understood files will be on your desk tonight sir."

Pikes was awakening by a strong smell of cleaning agents that singed his noise as he took his first breathe without the help of the breathing machine that sat behind his head he realized quickly that he was lying in a hospital bed, but he knew he wasn't in an ordinary hospital because there wasn't a window in the room he was in just white walls and a brown iron secured door with a tray slot attached to it. He naturally ran his fingers over his cheeks to pin point how long he had been at the place he was being held the excessive hair on his face let him know he had been there at least ten days because that is when he normally needed a shave before it grew out to the length he felt on his fingertips. The movement in his arm was normal as he investigated his entire body to see where he was shot during the gun fight that left him near death. Before he could get both feet to the ground, he heard the tray slot open as his folded police uniform was placed on the slot a tray would normally be put. He could not get to the door fast enough to see who had left the clothes besides, they had moved so fast even if he were well, he probably could have not caught a glance. Sitting on the edge of the bed Pikes pulled his pants on carefully looking for anything that did not belong he did this with each clothing item before placing them on wondering the entire time what his captives were up to.

"He is ready Askari."

"Bring him in."

Pikes was already on his feet pacing the floor when he heard the key latch to the door being opened which instantly caused his heart to drop. When the door open two black hooded armed men gestured for him to step out the room and when he did, they gestured for him to walk down a short hall where a door set ajar. When he walked into the room he noticed a black light bulb was illuminating the room from atop and the room was a replica of a county visiting room the only difference being the Plexiglas was black instead of see through and there was no way phone only an intercom box in which a voice began to speak asking Pikes to have a seat.

"It's fortunate that you were able to survive the medical to team had a slightly difficult time keeping your vitals up with the amount of blood you lost, but obviously they were very successful."

"With all due respect it is extremely difficult to thank someone for saving your life when they may have only done so to take it themselves."

"How asinine that would be do you honestly think that we would invest that much care and resource into someone we could have let bleed to death on the asphalt. I assumed you were sharper than that Pikes, but then again I can see how you came to that conclusion with what happened to Vasquez."

"Yes, Vasquez a family man who will never get to hold his little girls again because you killed him and left him in the streets like a dog."

"Actually, he was worse than a dog in that had loyalty only to his self not the ones he was entrusted to protect."

"What are you talking about?"

"All your partners were crooked Pikes; all of them did underhand things to those they were supposed to protect in order to move up in rank and make extra money on the side. It was necessary to cleanse them from the streets."

"So, what makes me any different than them?"

"Did you lose your hearing in the shooting?"

"No, why do you ask?"

"Because you seem to not understand what I am telling you, we don't have an issue with cop's just crooked ones. As long as human violence exists

Escape from Failure

there'll be a need for law that I am perfectly clear on the need for police officers in the community."

"So why did you bring me here instead of letting me die?"

"Because the community needs cops like you. Too many officers choose not to relate to the people they serve daily their too caught up in their own lives to take time to do what police work truly entails."

"How are you determining what officers are adequate and inadequate?"

"We pay close attention to all the offices that serve the 473 square miles and act on our findings accordingly."

"So, you expect by killing all the crooked cops that things will change for Blacks and Latinos in the inner city?"

"Of course not there are a myriad of factors that will need to change for us to prevail such as disunity caused by warring gang factions which I assume you already know we are taking care of with the elimination of those who rather destroy than build."

"Elimination is all I keep hearing you say. If you keep eliminating what will be left?"

"New thought will be left and with that new thought faith and hope will emerge providing those that have been stifled by violence to start anew."

"You have to let the system deal with the crooked officers what you are doing is against the law."

"Your department is bound together by a code of silence that protects these rogue officers. Not only do these officers get a slap on the wrist, but they get reassigned to other detail throughout the city where they cause even more havoc. They are often rewarded for their behavior as well promoted instead of demoted and you expect for us to sit around idle singing hymns and marching we shall overcome in the streets in hopes that these murderous officer get prison time that history has proven never happens as mourning families have to grieve over lost fathers and sons continually. All the law enforces agencies throughout Los Angeles have a long-standing history of shooting, beating, and killing minorities that will be stopped as long as I have sense to know that these things are unacceptable."

"Your words could not be more true, but you have to keep in mind the pressure that the average officer is under to perform in community where the mind frame is fuck the police it is not my job to baby sit 12 to 27 year old's on how to behave when they are out of control. A lot of parents in the communities that we serve have lost complete control of their children leaving us officers to have to deal with individuals who have no concept of authority whatsoever making it a highly lethal environment to work in which unfortunately breeds these rogue officers that come from various back grounds that have to tackle dealing with the Blackman and Woman whom more times than not live up to the stereotypes have heard about growing up in our suburb communities so most act in ways that they feel Black people only understand violence. Honestly, the violence of the officers is fed on fear. Many officer involved shooting happen more out of fear than any type of resentments towards the victim many just have an innate distrust that is ingrained into their psyche to approach Black people with caution, thus with gun drawn ready to kill to ensure their safety."

"I understand pressure, but I also understand loss of life and justice for all not just the elite or privileged. Why should we continue to be subjected to acceptable murder because perceived threats that I do admit exist, but it is upon the officers to understand the type of individuals they are dealing with when it comes time to apply for this line of work."

"From the L.A.P.Ds last reports there are 15,000 kids in gangs out of a million that is a staggering statistic as well as eye opening to the fact that there are only a handful of individuals causing the tension throughout the city. I say this to say let us continue doing our job and everything will eventually work out. You cannot continue doing what you're doing."

"Next, you'll be telling me to turn myself in, right?"

"Not necessarily because I understand where your heart is even though it makes me extremely uncomfortable that I am having a conversation with a cop killer."

"As uncomfortable as this may be, we are moving forward with our agenda. I only hope that you take what you have heard and influence others in your department, but most importantly I hope you turn a cheek to what you might see soon because any interference taken while performing our duties will be taken as an act of war."

"Do you actually think you are going to kill each bad cop in Los Angeles? It will get worse before it gets better if you continue this."

"Who will it get worse for the police or the community. Because if you are talking about the community then you are mistaken the damage is already done. I would rather go to war then to continue seeing my people killed in the street and killing one another because of imposed self-hatred that most are unaware of having. The days of sitting by silent on the side lines are over Martin Luther King said it best silence is betrayal if I knowingly allow this genocide to continue without a word, I am basically condoning it."

"Your mind seems to be made just know that there will be no good outcome to this."

"Not all outcomes have to be good to be effective sergeant."

After the conversation Askari informed his men to take Pikes away from their facility and let him loose. The team would continue to monitor his behavior from afar knowing that their meeting with him would leave him perplexed as to what action he should take next to prevent their plans from happening.

Chapter 22

Tragedy

Funeral services for Character ended quickly as three dozen of his homeboys along with family members came to pay their respects. Also amongst the mourners were F.B.I and A.T.F. agents who wanted to profile those in attendance which was why Shy Rock, Speedy, Camel, and Sharky were on the other side of town having a meeting on the school killing that left three officers dead along with one of theirs and two little homies. The killings had gained a lot of attention from the media, local enforcement, and federal agents to what exactly happened inside the school that left six men dead and one missing.

"The only thing I'm trying to understand at this point is why that crazy ass had a baby arsenal to break into a school" Speedy asked twisting a napkin in between his fingertips while waiting on his breakfast to come.

"That's the million-dollar question homeboy that no one has the answer to. Shy Rock replied sitting across from Speedy at Denny's. The most accurate story that I have heard is Character tripped the alarm at the school unknowingly and the cops came surprising them and then a gun fight ensued. Knowing Character, he was packing because of the East Coast Crips in the area, but that's just a speculation on my part the bottom line is this guy fucked up and brought heat in his death so let's take this as a lesson comrades to be very careful in our actions from this point forward because if the police hadn't killed him we sure would have. The only thing that does not add up is what happened to the other cop that was at the school. Damn what happened now?" Shy Rock said seeing a red breaking news alert flash across the bottom of the Joe Brown show.

"Channel seven is bringing you news from the ongoing search for Sergeant Roger Pikes who was found today outside of Centinela hospital unconscious laying by some bushes although reports are telling us that he is fully coherent and giving details of his kidnapping. Officers are elated that he is safe. A few months back officer Luis Vasquez was kidnapped in a similar fashion, but was later found dead at a local gas station that investigation is still being pursued by the F.B.I after L.A.P.D were unable to capture any suspects. Hopefully, Sergeant Pikes' information can give them the break that they have needed for a while to solve these horrible mysterious murders. This is Amy Powel reporting for Channel Seven news."

After the news report the four mafia members set perplexed at the information they had just heard they were under the assumption that the officer had crawled off somewhere and died the fact that he was kidnapped got them all to thinking that there was a lot more to the store that needed to be looked into because it was starting to look as if one of there was killed by an outsider and if so then there would be some get back coming their way courtesy of La Eme.

Death foreshadowed his thoughts constantly during the last hours of his capture even though the individual he spoke with behind the black glass seemed to be a man of his word he kept thinking in those long hours that he never promised they would release him alive, but yet there he was inside the police with a tape recorder alive surrounded by his collogues.

"Are you sure you are ready to talk Pikes." Sergeant Waters asked in between sips of coffee.

"Yes sir. I need to divulge as much as I can remember now while it is fresh in my mind."

"So, who are these men that kidnapped you and are they responsible for killing the officers at the scene?"

"They are definitely not responsible for the deaths of the officers at the school, but they are accepting responsibility for the deaths of Vasquez, Lee, and Fain as well as the attack on Rodriguez."

"Did they give you an explanation why they are doing these killings?"

"They actually did."

A look of surprise spread across the faces of the officers in the room they had been trying to figure out what was going on for almost a year and now the answers were about to come.

William V. Fields

"Their goal is to eradicate disunity amongst themselves as well as ineffective leadership that they feel has crippled the Black community almost beyond repair by cleansing the community of negative vises such as corrupt police officers, gangbangers, liquor stores, and corrupt politicians. They believe that as long as sub-standard living conditions exists so will genocide and poor education so they have taken it upon themselves to tackle these issues head on and unless we control our officers bullets will continue to find their way in places where recovery want be an option for them."

"So, they are threatening to continue to kill innocent officers at their leisure so why did they allow you to live?"

"They were very adamant to convey that they do not have a problem with police officers in fact under their plan they will encourage young people to become more active in the community by becoming police officers, politician, and judges. The reason they helped me recover from my near fatal wounds was to prove that their intentions are genuine and not that of vigilantes out to settle a score they don't condone any type of crime rather it be on their own or against an officer."

"Personally, they sound like terrorist. In your opinion do you think they pose a threat to national security?"

"Yes, because they have made it clear that they will eliminate whoever presents resistance to their goals."

"So, you feel we should get the military involved?"

"If we are unable to apprehend them ourselves they will give us no choice, but to involve other agencies yet it is premature to say that we will need assistance from the military because I am unaware how many of them there actually are."

"Did you get a chance to see what they looked like?"

"Of course not they were all camouflaged from head to toe wearing black mask so it was impossible to tell what nationality they were; I can only assume that they are African American because they seem to want better for disadvantaged, but specifically African Americans."

"Do you have any idea where they took you?"

"Absolutely not, I was unconscious when they recovered me from the school. They also drugged me before they dropped me in front of the hospital."

"I know that I am going to start sounding repetitive, but do you think that our officers are in danger?"

"According to my kidnappers our officers are safe as long as they do the job that they were hired to do which is to protect and serve."

"Did they abuse you in any type of way?"

"No, they treated me accordingly there was no mistreatment of any kind by them."

"So, in your opinion are we dealing with gang members with guns and a cause or something else?"

"The fact that they have eluded us for almost a year, killed four officers, and were able to conduct surgery on me confirms that these individuals have some type of military back ground they are not merely gang members with guns shooting indiscreetly. To approach them as such would be extremely detrimental to our officer's lives."

"Just for the record Sergeant Pikes you are unable to give a description of the suspects?"

"Yes."

"You also have no idea where the suspects are located?"

"Yes."

"You feel that these men possess some type of military training?"

"Yes."

"Do you feel the suspects are a threat to national security?"

"No."

William V. Fields

"We all appreciate you coming down to conduct this interview after what you have been through. The information you have given us will give us enough to at least start a profile and lead us in a direction to get these suspects off the street. When you wrap it up Pikes come by my office?" Sergeant Waters said walking out the interrogation room.

"Come in. Waters said hearing a knock at his door. Have a seat Pikes. Of course, I could not help, but think during the entire interview that you had warned me about what was to come prior to your kidnapping taking place and honestly, I feel foolish for not listening to you. Now the only other question I have now is do you think we can catch these suspects without any other bloodshed?"

"Absolutely not they made it clear that compromise is not an option."

"So how do you suggest we lure these suspects out to take them out?"

"The only way to lure them out is to show admittance of rogue cops within the brass and knowingly use them as bait. It would never work because they operate in small units that are assigned to different task. So even if you draw them out there will be losses on both sides."

"How is it that you know they work in units?"

"Because they mentioned that they had been monitoring me as well as other officers. So that inadvertently let me know that they work in assigned units like our structure."

"So, it seems that there is no tactical way to approach this without casualties on both ends which will be a benefit for them. There must be away to draw them out."

"Wait, watch, and follow leads closely until we can find out where they are located because to come at them any other way would be as you say to their benefit."

"I have to prepare a report on your kidnapping to take to the Chief tomorrow I will recommend that he assign you to the case of finding these suspects before another killing happens. Most likely you will be working with the feds on this case."

"Before I go have you heard from Rodriguez lately?"

"Last I heard he was still under suicide watch at the hospital."

The day felt like it would never end Pikes thought to his self as he turned the key to open his car door his thoughts were scattered some question whether he was doing the right thing pursuing his captures because in a way he felt their plight to want better lives for their people, but he knew killing wasn't the answer yet his collogues killed under the guise of I feared for my life. He was confusing his self with his own thoughts and figured he needed to just go home and get some rest.

***

Toy Box had been dating Pastor Robert for the last few months since she started to attend his church, she found out quickly that he had a thing for troubled women especially with kids. After observing what he was into she dressed accordingly making sure she sat on the third pew next to the edge so that he could get a full glimpse of her juicy thighs every Sunday morning. He first approached her in the parking lot after service asking her if she was going to make the church her permanent home in which she replied maybe. It didn't take long for them to exchange numbers and begin talking regularly with conversation that were as simple as him telling her his plans of starting his own ministry in the Inland Empire were any Black pastor could make a fortune for Gods work amongst the diverse people who needed motivation through the word of God. He had even suggested that she could be the first lady of the ministry if she did exactly as he said which entailed her giving her body to the body to him as a faith sacrifice that would show her belief in the mighty word. For hours he would try to convince her that women were made to service the pastor because he was chosen by the Lord and in turn they would be blessed financially. Through their conversations Toy Box could see how his spiel worked on troubled single mothers who had been deceived by men all their lives except the pastor the one man they were train to trust it sicken her to know that he was using his power to take advantage of not only women, but poor people giving her every reason to want to kill him even though her mission didn't entail that. She was to find his angle so that the group could use it to discredit him and get him out the church because he was the main vocal preacher that was against their movement. Askari knew that if he didn't keep tabs on Robert that he would eventually go to the police about what was going on in the community concerning the churches private funding the only thing that was stopping him as well as the other pastors that were against what he was doing was greed if they alerted the authority to what was taking place it could lead to their financial indiscretion coming out something that none of them wanted, but since Robert had the most influence amongst the congregations he needed to be made an example of.

"Sister Toy how long have we been conversing?"

"About four months are so."

"Is that all it really seems like we've been connected forever. Probably because I have been able to help in your spiritual development since we have met."

"Yes, I agree."

"Well the reason I called you today is I found a building in the I.E that is suitable to where I want to start my ministry and I would like for you to go with me this weekend to go see it. I already have a room reserved that we will leave from in the morning."

"Okay just give me the address so that I can meet you there tonight."

After getting the room number and address Toy Box immediately contacted the group so that they could set up surveillance in the hotel room. One of the many benefits of owning a cleaning service was the multiply contracts the company had with various companies that allowed them unprecedented access. Once the room number was known the surveillance team went to work rigging the room with mini high definition cameras everywhere. Toy Box arrived at the Hyatt in Downtown Long Beach around 7:30 p.m. she quickly noticed the pastor's green jaguar parked in a reserved space and took a deep breath before signing. She made sure to avoid all camera angles as she made her way up the stairs to the room which was on the 5th floor overlooking the ocean she reached in her purse to get the duplicate room key the group had given to her earlier it felt slightly awkward carrying a purse she was more accustomed to carrying guns so it took a little getting used to make it all flow naturally. Robert eyes got big when he saw Toy Box come into the room, he had been there for hours prepping the room with floors, candles, and incense. He had done this before so he knew the routine when it came to women with nothing, but their faith left although he was slightly disappointed that Toy Box was wearing jeans and a shirt usually the women came with provocative out fits to only play hard to get.

"So, did you have a hard time finding the hotel?"

"No, I use to work as a security guard here and around the area."

"Amen. What made you stop do security?"

"I couldn't get a guard card because I have a felony so eventually the company let me go."

"Do you care for a little wine?"

"I guess."

"Hay don't feel uncomfortable a lot of Christians forget that Jesus turned water into wine; nothing is wrong when it is done in moderation."

"Then pour me a glass."

"That's the spirit you need to learn how to relax you are always so tense. So, when I told you about the new church what went across your mind?"

"Exciting thoughts of all the people we could bring to the Lord."

"Amen sister. A lot of people really do not realize that it is hard work being a pastor with all the temptations in the world especially with the flesh being so weak. I have a confession Toy I need you to help me purge my sexual demons."

"How can I do that?"

"We must have sexual relations so that I can have a pure mind and spirit when I am on the pulpit delivering the word. It is my understanding that one must be pure and have one by their side in which the deed can happen."

"Shouldn't we be married first? What's the difference between this purification you are talking about and fornication?"

"A man chooses his wife by the fruit she bares. Fornicating is two people having sex just for pleasure. Purification is the process of keeping me pure of mind and spirit."

"I thought prayer was supposed to help in those areas."

"The flesh is weak and needs purging."

As they went further along in the conversation Robert started to remove his clothing until he was standing before her with his black briefs on clearly aroused.

"Are you ready to bare your fruit for your future husband?"

"Yes, let me go to the bathroom first to freshen up." Toy Box grabbed her overnight bag and headed towards the bathroom. Once inside the bathroom she placed her bag on the sink and reached inside for her ten-inch strap on with a smirk across her face. When she stepped out the bathroom all she had on was a red bra with the strap on extended out with only the black straps holding on to her outer thighs for support. Robert was sprawled out on the bed by this time completely naked running his fingers along the top of the bed spread. The sound of the bathroom door turned his attention to Toy Box who was ready to turn the tables on the pastor, but even she was not prepared for his reaction. Toy Box had never penetrated a man before, but she had always wanted to do it to certain males throughout her life especially her dad who was too busy chasing skirt to be a father he had slept with her aunt which caused a permanent rift between her mother and sister as well as the family with different relatives taking sides which further separated her already fragile family. His absence in the house hold made every situation that came along with being a lighted skinned Black girl worse there was no protection from older men in her community who routinely preyed on young girls for sex where it is regular practices for a man to have sex with a females ten to fifth teen years their junior with without a second thought because it was condoned behavior that no one berated especially in the gang culture where older gang members routinely had sex with young girls from junior high to high school it was often times seen as a badge of honor to them to knock down a young girl to be her first before she got passed around by others in the neighborhood. Fortunately, that did not happen to her, but enough of her home girls where ran through by local predators including her sister for her to have a firsthand account of the damage caused by underage sex with grown men. Even though she never gave in to sexual relations with the males in her community like her home girls they all shared the common bond of not having a father in their lives. As she gazed upon Robert's naked body, she could not help but feel disgust in her stomach for another predator.

"I see you come baring a banana for pastor to eat. You must've read my mind." Robert said casting his eyes on the tip of the penis head before dropping to his knees to perform fellatio on the strap on as Toy Box tried with all her might to keep a straight face this was not the reaction she had expected, but she went with it palming the back of his head as he went to work with the experience of a man who had done the act before. Before she knew it, Robert was on all four at the edge of the bed with his ass touted ready for intake. Toy Box was slightly disappointed at how easily the ten inches went into his rectum she was honestly expecting some type of resistance to the penetration as she placed her hands around his waist thrusting away until he ejaculated on the covers. The men doing the recording were back at the station could not believe what they had witnessed their jaws were to the ground as they kept repeated simultaneously saying this is crazy! When Robert finished ejaculating Toy Box pulled out and went to the rest room to get dresses and dry off the sweat she had worked up routinely from using her strap on although she had never went that vigorously before. Seeing Toy Box come out fully clothed Robert had a slightly baffled look on his face.

"That was amazing! I truly feel purified now. How did you know that I craved to be ravaged?"

"Weak flesh breeds strange desires in the soul."

"Okay. Why are you dressed?"

"I realized that I left one of my other toys in the car when I was going through my bag."

"Don't be too long."

"I'm sure that want be a problem for you pastor."

After thirty minutes went by Robert got dressed and went outside to see what was taking Toy so long. He canvassed the entire parking lot before accepting that she had left. When he got back upstairs to the room, he called her on her cell phone, but she did not pick up. Twenty non-responsive phone calls later he accepted that she was not picking up the phone. When he awoke Robert began his morning like every morning with a prayer to prepare for the day; he knew it would be a long drive out to the I.E., but he was prepared for the drive that would help clear his mind of the night before. Halfway down the 10 West he called Toy Box's phone again, but still did not get an answer. Oh well he thought he had seen them come and go most of the time they left the church too, but there was always one insecure single troubled female that would take the place of the fleeing. By Sunday morning Robert had forgotten about the tryst with Toy Box he was back to his energetic boisterous self-bouncing his shoulders to the choir's rhythmic sound behind the podium. It was Easter Sunday and the church was packed it was one of the only Sundays where gang members came to church dressed in their loud Easter suits giving the illusions of colored eggs in a carton as they sat packed into each pew. Once the choir finished their song Robert addressed the congregation.

"As I scan the congregation, I see a lot of visitors in the pews hopefully by the end of this sermon you will no longer be visitors at our church. Know that you can always call Gods house your house."

"Amen!" A few people yelled out at the pastor's words."

"Thank you, Sister Royce, always a great supporter of the gospel. Today's sermon is about being a supporter of God's almighty word. One thing that I come to realize in this life is that we all need some support at some point in our lives and there is nothing wrong with that depending on where you are getting your support from. Ya'll do not hear me up in here today! Ask yourself is Jesus really your support system or just a plan B someone you go to when all else has failed? Example most of you don't call on Jesus for support when you are having a bad day and the reason why is because you know that all you have to do is call upon Mr. Newport or Kool's to get the support you need to get through any particular situation and don't let the situation be too much for the cigarette to handle because the chronic man are smoke shop will be

Escape from Failure

the next stop on the way to support that is only temporary. Ya'll do not hear me up in here! Or let us say that it is Saturday night and the kids are off with your mother and you do not have a thing to do who do you go to support? I know the club with your worldly friends where ya'll are supposed to be having a good time, but you need some Patron to move you along to give you just a little more support. Ya'll do not hear me up in here! The only support that is going to help you get right is from Jesus and nothing else not money, alcohol, or drugs! In correlation to that know that the Lord loves a cheerful giver you must give to receive. I will be passing the collection plate around right after I play a short video of our up and coming events next month.

As the video started up the pastor made his way up to the podium to watch to three seventy-five-inch screens that were positioned at different angles in the church so that all could see no matter where they sat.

"I see you come baring a banana for the pastor to eat. You've must of…."

It took about seven seconds for Pastor Robert to realize what he was watching because he had removed it from his thoughts, but when he realized what was actual playing on the screen he yelled to the audio technician who was normally in the corner to cut the video, but he was not there forcing him to try to find the switch to the video feed which he was having a very hard time doing because Askari's men had redirected the power source so that they were in full control of it. Once Robert figured out that he couldn't cut the video he made a b line to hidden door that lead to his office which was futile because it had also been rigged not work properly so after a few hard nudges Robert had to choice, but to walk up the aisle to the front with shouts of Lord Jesus by the elders of the church who were watching the video in pure mortification at the pastors support system as he walks speedily towards the entrance with his head ducked down covered by his right hand. Relief overcame his embarrassment as the sunlight touched his face only to return once he realized that his car keys were in his office the only decent thing he could do at that point was walk down the street until the church let out to retrieve his keys. Inside the church reactions were mixed at the scene they had just witnessed.

"That's why a nigga doesn't come to church." KP said adjusting the tie on his shirt next to his grandmother.

"Will you watch your mouth you don't speak like that in the Lords house."

"I don't see why they are doing way more foul stuff that needs to be addressed."

"This is truly a tragedy."

"Amen to that." KP said scanning the church for any potential cheeks he could stalk.

The scene at the church spread throughout the streets like a hot std fast and relentless it was the talk of the town for months and of course Pastor Robert never showed his face in Los Angeles again instead he relocated out to the I.E. where he started up a new ministry were his main focus was follow the message not the messenger. Robert's humiliation was only part of Askari's plan the news of his disgrace was more of a caveat to all the other preachers that they would be held accountable for all their action as long as they kept the title of a spiritual leader within the community more so the news reached the ears of the local politicians who quite as kept had strong ties to the church community especially when it was time to rally votes for reelection. Too most it was a funny sight to see the pastor fall from grace while for others it was retribution for financial, physical, and spiritual abuse that he had caused during his reign. Askari on the other hand was always looking at the ramifications of every decision he made in regards to getting rid of those that he knew made things worse for his people he was conscious that every move would garner a response of some sort that would advance the movement or derail it. Up until this point he was pleased at the results he was seeing throughout the streets more kids were getting involved in community activity without the fear of being ostracized by the local gangs in the area through K-Stones programs kids were getting the needed after school tutoring that they needed to help them succeed in school which improved their confidence as well as G.P.M across the board. Their parents were also getting much needed counseling on parenting skills and job placement too often males and females had children with no blue print whatsoever of how to parent it was definitely lost to them which could be seen in the behavior of the children sadly the parents lack of parental experience caused them to treat the child violently because that's what the parent learned from their parents how to set a child right. It was no secret to Askari that abuse ran deep in the ghettoes which nurtured seeds of hatred in the receiver which was most often a child. He knew it was fruitless to help the children without reaching out to the parent who was raising the child who also needed to reinforce every principle that the children were learning in the programs that K-Stone and his self were funding throughout the week. Most single mothers poured the sickness and pain that they endured in their lives right into their own children with little to no regard to the dysfunction they were creating in that innocent being who only wanted a chance to be great. It was Askari's belief that all children start out great capable of great feats until someone around them told them differently setting them off the course of their true purpose into a life of low self-esteem and constant self-doubt that was hard to climb out of once it was ingrained from birth that they weren't shit. So, the solution that so many non-profits overlooked when helping children that his program did not was the mindset of the parent needed to be examined to establish true success with the child's developmental build up to greatness. What was most disturbing to Askari was seeing abusive mothers involved in the nonprofit programs trying to help other people's children when their households were in shambles thus preventing them from identifying the neglect of parents because it would in turn shine the light on their abusive ways which only created a faulty system that turned a blind eye whenever they saw their own wicked behavior in another which only hurt the child in the end. Through his guidance these disturbing practices were being eradicated whenever an individual was identified with the trait overall there was beginning to be a glimmer of hope in the streets that was absent upon his release.

Chapter 23

Self-Hatred

Walls that were once accustomed to having graffiti sprawled on them for years were now bare giving once shamed communities a sense of pride again in how their neighborhoods reflected them as a whole a definite mile stone to be elated about even though it took most in the inner cities a while to fully appreciate clean walls again because they had grown immune to their intruding presence for so long bringing down property value and costing the city valuable resources on graffiti removal. This small, but much needed victory did not come without a cost there were still a few individuals who were wall banging and Askari knew who they were because they left their gang monikers on the walls symbolizing their defiance. He had managed to get through to the majority of the gang members that took pride in striking up on walls some he even recruited into the group assigning them to seek out and find others who shared their artistic desire. Unfortunately, some chose to go against the grain of what he was trying to do and paid with their lives much like the current individuals were aiming to do. In a small way he admired their defiance for it was only revolution with no direction yet he despised their desire for destruction when it served no purpose he was aware that most people did certain behaviors for so long that they ceased to question it which often times created problems. The majority of the gangs throughout the city had agreed to stop the gang related killing all together some by choice, but most by force with the help of the groups outside members coupled with fellow incarcerated members enforcing the groups policies inside the prison and jails it was becoming deadly to be known as a gunner a once lionized title that carried fear and respect now cared death and dishonor on the streets as jails became death chambers for individuals coming in with a murder *beefs*. HCG's territory spanned from the forties all the way to the hundreds down Hoover Street comprised of eight clicks that all had separate reputations that they were known for. In the pinnacle of their reign they were fear by most gangs through Los Angeles for their perpetual violent behavior that was passed down from generation to generation without fault, but like most gangs they eventually fell victim to their prominent members getting murdered, getting life, or turning snitch all these circumstances eventually left the gang in shambles a mere glimmer of their former glory in fact their only savior was there reputation which kept certain enemies at bay when the gangs were still warring with each other. Out of the eight clicks only one was going against the new mandates set down by Askari the 83. Being that the taggers were so sporadic in their graffiti the group in charge of catching them wrote rival graffiti on the wall in hopes they would come out to cross it out giving them the opportunity to take them out.

"Groove did you see what those boys wrote on the wall?" KP asked walking down the street in the direction of the wall he intended to graffiti on.

"Hell, yeah that's why I ain't with this punk ass peace treaty they got going on right now in the streets. These niggas are acting like weenies all of a sudden like they then forgot what it means to groove."

"For real though, wait hold up there goes one time in the alley. Alright they kept it grooving let us go whack this shit out."

As KP and Kool Aide shook their spray cans in preparation to deface the wall two snipers were in position ready to pull back on the trigger as soon as the paint from their cans touched the walls. Both snipers were looking through their scopes when they heard police radio's running interference with their line of communication causing sniper one to signal the second sniper to fall back to see what was going to happen. Before KP and Kool Aide could respond the light of the helicopter was locked in on them giving them only one option, Kool Aide ran to the left while KP headed for the right hearts beating rapidly as they tried to escape the light of the helicopter that corralled them in the direction of awaiting C.R.A.S.H officers who had cornered off both directions prior anticipating they would split and run. When both of them heard the dogs barking they both stopped simultaneously knowing that there was no getting away as the officers commanded both of them on opposite sides of the street to lie on the ground where they were handcuffed and brought back together to talk to sergeant Pikes. Pikes did a slight glance over of the highest set building in the area and knew in his gut that the men who had kidnapped him were watching from afar.

"I saved you guy's life tonight. You might want to tell me what exactly is going on in the streets."

"What you mean you saved our lives? You did all this bullshit for some graffiti!" KP asked while trying to catch his breath.

"You don't even realize that this was a trap to kill you in order to stop you from defacing the wall."

"If it was a trap why are you arresting me and not the ones who set it up?"

"To catch them would've meant that I would have had to let them kill you. I prefer to not use live bait to catch these people. Now do you have any information?"

"No. I ain't a snitch."

"Take them to the county." Pikes ordered his officers.

As Kool Aide was getting escorted to the squad car, he collapsed falling to the ground he had been shot through the neck by one of the snipers killing him instantly. The snipers had found a different position among the building determined to finish their mission but were unable to get a clear shot on KP who now being covered by the officers to prevent him from being shot.

"Is everyone safe?" Pikes asked clutching an assault rifle not knowing where the shot came from. His mistake was he assumed that they had left once the officers arrived, he learned a lesson that night to how relentless this group he was hunting was. Back at the station he tried to convince KP to talk to him after the death of his friend within the interrogation room.

"The charge that we have you in here for will only have you in the county for a few weeks at best. Once you are back on the streets, they will kill you; notice I didn't say try because they are relentless when they after someone they will kill you just like your friend."

"Do I look scared?"

"No, but I know you are. I'm not asking you to snitch I just want to get these people off the street before they kill another one of your friends or you."

"Look man all I know is that no one knows were these niggas came from they just started pushing this cold line about Black Power and Blacks need to stop killing each other and if they didn't then they would start getting rid of the trouble makers. All the other gangs have agreed to stop killing as long as whoever is pushing the line doesn't push a line on them."

"So, let me get this straight no one has seen them before or met them personally?"

"Not that I know of there like shadows."

"Then how do they communicate their messages?"

"Through flyers and I almost forgot they pay certain niggas a visit if they feel that they are calling shots in their sets and send messages through them that's all I know."

"Thank you."

After a day and a half KP was transferred to the county jail downtown to await a hearing on his vandalism case that would most likely be tossed out. When he arrived on Baker row, he was put in the cell with two of his older homies that he had only heard about they were both down from Folsom to testify in one of their other homeboy's defense. Just staying in the holding station a few days left KP feeling food deprived so of course when he saw the bags of food poking out from underneath the bottom of the bunks his stomach grumbled. It was amazing that even in jail there was a hierarchy of sorts from how much canteen a person had to how many visits are mail they received weekly the amount of bags underneath the beds let KP know that his homies had to be the *man* or had family that was super looking out for them.

"I see ya'll on fat down there want you look out for your boy."

"Grab whatever you want homie it's all good. One of the older guys said in response while moving the bag of food from underneath his bunk. So, what kind of case are you fighting lil homie?"

"Some punk shit groove they caught me writing on the wall."

"You still writing on walls, I thought there was an understanding in the streets that cats were going to stop wall banging?"

"They do, but I ain't with that peace shit I do what I want to do."

"Why is that?"

"Because ain't no nigga about to tell me what to do."

"But the police tell you what to do and you do it what's the difference?"

"The police are different there the police I have to listen."

"Who taught you that concept?"

"I don't remember it's always been like that for all I know."

"So, you have grown up to fear and respect the cops, but not your own kind. Don't you know that the groups behind the changes you are starting to see in the community want better for the people?"

"How they make it better niggas can't make shit well it's too fucked up."

"Where are you getting this information from?"

"From shit I see I have never seen a nigga change shit."

"You are right about that a nigga can't change anything, but a man can if given the opportunity which history has proven time and again. Instead of going against the grain want you join along in the movement."

"To keep it real I don't want to be a part of the movement. I do not want to go to school or stop selling drugs I like what I do. They are preaching that Black power Black is beautiful shit on these flyers floating through the set and that's cool if that's what a person wants to be on, but me I'm on some nigga shit straight up."

"What exactly is nigga shit?"

"Talking shit, waking up late, smoking weed, popping pills, fucking bitches, having kids that I don't plan on taking care of, buying new clothes every week, driving the tightest whips out at the time, and doing what the fuck I want when I want that's nigga shit."

Escape from Failure

"Where did you learn this nigga shit?"

"From watching other niggas."

"Obviously, you have watched niggas your entire life so you know where the lifestyle will lead yet you still want to proceed forward with this behavior when other options exist."

"Look homie I know that whoever is behind the street unity has good intentions there just not good for me change isn't for everybody."

"I strongly disagree; brother you can change if you want to."

"And that's the thing I don't want to. Besides why do you care you have life what does it matter if things get better on the streets. It wants give you a release date."

"After twenty-five years in this system release dates cease to matter anymore and to answer your question it does matter to me that the streets get better I am tired of seeing young brothers getting life or having to take outrageous sentences to avoid getting a life sentence. If the streets get better, then fewer brothers can miss this dehumanizing environment that can rip one's soul out. I have kids out there as well that I want a better life for because it is them that I worry about not some perceived enemy in here. Overall, I can live vicariously through the triumphs that are people should have been making. This movement is truly beautiful brother unfortunately you don't want to see it therefore we cannot allow you or anyone else to jeopardize it."

KP's response time to his homies words were too slow and before he could utter a response he had received a left hook to his chin which dazed him preventing him from blocking the larger man's next punch that landed on his right eye causing him to see a flash of red. Before he knew it, he was lifted off the ground by the other guy in the cell into the air by his left leg and arm over the men's head and then rapidly brought down over his knees. He could not hear his spine crack, but he knew there was extensive damage to it when he could not get up off the ground without pain shooting up his lower spine. Seeing that he was unable to walk they left him to crawl on the ground as they placed bars of soap within two socks before tying knots in them. KP pleaded with them as they walked towards him with the filled socks in hand as to why they were beating him.

"Because you refuse to stop your behavior, do you expect for us to stand by while you stand in the way of our people's rebirth with no regard to the damage you are causing with your actions. You are a disease that caries self-hatred which is highly contagious therefore you must be purged from the community for it to strive."

KP looked up at them from his crouched position on the ground with confusion before closing his eyes as the first sock came across his head. When the men were finished beating him to death all the soap in the sock was broken into pieces leaving his entire face and skull dented in. When the guard came for the nightly count and mail pick up later that night he hit the alarm before throwing up in the corner of the tier the sight was similar to Emmett till, but worse it was an image that would haunt the deputy for life. The news of KP's death had reached the ears of Askari and Pikes simultaneously rousing different reactions. Askari's found no more enjoyment in KP's death then an owner of a racehorse having to put down a good horse with a bad leg, it was unfortunate yet necessary. Pike's first emotion was anger at his self for not thinking ahead to prevent KP's death, but his anger soon melted away into a new understanding of how far the groups influence spread. Their movement was further along than he had thought, but now he felt like he had two of their members in custody a first since the cop killings had begun his only hurdle would be to make them talk a task he knew would be incredibly difficult to do with two individual who had life sentences already there would be no leverage for him to yield to get them to talk unless he was somehow able to commute their sentences down for corporation a million thoughts were going through his head, but he knew he had little time to figure out a way to extract information from them.

***

Askari was ending prayer in the back yard where he had built a small sanctuary where his members could go for prayer or reflection if they needed to it set all the way in the corner on the left side of the yard and was big enough to accommodate three people at a time-Ball was approaching the sanctuary as Askari was coming out with a look of urgency on his face.

"Our cameras have picked up a gang related killing on Crenshaw Blvd. It is apparent that the sixties have killed one of their rivals in the area."

"Was the individual a reputable?" Askari needed to know the specifics in order to knowhow sever retaliation might be.

"Yes, it was AK from BPS."

"Okay get the groups together we will have to neutralize this situation."

The death of KP within the county jail was the last show of power that the Hoovers needed to see to get on board with the other gangs throughout Los Angeles county to stop killing one another under this agreement Askari had vowed to the gangs that any gang that violated the peace would be taken care of by his group. Even with all the programs and help he provided for those who agreed to his group's terms he knew that eventually some group would test the water forcing him to show the power of his group. Before approaching his soldiers to give the orders he sighed in sadness for it was never his intentions to slaughter yet he was fully aware that ignorance ran deep within the ghettos making decorum a foreign language to those who only understood acts of violence. Looking from the podium upon the crowd of warriors that lined the underground room Askari could feel their energy radiating as uncertainty laid in the air all of them were aware of what the night would bring for they had trained for this occasion for months knowing the day would come, but hoping they were wrong nevertheless they knew their duties and were fully prepared to carry them out as they stood at attention in straight rows waiting for their orders.

"Victory was not so distant a taste in our mouths as we celebrated two months of no gang violence in the city of Los Angeles. It was a history defining moment that I can say left all of us reassured that our efforts have not been in vain. Collectively it lifted our spirits and gave us a glimpse of what type of environment we can produce with our actions. When we partook on this journey, we were all aware that our biggest enemy would be our own people. We were never disillusioned that the White man would give us much grief in the beginning phases of our uprising we knew in our hearts that the enemy was amongst us in plain sight. Earlier this morning I received confirmation that a faction of the Crips has chosen to go against the group's agenda. They are aware that this decision will be taken as an act of war against the Black community that this group has sworn to protect. We will annihilate this faction immediately to send a message that we will not tolerate this type of defiance whatsoever. Each group will have assigned targets depending on the special training you have received we will commence on the targets in the tomorrow at their hood day that is being held on the outskirts of town Friday June 10th at Wilson Park in Torrance. They have chosen this park because of its exclusivity on Fridays so there will be little to no civilians in the park when we engage. This park also has an artificial lake that we will be utilizing as well. The directive is to push the targets towards the lake where are aquatic unit will neutralize them, we will also be taking full advantage of the trees in the area as well as the several mini trains that run through the parks. Our explosive units will go out tonight to place C4 on our target's vehicles. Meet with your respective unit leaders so that you can be further briefed on your individual duties."

Abidemi, Akachi, Jelani, and Ekwueme were mixed amongst the crowd of soldiers ready to debrief their individual teams on what was going to take place. Before now all their missions had been covert or small scale attacks this would be there first major attack as a group and it was imperative that it be successful for the time would come that they would possible find themselves going into full scale war with the government over their beliefs. It was a day that Askari dreaded because he knew he would lose a lot of his soldiers if it came to war in the streets, but he knew that before the government would agree to their terms they would first try to neutralizes them under the guise of being urban terrorist. Comprise would only come when they were unable to just dispose of them so he knew that he had to keep pushing his units to get them ready for the day when the streets of Los Angeles would be reminiscent of the Watts and Rodney King riots when the national guard was called in to suppress deemed threats. Change was among them he just needed to make sure that they survived long enough to secure it permanently in their community.

June 10th had rolled around with the Rollin Sixties in full force wearing their gang colors with extreme pride. Most of them had barely made it to the Slauson Swap meet that morning to get their t-shirts scribbled on with their neighborhood idioms celebrating their hood day. It was amazing that they

Escape from Failure

took so much pride in a faction that caused so much pain. White t-shirts and NY hats could be seen up and down 10th avenue, Brynhurst, and side streets of Crenshaw Blvd. Vehicles from Cutlass on 24" Rohana rims with Pirelli tires to Range Rover on 22" Klass KF1 with Toyo tires filled local gas stations as members from the gang filled up on gas and blunt wraps for the long trip down Crenshaw to Wilson park. The stench of marijuana and burnt tires from the gang members burning rubber in the streets could be smelled up and down Crenshaw as their caravan journeyed out of their neighborhood into the Torrance area where they knew they wouldn't be able to smoke their blunts without alerting the cops. Askari's surveillance team was monitoring the group's movement as they traveled further into Torrance near the park alerting the different units that their targets were approaching. There were about twenty-five trees in the park, but only fifth teen sufficed for the snipers to be able to hold a solid position while maintaining appropriate camouflage to execute their objectives five of the fifth teen were large enough to support two snipers. The aquatic unit consisted of eight members who were already in the lake camouflaged amongst the seaweed and algae so that they could peer out to see their targets. Parked around the park were twenty bullet proof vans that held twelve members each who would act as ground units to flush the gang members into the middle of the park by the lake so that they could get better kill shots by shooting down wards. Toy Box lead a group of women who would corral certain members that managed to get away from the attack in all seven of them were already spread throughout the park ready to mingle with the gang members to give word on when it would be best to attack. Unlike the men who carried assault rifles Toy Box and the women carried two FNH handguns apiece which they concealed on the side of their waist. The groups were given their last alerts around noon as the gang members piled into the park parking lot music blaring Nipsey Hussle oblivious to what was coming their way.

"Did you peep those bad bitches in that Porsche truck?" Khaki Blue asked his homie as he tried to find a parking spot amongst the confusion.

"Hell, yeah a nigga going to have to holla at those cakes when we get in the park."

While the members of the Rollin sixties gathered their lawn chairs, domino sets, and food out their vehicles Askari's men waited patiently as the inside of their stomach clinched up tight as the impeding attack loomed near. On the other side of the park a few miles over Askari lead a small explosive team that were placing explosives around the police station to create a diversion when the shooting began at the park. He also planned a fake bank robbery at the local Chase bank to create a hostage situation to draw all the Torrance P.D. out to various calls to prevent any of their officers from being wounded in the attack. Around 2:30 p.m. all the members of the sixties were in the park drinking alcohol out of brown bags and lighting the air up with Kush while a mixture of rap music played from their vehicle stereo systems. Although a lot of their key members were in attendance a few were nowhere in sight.

"Code drive, I repeat code drive." Toy Box said into her blue tooth signaling all the members to prepare to move in shortly. All the snipers had key targets that they were instructed to take out first before giving cover fire a tiring task for some who had to follow their target s with binocular the entire time they were at the park. The police received a call regarding a bank robbery shortly after Toy Box gave the code and two minutes later a bomb exploded on the north side of the Torrance Police station injuring no one, but causing immense damage to the building with these two incidents taking place The Torrance police were solely focused on attending to the two crucial situations taking place giving Askari's group ample time complete their mission. Once the call came through of the explosion the twenty vans that were on the outside of the park went into position with doors flying open as the groups file out the back military fashion approaching the group from a tactical position to ensure their men didn't get hit with friendly fire. The snipers moved in the same rhythm taking aim of their targets between their sights before squeezing on their triggers all the targets fell as planned taking shots to the chest and head before the snipers started to train their fire on individuals in the crowd who were now panicking trying to take cover not know where the shots were coming from as they heard loud crackling sounds from assault rifles as the ground unit descend upon them taking kneeling position as they mowed down the crowd of gang members who were helpless to the power coming from the guns that kept firing without stop. A few gang members managed to get cover and return fire but were of little match of against the machine guns that were eating away at the concrete tables a few tried to hide behind to no avail. The ground troop moved in as the sniper units cabled down from the trees to meet with their getaway vehicles they had served their purpose and it was time for them to fall back as the ground troops advanced forcing the remaining gang members down the hill towards the lake. A few gang members managed to get to their vehicles to get away but were blown up in the process as the second explosive team ignited explosive that they had put underneath their vehicles the night before. Hearing and seeing the explosion in the parking lot sent further fear through the gang members as they tried desperately to get away from their attackers. As they got closer to the lake the ground troops started to pull back return to their vehicles leaving the aquatic team to clean up the few that remained.

"Cuzz what the fuck... Khaki blue said holding his 9mm tightly with only a few bullets left in his clip. Who are these niggas shooting at us?" He asked his homie right beside him who was unable to respond due to his chest being opened by one of the members of the aquatic teams M16 rifle. The eight men in the water emerged systematically as they had been train finding their target and firing without second thought. The thirty members that managed to make it down the hill were slaughtered by the team in less than minute as Toy Box and her crew of ladies pistols in both hands killed everything left breathing with a shot to the back of the head before Toy Box got to Khaki Blue he squeezed off the last rounds in his pistol hitting her in the chest four time sending her to the flying to the ground before returning fire that tore the side of his face off sending parts of his braids flying on another dead body. Toy Box was out of breath from the bullets that hit her body army, but she quickly shook it off and got to her feet returning back up the hill which was completely cluttered with a sea of over a hundred bodies of men in women soaked in bloody clothes atop of one another. She took a quick once over of the scene and did not see one chest gasping for air as she maneuvered her way through the dead bodies to her getaway vehicle that set on the other side of the park. The police got the call of multiple gun fire from surrounding residence that were too frightened to call while the gun battle was taking place. S.W.A.T. was unable to answer the call as they made their way to the entrance of Chase bank for thirty minutes they had not received any communication from the would be robbers inside forcing them to approach the entrance to see if the hostage were safe. Upon looking in they noticed that all the hostages were tied to the floor with one-gun man standing with his back to the window prompting the officers to take the shot and move in. When they entered the bank, they followed their normal procedure of securing the scene by making sure the suspect was down first before checking on the hostages. When the S.W.A.T. team stood over the body of the suspect, they all felt an empty feeling inside and then perplexed when they realized they had shot a mannequin. In that moment they all understood that they had been played which infuriated them all. The bank robbery and bombing served its purpose for Askari's group in providing a smoke screen for their getaway. Back in Altadena Askari walked amongst the groups as they organized their gear and weaponry in the armory they were proud of themselves for executing the mission as planned as was he yet excitement was not in the room at all for in their success they were all aware that it was ultimately a failure. Through their actions they had eliminated potential fathers, educators, and mentors for their community. Although it had to be done it was a bittersweet victory that would serve as the catalyst the group was seeking. Individuals in the ghettoes were so taken aback by the show of power in Torrance they knew it was pointless to go against the structure of the group in any way exactly what Askari wanted. Immediately after the killings at the park gang related murders throughout the city dropped to zero the fear of having a June tenth happen to their sets was apparent. In the absence of gang activity, most of the gang members sought after the programs available to them in the communities that they would have normally ignored. Single mothers were also attending parenting classes so that they could be better parents to their children; through the parenting classes they learned that they had to build their children up in all areas for them to be truly successful to tear them with physical and mental abuse would only set them up to continue a cycle that the group was aiming to stop. So seven days a week the classes would be held with the women having to attend at least four times during the week were their progress was monitored by a plethora of exercises that included role playing activities to show case what they had been learning the program didn't have a completion date because Askari was aware that most women and men within the community didn't have any idea of how to be actual parents most assumed having children made them a parent. Progress for some was very slow which was definitely understandable because they had been accustomed to doing their behavior for so long yet all of them started to slowly come around when they saw the results in their children's confidence and academic performance in school. To rebuild the community Askari knew he had to start from the ground up which meant he had to get the women mentally right by building on their self-esteem which would affect all other aspects that took place in the rebuilding of the community. Education would be the second factor for it would make people start to think and value not only their life, but others. Finally, the community was like play dough in his hands ready to be remolded into greatness, but of course the old platitude range true that with one great accomplishment came even greater challenges.

Chapter 24

Two ears one mouth

"June tenth will be synonymous with tragedy forever for the families who lost their loved ones to the brutal massacre that left over one hundred gang members dead at Wilson Park in Torrance. For two weeks now officers have conducted a multiagency investigation but have come up with next to nothing on why or how this massacre happened in their city without having a single witness to the crime. Which is sparking outrage and accusation amongst the families of the victims killed who believe that the police have something to do with the murders in retaliation for the deaths of four unsolved officer related killing months ago. Black leaders are also up in arms of the killing which they also deem as some type of get back. Although they are at odds over the massacre both sides agree that the individuals behind the killings were professionally trained a fact that has the community at large afraid that there are individuals walking the streets who are capable of such acts. The families of the murdered victims plan to march in a few weeks to bring more attention to the tragedy so that the police will not falter in their efforts to bring justice. This is Amy Powell with Channel Seven news please continued to stay tuned as we bring you up to the minute updates on this tragedy."

Askari clicked the mute button on the remote as Carole lay on his chest he knew that she had been antsy wanting to comment on the murders that had taken place in the park which was not surprising; it was a hot topic at probably every ones table the last few weeks.

"Skari I can't believe she didn't mention the instant drop in gang murders since the massacre took place. I don't think the police have anything to do with the murders personally, but I do feel they are overlooking a lot of critical issues in the wake of the killing."

"Definitely, there hasn't been one gang related death in almost three weeks or act of violence reported on in Los Angeles or the neighboring cities which is incredible being there should have been some type of retaliation after the death of all those gang members."

"It's funny you say that I interviewed this older lady in the Leimert Park area for the senior living section in the paper who has been living in the area for her entire life and she was adamant about the change in the community over the last few months before the killings at Wilson. She said she realized that something was amidst in the area when the graffiti that normally covered the apartment walls across from her house had disappeared completely. She went on to say that she was positive that the city was not cleaning the walls and that gangbangers had just stopped writing on the walls. Which was odd to her because they were still hanging out all the way until they were killed in June?"

"Obviously, you feel that if this older lady can see that there are changes happening from within why the police aren't focusing on this shift."

"Absolutely, the officers in charge of this investigation are obviously jaded by all the gang violence that they have seen over the years that they are missing what is right in their face."

"So, what are they missing?"

"Whoever is responsible for the June tenth killings are probably responsible for the changes happening throughout the city? Gang members are not about to just stop writing on walls and hanging out for no reason. I've been around long enough to know that graffiti is the gang members main form of communication and authority in their neighborhoods; to give that up voluntarily is unheard of unless they were being forced to or came to some type of compromise with someone not to do it which leaves the question what are they gaining by stopping."

"Maybe they just got tired of defacing their own communities. Maturity can happen at any age if a person is receptive."

"Probably one or two got some sense suddenly, but not all of them at once. I am going to find out what is going on. I'm surprised that you haven't heard anything from your employees about what is going on?"

"Most of my employees don't communicate with their old neighborhoods much so they know just as much as you do. All I can tell you is to be careful in your investigation because if this group of people is as organized as you may think they may not take kindly to you asking questions."

"Skari I have investigated these types of things before in other countries, so I know how to maneuver without being detected."

"Of course, just be cautious new groups tend to have something to prove I wouldn't want you be used as an example."

Askari and Carole had grown extremely close over the last few months as their wedding ceremony drew near, she had even taken to calling him Skari affectionately because she felt his name sounded too militant. Despite their closeness he knew she was completely unaware that he was a part of the group she wanted to investigate. With her intelligence he knew it would not take her long to come close to figuring out he was in fact running the group. Even though he ran an entire underground organization he was still perplexed by man and women relations because he had spent most of his time studying war, social systems, and psychology. Personal relationships were not at the top of his list so he found his self-vexed to rather he should tell her or let her find out on her own. Both presented difficulties of there on so he decided to go with the latter and handle the situation when if it arose.

***

"Supposedly the group behind the Torrance killings wants to have a sit down with us." Shy Rock said addressing his homies in Sizzlers.

"How the hell did they get in contact with you?" Sharky asked cutting into his steak.

"Through a mutual acquaintance they want to discuss a few things with us as soon as we pick the location."

"You trust these guys enough to meet with them how you don't know it's the police trying to set us up?"

"Because I know and trust the individual who brought the information to me."

"You clear this with La Eme?"

"Yesterday homes."

"Then let's set the meeting up ASAP so that we can handle other business."

Baby Boo from 83 Hoover had approached K-Stone a week ago inquiring why the Black gangs had to stop writing on the walls if the Hispanic gangs continued to do so he felt as if they were being punked and that other gang members were also wondering what was up with the Ese. Of course, K-Stone brought this news to Askari who extended an invitation for a meeting. It only took a few days for the meeting to be arranged they would all meet at the Magic Carpet hotel around ten p.m. Shy Rock, Sharky, Speedy, and Camel would all be in attendance along with Askari and three of his men. Both sides agreed to show up without arms and agreed to pat each other down once they entered the room. Askari chose to bring three of his members who were known for their combat skills incase hand to hand combat was needed. Once all the men were in the room Askari seated himself as his three men stood behind him Shy Rock took the same posture before the men began to speak.

"I appreciate you meeting with us under such short notice. I greatly hope that I haven't inconvenienced you in any way."

"No inconvenience at all I am curious to why you wanted to meet with us."

"Before I began let me say that we come to you humble with the community as a whole and everyone in it our concern. With that said have you been conscious to the recent decline in gang related deaths and total stoppage of graffiti?"

"I had wondered why the Blacks had stopped writing on the walls and killing each other's, but honestly it was only for a short while, so I didn't give it much thought."

"The reason behind the sudden decrease is because all the Black gangs have taken a vow to stop killing one another and destroying the community. In correlation to that we want to ask of you to also comply with the graffiti vow because it is slightly frustrating to some for them to maintain the walls while others continue to vandalize them."

"Your request is a very complicated one being we don't work that way with Blacks."

"I understand your policies in concerns to illegal dealings, but this is for the betterment of all people not just Black people. If we start to build up our communities, we will attract better jobs into the community as well as reverse the effects of gentrification on our people right now are communities are prime real estate most just don't realize it."

"I hear you, but you're asking me to stick my neck out on the line because you feel that the graffiti is bringing the value of property down."

"Perception is everything when people see themselves as living in the ghetto their entire aura exudes that energy causing stress to be at the for front of their day to day activities. On the other hand, you get that same individual to take pride in where they stay you start to see less litter on the streets, lawns that were once brown start to look green, and houses that where decrepit start to get upgrades. We want the residents who live in South L.A. to feel as safe in their community as they would be venturing to Beverly Hills for a night on the town and all that begins with taking care of what we got and making it better. So, I am asking you to bridge the gap between our people so that even we can stop looking at each other as the enemy."

Shy Rock listened intently to what Askari was saying and had to admit to his self he did not expect for the conversation to go in this direction. He realized thirty minutes into the meeting that he was sitting amongst greatness. Askari remind him of the days of old when Black and Brown where slightly united in their fight for civil rights, but somehow along the way they lost that connection. In his heart he understood what Askari was trying to do, but he was skeptical about how it would go over with La Eme.

"You remind me of a militant Cesar Chavez I can feel your heart, but I cannot honestly tell you right here right now that I can make that type of call without talking with my carnals. I will take with you have told me back to them and get a response."

"All I can ask for is consideration I will be in contact with you."

After the meeting, the men with their separate ways to only meet up in different areas to discuss what had happened.

"So, do you think they will get on board Askari?"

"It's hard to say they are under a different structure then we are. For the sake of us all I hope they do. The ones we will have to watch are Camel and Sharky their body language told me a lot about how they felt about our goal unfortunately they have that hate in them that leads to death when we get back to the facility make sure you put together a team to track all of their whereabouts in case we have to adjust their thinking."

On the other side of town in Shy Rocks back yard the men discussed how they felt about the request Askari had put on the table."

"That ese speaks from his *corazon* so I know his words are sincere about uniting our *gente*, but we must first present this request to the carnals ."

"Ese are you really considering cooperating with the *mayates*? We are having a hard-enough time bringing our own together to start trying to build with another race let alone the mayates. Half our race thinks their *gavachoes* or *mayates* anyway if you agree to do this it will make the lost Raza even more confused." Camel said angrily with the thought of Shy Rock bringing Askari's proposition to La Eme.

"Camel your letting your anger and past experiences cloud your mind holmes. What Askari intends is for a cleaner environment for our *gente* to grow up in that's all so that for both groups its *firme* to grow up in succeed."

"*Chale,* but I still don't trust them no matter what they say."

"Why is that?"

"Because deep down inside we can never be equal they will always sale us out when the chips are down or jump us when they are deep. I know how they operate holmes. They treat each other like shit their so confused that they even treat us better sometimes then they treat their own. So how am I supposed to align myself with a race of people like that?"

"The same can be said about our people as well. Chicanos are referring to themselves as niggas now and wearing saggy pants some even sport braids, but you know what that lets me know ese, that there is still opportunity to bridge the color lines."

"What you just said is exactly what I am talking about why would those Chicanos give up their *estilo* for that of the mayate?"

"I'm not trying to tell anyone how to live holmes my only concern is that our gente are safe and have every opportunity to not end up like us. Do I want them to preserve our culture of course I do, but I am aware that this generation of Chicanos and Chicanas are different from ours which can only be expected since we played a part in confusing them with our actions? Regarding the proposal from the Blacks it falls right in line with La Eme mission to shift the goal of our young we could kill two birds with one stone with the right decision."

"Enough talking take the issue to La Eme, there are other issues that we need to keep in mind like the death of Character. Is it just me are do the shooting at that park and the one at Fremont seem similar?" Sharky asked blowing cigarette smoke from his nose.

"Are you saying that Askari may have killed the carnal?"

"The *placas* never caught the individuals responsible for the murders of the homies are the people in that park. Everybody knows that the placa who was kidnapped was taken by the group that killed those other placas."

"But why would they kill Character?"

"That's what you need to find out before you jump in the bed with those mayates."

Monday afternoon Shy Rock received a phone call from Smiley who was doing a life sentence in Pelican Bay with word from the request that Shy Rock had put in a week ago.

"The carnals have mauled over your request to deal with the Blacks on the graffiti issue and we will send word that we will comply with the Blacks on this one issue because it serves as an advantage for both sides to stop putting our business on walls for the placa to see." Shy rock was shocked he knew for certain that the carnals were going to shoot the proposal down so many of them were prejudice that the mere mentions of Blacks brought up anger. Within two weeks the new order had been sent down and was being enforced in all barrios throughout L.A. which didn't sit well with Sharky and Camel who prompted their young homies to go out and kill Blacks in retaliation for not being able to represent in a way they had been doing for years. When word got back to Askari of the first murder done by the 12th streets on a young Black male under the tutelage of Sharky he immediately came to Shy Rock to diffuse the situation. Shy Rock was just getting in closing the door behind him when he realized it was too late to reach for his gun the Black figure that was sitting on his couch already had the drop on him.

"I come only to talk." Askari said standing up from the couch.

"You could've just called me on the cell."

"What I have to discuss warrants a personal visit."

"Speak on it." Shy Rock said taking a seat across from Askari.

"I've received confirmation that a member from your group has orchestrated the murder of a young Black male last night in Pomona are you aware of this murder?"

"Yes, I heard about it on the news. How do you know that one of my comradas was responsible for it?"

"Outside of stopping Gang members and taggers from writing on the walls we also have an agreement with the former gang members that they will not kill one another or other people within or outside their communities; under the agreement my group has vowed to protect anyone that harm has come to rather it be them or their family members in a we are the security for the community. We are not on a Black Power trip, but we are definitely about uplifting are people so that they can make better decisions in life and we accomplish that by making them feel safe a feeling that has been foreign to them for far too long so it is imperative that you know that this has nothing to do with race."

"I respect you for coming to have a face to face with me before acting on your findings. Sharky has a vendetta with Blacks that goes back to his junior high school days when Blacks use to beat him up; he never figured out how to separate one bad group from the entire bunch. He like most homies have taken one or two bad encounters and has deemed your entire race as no good because of a bruised ego that should have healed years ago. I understand what you are trying to do and I highly respect it, but there is nothing I can do to another carnal for taking a Black life if anything he will be given more respect for it, but to put it plainly and this pains me to say there'll never be peace among our people because you have too many fools that feel they are better than the next man and that their way is the only way which causes rifts between our own as well as with other racial groups. My mission this time around was to try to stifle this way of thinking, but sadly it is too ingrained for me to stop it on my own. Individuals must want to change for progress to happen. Egos have to be shed and angered released in a healthy fashion then the transformation can take place between the races Askari."

"We are one brother for your thoughts are mine. I know you cannot touch Sharky without bringing death to your doorstep and you have been around long enough to know I will not let him live. When the gun smoke settles it will be me that comes for you and no one else my brother do what you must and know there is no love lost no matter the outcome."

"Spoken like a true warrior I will see you on the battlefield."

Askari left as quickly as he came, he had dispatched a unit to kill Sharky hours ago and was headed back to Altadena to get confirmation of his death. Sharky had been driving through Pomona for a large part of the day picking up money from different stash spots in his neighborhood. On his way to the liquor store he spotted Askari's men tracking him in a black Altima through his rearview mirror he had seen the car hours ago but paid it little attention until now. He knew if he didn't go into the liquor store that that the men would just keep following him until they got him cornered in; so he stuffed his 357 Taurus into his waistband and made his way into the store peering at the men through his Ray Ban's sun glasses. There was only one way to go so Sharky walked to the liquor aisle grabbed his self a can of 211 and guzzled it while the cashier watched him on the video camera. The cashier was about to tell him to pay as he walked out towards the exit past the register but was silenced when he saw the young shaved head Mexican pull out the biggest revolver he had ever seen. Sharky picked up speed as he ran out the door making a quick break towards the Altima with his arm firmly extended finger on the trigger squeezing as soon as he lined up the head of the passenger with his sights. The first shot found its target splitting the man's head instantly after the first shot Sharky squeezed off three more into the front wind shield shattering the driver's side as he found cover behind a mailbox. Sharky was unsure of rather he had hit his target or not, but aware that he only had five more bullets left in his revolver to kill his target. Regardless to whether he was dead or not he knew he had to get to his car before the police showed up, but knew that wasn't much of an option once he heard the sirens blaring forcing him into a do or die situation to move from behind the mailbox and possibly get shoot or to wait for the police and get shot he figured he had a better chance with option one, but soon paid the price for the error with his life as the driver of the car tore into his chest cavity with a Famas F1 assault rifle that careened his body for a few seconds before releasing him to the ground. The driver of the car knew he had limited time as the sirens became louder, so he released the pins on the hand grenades leaving them throughout the car to explode while he ran through a nearby alley to find cover. Once he had gained distance from the scene, he called into the headquarters to arrange a car to pick him up so that he could debrief on the situation. When the officer arrived on the scene, they quickly exited their vehicles guns drawn to secure the crime scene while approaching units called for the fire department to put out the car fire. Pomona PD was on high alert along with all the other police divisions since the Torrance massacre prompting them to call in the F.B.I as soon as they realized that the deceased was a Mexican mafia figure.

"This was obviously a hit no one would just kill a La Eme member like this. Agent Klien said knelt over the body of Sharky pinpointing bullet wounds with his ink pen. Salvador Marquez is the man lying here dead, but you detectives probably know him by Sharky?"

"True analysis he has been terrorizing this community for years along with his family. Shit the only break people got around here is when he went to prison for five years, but then he returned a carnal making it near impossible to pin anything on him."

"Well someone got to him and their running around in the streets as we speak. Did the fire fighters find anything in the burning car?" Klien asked one of the detectives walking from the direction of the vehicle.

"Just the passenger of the vehicle charred beyond recognition."

"From right here I can see a grenade that didn't detonate. Someone call the bomb squad and evacuate the residences until they come, we don't want to take any chances with this especially after what took place in Torrance." The officers at the scene quickly went into action alerting nearby residences of the threat. The bomb unit did not take long to get to the scene and gear up although it took a while for their remote-controlled robot to retrieve the grenade for explosion which barely made a sound from within the protective box.

"So, it's safe now guys? Klien asked the bomb squad as he walked back over to the car to investigate the items removed by the bomb squad. Okay gentleman we have a charred vehicle which was obvious blown up with grenades by the driver of the vehicle who is not here at the scene. We also have a slightly burnt fusil assault rifle which is native to the French Foreign Legion or French Army sitting at a crime scene in Pomona. This type of weaponry is used to wage war much like the bullet casings found at the scene in Torrance it is possible that some illegals from Mexico have done this they are highly capable of getting their hands on these type of weapons. Detectives you may have a drug war on your hands."

"Agent Klien one burnt bizarre weapon signals to you that there is a drug war taking place in our streets?"

"No, but the fact that there is one dead mafia member, one dead unidentified person, and discarded war weapons around the crime scene tell me that this isn't a typical drive by shooting. These individuals who came for Marquez came to kill not only him, but whoever stepped in their way too. From my years in the field this points to the Mexican Cartels type of behavior. I will get in touch with immigration to see if there has been any influx of immigrants

Escape from Failure

from Mexico lately that will at least give us some type of clue to work with until something else shows up on this.

***

"Hold up cuzz this my nigga from out of Texas." Uzi said as he passed the blunt to one of his homies.

"Uzi, it's been three months since we have gotten any tangible information from you. We did not let you out for you to relax on our dollar."

"I feel you, but what you think a nigga out here doing? The streets are on fire with one time right now making it hard to move ain't nobody doing much of nothing outside of drugs."

"Look I know you are from South L.A., but I need you to venture into Pomona to see what you can find out on any murders or drug transactions that have taken place within the last month."

"I'll put my ears out there to see what I hear then I'll drop something on you."

"Make sure it's soon Uzi your importance to this investigation is starting to be questioned."

"By whom, I thought you were in charge."

"I am, but even I have to answer to someone. I'll meet with you in a few days at the same spot we always meet have something for me." Klien was desperate he needs some type of break that would lead to the arrest of a significant figure that could shed some light on what was going on in the streets.

Most back streets in Carson were quite providing the best places for informants to debrief. Klien had grown up in Fresno where he graduated from Fresno State before joining the F.B.I he was a typical White kid by most people's standards. Two parent home moms was a nurse his father a cop he played football for some years before tearing a tendon in his knee. He was always privy to why he joined the F.B.I, but most in his family thought it had something to do with his best friend being killed by the Fresno Bull Dogs when he was a teenager. After the death he had become a bit withdrawn from family and friends and before they knew it, he had up and left Fresno never to return in pursuit of his career as an agent. His collogues respected him although known really claimed to know him on a personal level he was most alive when he was cracking a case is all they knew and his amazing knack for turning out gang members into the F.B.I. best informants. From his experience it was always easy to turn out Blacks because most of them didn't have any type of real foundation or principle to stand on expect gang principles that mostly went out the door when they were facing a life sentence. Money was another motivating factor for them he had learned during the years they would give up anybody for a little money or to get their car out of impound and Uzi was no different to him he had seen all types crumble under the heat of a light late at night killers, drug dealers, and young to old gangsters. He had put so many under the prison because of informants he practically relied on them to do his job. He could hear Uzi music from around the corner before he hit the block he was parked on. He had to admit that he had met some pretty gone individuals during his time with the feds, but Uzi proved to be the most gone of them all he was even slightly more cautious when he was around making sure the button to his pistol was loose. He popped his door loose as he approached his side door smelling the aroma of weed as he set in the passenger seat.

"Why you always looking all tense every time you see a nigga?"

"Because I am still the police and you come around me as if smoking weed is legal."

"Klien sometimes you are on some real soft shit won't any of that matter when I hit you with this info. I have a few rats that stay in Pomona as well as some peoples from Pomona Piru. A little boy got killed a few days ago it was all on the news and shit you probably heard about it. Well the little nigga was related to this *rat* I be bashing out there so she was all emotional after she *domed* me off telling me about how this group of niggas took care of the entire funeral cost to bury the little nigga after the 12th streets in the area killed him for no reason. So after I leave the broads house I shoot over to my peoples house from Piru to see what it do and they tell me that some fool named Sharky from 12th street got chopped down coming out the liquor store for killing the little nigga a few days ago. So, I asked my folks why they did not ride, and they told me they did not have to the group took care of that type of shit. So, both people I talked to kept talking about this group like they were the illuminati or something. That's all I know besides that the streets are dead out there ain't nobody doing nothing just going to school and staying out the way; I've never seen so many niggas going to school and marrying their baby mommas in my life it's crazy."

"This group you keep hearing about has anyone seen them are they former gang members?"

"My peoples from the Ru gang say some nigga with a mask had a sit-down meeting with their big homies about the gang related killings having to stop, but that's the description that they know of."

"A mask...."

"Yeah, that's what I said, but they say he wore the mask to protect them in case the police tried to make them question them about him or the group."

"Uzi you have to infiltrate this group so that we can stop them."

"What the hell you think I've been trying to do. It is not like they are having open recruitments. I've been hollering at all my leads and turning up blank either people don't or they not saying anything period."

"Alright I have to go, but I will be in contact with you so make sure you answer your sell phone when I call or text you we need you to come through on this Uzi there will be a nice reward if you do enough for you to retire and start a new life."

"Niggas like me don't start new lives just break that bread off when I come through save the picket fences for your White ass."

Klien knew that the group would probably never pull some one as gone as Uzi yet it was his only resource at the moment he figured at least he had a lead on the case now he just needed to touch bases with Pike who had been insisting that there was some type of underground Black militia behind the deaths of the C.R.A.S.H officers as well as the transition in the streets. Klien realized that it was time to open his ears and listen to Pike who has been on the right track all along.

William V. Fields

Chapter 25
Old Ties

"Some people in this city believe that race relations are dictated by the police that service the community, but I feel that is a fraction of the iceberg in terms of how social development is created in the community. You have to take into consideration the level of college graduates in the area as well the poverty line and the list goes on in the number of factors that decided the vibe an area will have." Carole said sitting down to talk with Pikes about the ongoing investigation within his office.

"Actually, I concur with your thoughts on the matter. There is always more than meets the eye. Take this investigation for instance there have been numerous stories for months about what happen to the slain officers, but none of them have been accurate. For instance all the officers were singled out and targeted none of the killing were random acts of violence and from the little evidence we could accumulate we understand that these were military style murders, further more when I was captured by the group they let me know what their intentions are..."

"Wait...wait you were captured by this group?"

"Yes, when the school shooting took place a while back and I came up missing the group responsible for the cop killings had been following me. They rescued me after I had been shot and was lying in a pool of my own blood about to die..."

"Wait... and I'm sorry to keep interrupting you, but why was none of this mentioned in the news?"

"Because the department didn't want people questioning the motives of the group that had saved me, if the details of the story had been fully disclosed there would have been mass confusion of rather this group is bad or good. The police department does not need that type of thinking going on in the streets further confusing people. This group has murdered police officers' period. If people start to overlook that point because they have stopped gang members from killing each other who is to say what else, they want try to prove a point."

"I heard you say that these officers were targeted; my question is why?"

"Plainly put they had past that came to haunt them they were not angels by a long shot. All the officers had one complaint, or another filed or attempt to file on them for various reason involving the public."

"So, have you tried to track down the individuals that the officers had negative run in with over the years?"

"Of course, but it is a very tedious process to go through each and every arrest or complaint filed and then put a tale on each one to figure out if they had something to do with the crimes plus our budget is tight in all areas despite the importance of the case."

"Tell you what Sergeant Pikes hand over some of the names you have and let me investigate in my spare time to see what I can get for you."

"What you're asking to do is very dangerous more so what is in it for you?"

"I want first run at the story when it breaks. I am sure you understand how huge this is going to be when it all comes to the surface. A lot of lives are going to change as well as the entire social system because of what this group has done single handily to try to better their community. I also want to interview these individuals when captured to understand their ideologies on life and why they chose this path instead of another."

"Be careful what you ask for I have an idea that the individuals we are looking for are not hiding like some would want to believe, but in plain sight amongst waiting for the right time to complete their plan."

"Well I intend to find that out with your permission of course."

"I will give you a few files to get you started, but this is to be kept completely confidential no one else most know about this and if any of it leaks out I am assuming you already know the routine of those consequences. Miss Perking I am aware that you are accustomed to working in tense environments from the stories you have had to cover, but this is a slightly different situation because we as a department have never dealt with a situation like this before. Be cautious in all you do is what I am saying.

"Thank you I will…Well it seems you have a lot of interviews today I will get going." Carole said seeing the silhouette of Klien in the hallway before he came through the door.

"You're the last person I ever thought I would get a call from." Pikes said as agent Klien took a seat in his office.

"My sentiments as well I tend to keep fed business between feds because our ways of solving cases is slightly different from local authority. My father was local authority up in Fresno so I know the mind set when it comes to solving cases for your type you enjoy by the book if possible as we on the other hand rely on various techniques to solve crimes and case. The main difference in what we do and what local authority does is we take down whole organizations while the local is content with a gangbanger or two. By now I know you have caught wind of the murder of Marquez in Pomona?"

"Yes, I have." Pikes said annoyed waiting on Klien to get to point of why he was in his office. He was still upset about him and his partner releasing Uzi back onto the streets.

"I received information that the group that kidnapped you was also responsible for killing Marquez because he was responsible for the death of a little African American boy prior. For a while I was slightly skeptical about your story of a sub-group that was out to take control of the streets by eliminating gangbangers and crooked cops, but now it is apparent you were right all along. So, I am here to extend the branch so that we can get these individuals off the street. Both are skills are needed to catch these killers what do you think?"

"How are you certain they killed Marquez?"

"Because a reliable source told me; if we don't find this group before the mafia does it is going to be a lot of bloody white sheets in the streets."

"Marquez death has already made wind to the Mafia members that call the shots by now. All we can do is wait for it to happen and counter act the actions of both groups. I will go to the Chief and let him know what is going to possibly happen and that we need officers on standby for this potential threat. Make sure your men are ready as well." Pikes understood the severity of the violence that could take place if a war happened on the streets between the Blacks and the Mexicans, but in his heart he knew he could not stop it only pick up the pieces and move forward after the bullets started to fly. When he arrived at the Chief's office, he was just ending a meeting with Sergeant Waters who had a look of disdain on his face as he walked past Pikes."

"Chief I apologize about just showing up in your office without announcement, but I have some urgent information for you about the group that kidnapped me."

"Finally, hopefully it's about their whereabouts."

"Not exactly, but it is close. Agent Klien just left my office after informing me that the death of a Le Eme member last week was a result of the group that kidnapped me. In short we should prepare extra units for what could take place as a result of this."

"Your tone is telling me that this is going to happen rather we prepare for it or not. You have been most accurate about this case the entire time and it is about time that we get justice for our fallen who were victims of this heinous group of individuals. Too bad I want be able to spear head this one with you being that I am leaving for another position in Washington."

"Sir...what are you talking about...it was you that said you were not going to go anywhere with all the changes that are going on with the department. What happened to the tipping point?"

"The tipping point is now Pikes you are about to crack one of the biggest cases that has ever befallen our department. Clifford will be your new Chief and I am confident that he will be very productive in his new position."

"So, when were you going to make this announcement to the department?"

"Later today at a press conference, but I will not step down until two weeks from now. You look out of sorts Pikes are you alright?"

"Just a little taken aback I thought you were here for the long haul is all."

"Me too, but I have come to the conclusion that I have done all I can do with this department, now excuse me I have a dinner I have to prepare for."

***

Waters could not stomach another year of being Sergeant especially under Clifford's tutelage he wanted to be Chief so that he could enforce the type of policing he was taught by the likes of William H. Parker aggressive and proactive. The department in his opinion had gone astray in all their people pleasing tactics thus allowing rebellious behavior in the communities they worked in to take root. It was time for a change, and he knew the only thing that stood in his way was the doorbell to Deputy Chief Clifford's house. Waters seldom came over to Clifford's house, but over the past few months he had been made privy to the Chief stepping down putting him in a position to take over the department and run it correctly. It had been a mundane process working with Clifford every other week to get close to him, yet it was necessary to gain his trust by showing interest in his re-entry programs for parolees. Clifford had invited him over a week ago to go over the final plans for the re-entry program, so he was expecting him.

"Waters thanks for swinging by I know you were swapped at the office with paperwork. What's the alcohol for?"

"To celebrate your completion of the re-entry program of course, what else would it be for?"

"That's what I was wondering because I can't drink alcohol, I have diabetes."

"I was completely unaware of that with all the bottles you have on the cabinet."

"Those are from years ago when I use to drink and gifts from friends, I just haven't had time to through them out."

"No need to waste I'll come relieve you of them next time I come by."

"Fine with me, so let us pick up where we left off last week because I know your time is short. I recently got in contact with Steven Bradford an assembly man I went to school with years ago who shares the same passion as me regarding giving people a second chance at life. He is pushing a Re-entry Employment Opportunity Act which would prevent employers from denying employment based on a felony unless it had a direct conflict of interest with the job. For instance, drugs addict working at a pharmacy or a sex offender work at a pre-school. I think so often society here re-entry program and they automatically think harden criminals are going to be working in their homes and handling their credit card information when that is not the case. Harden criminals don't want to work so why punish those that have changed their lives forcing them to go back to being harden criminals because they are frustrated they can't get a job that they know they are qualified for."

"Hold that thought let me use your rest room for a minute." While in the bathroom Waters took a deep breath before he placed his leather gloves on and poured chloroform into a white cloth he had in his back pocket. It was now or never for him. Clifford was hunched over looking at some paperwork when Waters came up behind him and placed the cloth over his nose giving him little time to even fight back as the chloroform took effect quickly. Waters gentle laid Clifford down on the floor before going to get the Ever clear grain alcohol he had in the brown bag it was the highest proof he knew existed that would put Clifford into a metabolic coma the fastest. Once he was laid on the ground Waters twisted the cap off the bottle and started to pour it down the throat of Clifford. Clifford was unresponsive after an hour giving Waters time to set the scene for an apparent drunken suicide. He poured the remainder of the alcohol on his clothes and paperwork on the table then he scanned the room and made sure everything was in order before leaving the house. After two days of being a no show to work Chief Williams called Clifford's family asking if they had heard from him within the last few days. When he heard no, he sent a unit to his home to investigate and shortly after homicide was on their way to investigate his death. The coroner looked over the body any deemed it an accidental death to spare the family the embarrassment of a suicide accomplished curtsey of the Chief who felt it was unnecessary to end Clifford's legacy that way. The service was held at Crenshaw Christian Center in the heart of south central with hundreds in attendance to pay respects to a great man. Heart wrenching words were said by many in the brass as well as those on the other side of the fence who

Clifford had helped along the way; Waters even managed to say some words about how close the two had gotten over the last few months. The day was a sad one that left all in attendance feeling empty at the loss of a great man while the conscious were aware that a shift of power had just happened. Shortly after the funeral Chief Williams announced his departure to Washington for another career that involved private security. With the sudden death of Clifford Waters was promoted to active Chief of the L.A.P.D. he would be sworn in shortly after in front of the media as the new face of the police department. Waters primary agenda was to capture those responsible for the unsolved murders of all the slain officers who had been killed prior to him becoming Chief.

Officer Rodriguez was near death from an infection that had started to grow in his right leg from unknown bacteria the doctors were unable to counter when Waters had arrived at the hospital to see him. It had been awhile since he had been to visit him since the suicide attempt a few months back; Waters stood looking through the two-way mirror as the nurse opened the doors to his room where he was laying in the bed incoherent.

"It pains me to see what these bastards have done to you, but I will avenge this tragedy."

"Franks." Rodriguez managed to say once he realized Waters was standing in the room or so he thought the drugs they had him on currently kept him slightly delusional the majority of the time, but they helped him focus to the point where he could revisit each and every arrest he had made up until his attack. In his drug stupors he would determine who could have been responsible for what had happened to him and his conclusion was a young Black male named Timothy Frank who he had sent up to prison years ago. All his training in the field had pointed to Franks as the master mind he was just unable to prove it in the current state he was in nearing death with no way of writing out a lead or expressing it without someone thinking he was crazy. While Waters stood over him shaken his head in pity Rodriguez finally understood the anguish, he had put so many through with his illegal policing that had put many innocent men behind bars with the chips stacked against them. As Waters left the room, he asked the nurse if he had been drugged before him coming to visit.

"No Chief we usually medicate him every four hours. May I ask why?"

"It's as if he didn't recognize me, he kept calling me Franks.

Chapter 26

Green Light

"Come here *mijo*. Shy Rock said beckoning Shy Girl over to the table to finish their game of spades.

"Let me chop the avocado for the dip first."

"*Chale!*" So, what did you think about the funeral for Sharky?"

"Nothing, it's was just like all the rest black clothes, shoveled dirt, and vatoes talking shit about what they're going to do when they leave the service."

"It's typical, but that's the way it has been for years' regression instead of progression. So, what's the score now?"

"Two one you up."

"Prepare for number three baby doll."

After a couple more games of spades the Shy's headed to the bedroom where Shy Rock took off his shirt before lying face down in the bed waiting on Shy Girl to give him a back massage before she straddles him she went to the front of the house to unlock the door."

"What did you forget?"

"My lighter it was in the kitchen." Shy Girl said getting on to his back.

Shy Rock was enjoying the massage that was easing his sore muscles when he noticed that Shy Girls lighter was sitting next to his house shoes. Immediately he knew what was coming next as he twisted around with her on top of him to lock eyes with Speedy who was standing in the doorway with murder in his eyes giving Shy Rock little opportunity to squeeze off a shot from his 44 snub nose revolver before the fire of Speedy sawed off shotgun lit up the room as Shy Girl took the major portion of the blast to her back knocking her off of Shy Rock face first onto the floor giving Shy Rock the opportunity to dive to the corner of the room where he pulled the trigger before having an actual aim on his target to clear him out the door way. To his surprise he had actual shot Speedy in the stomach knocking him onto the floor as well. Shy Rock took deep breathes as he tried to gather his breathe and thoughts. Shy Girl was still alive laying on the floor with an exposed bloodied back he didn't waste any time in shooting her in the side of the head before he trained his weapon on Speedy in the middle of the hallway whose eyes went from murder to compassion that Shy Rock was in short supply of as he gave Speedy the same fate as Shy Girl. With all the commotion he knew one of his neighbors would call the police so he decides to go out his bed room window to go around the side of his house to his back yard as he stuck his head out the window all he saw was a flash of light before his face was removed by Camel's double barrel shotgun which left his body hanging in the window before Camel dragged it out to the outside where he spray painted mayate lover across the front of his body in black.

"Well we have a piece of the victims jaw over here on the fence along with the remainder of his teeth in the dirt." One of the detectives on the scene said snapping pictures of the scene.

"Your victims name is Benito Hernandez, but best known as Shy Rock one of the leading members of La Eme until now. On the inside we have Jose "Speedy" Ruiz also a member and one unidentified female. All the victims were from eighteen streets which is evident by the tattoos on them all. Motive would probably be the message left on the stomach of Mr. Hernandez which means the hit man or men have gotten away which is beginning to become a trend around here detectives." Agent Klien knew that something was going on with the Mexican mafia he just did not understand why they had killed one of their own even though the cause was scribbled across the stomach of the victim. In the back of his mind he wondered if the Black group had set this up to start a race war between the two groups.

"So, Pikes what is your take on this scene?"

"Klien I know what you are thinking, but the group did not do this it is not their style. This scene reeks of desperation and shooting to survive. There was a target, but a lot of screw ups in between it all. Although I do agree with you that something is brewing around here."

"After your detectives wrap it up, I'll meet you back at your office for a meeting." Agent Klien said walking to his car.

Escape from Failure

***

"Carnal on July thirteenth we are putting a green light on the mayates, it is time to eliminate this pest and take control of all the available resources in the community and avenge the deaths of our canals who have lost their lives fighting for La Raza. All the comrades know about the plan and are ready to move forward." Camel relayed the message given to him by top members of the mafia verbatim after the murder of Shy Rock to a group of comrades from various sets throughout Los Angeles. He was ready for the killing as he stood before the crowd with pride in his eyes at their lionization of him. The mafia had enlisted members from Mexico to come over and assist in the attack as well the majority of them spoke no English, but they knew how to kill as they crossed the borders in droves with M72 antitank weapons, K400 fragment grenades, and Barrett sniper ready for war.

Triple homicide leaves two Mexican mafia members dead in a South L.A. home over the weekend prompting authorities to beef up their patrols in the area known for perpetual gang violence. Askari sighed as he read the Los Angeles Times article in his living room about the weekend slaying. His only liaison to the mafia was now dead because of him and repercussion were soon to follow as a result of the death which was clearly a sign to his group that there would be death coming their way as well. The last thing he wanted was a war between the two groups because their ills were mutual on so many levels that it was pointless to war, but he was well aware that hatred was often brewed in the same vein as hurt and ignorance two forces that were hard to extinguish within an individual that thrived on them and was short sighted in their views of life. He had recently put in an ordinance that would arrive on a ship shortly so if war were needed to bring understanding then he was well prepared. His thoughts shifted as he heard keys fumbling at his door, but were soon put at easy when Carole walked through the door caring a tall stack of envelopes which she put down abruptly at the kitchen table before Askari could assist her.

"You should have called before you walked up here with all those files, I could have carried them for you."

"I didn't want to bother you; besides, I haven't been to the gym in a few days I needed the exercise."

William V. Fields

"Carrying all those files will definitely give your shoulders and arms a workout and if you plan to read through them all it will give your brain a workout too."

"I know I just left the 77th division station talking with Sergeant Pikes of the gang unit and he gave me all these files to sift through to build the store I am going to write on the murders that have been taking place throughout Los Angeles the past few months."

"I see so you're a detective now."

"No way I just like to give accurate reports that depict the true story instead of assumptions especially on cases involving life and death issues."

"I am surprised that the Sergeant allowed made you privy to that type of information let alone walk out the station with it."

"It wasn't easy, my reputation sealed the more so then anything else. The sergeant knew that I would really dig which could in turn help his investigation that the police are desperate to solve. Especially since the sudden death of Chief Clifford and the departure of Chief Williams there is a lot of configuring going within the department that you probably know already from reading the paper."

"My main concern is your safety. Just make sure you don't go into any dark alleys trying to apprehend criminals."

"Least of your worries I would chase a dollar in the wind down a dark alley. I notice that your baggage is packed are you going on a trip?"

"Unfortunately, I have to go back to Africa to renegotiate the prices of the material that I have been getting over there my contract is coming up for review."

"How long do you plan to stay?"

"Just a few days to see what's new in terms of cleaning material and close the deal on a longer contract because I have been satisfied with the service the company has provided me with thus far."

"Too bad I want be able to go I have to get these files back to Pikes by next."

"Why does he need them back so soon?"

"Because I am not supposed to actually have these files in my possession some of them are considered classified."

"So, he put his career on the line to give you files that he feels you can find information in that his officers haven't been able to do."

"Honestly, he is on edge the department has gotten nowhere with these cases that have been on the news lately. So, he felt that a set of new eyes could spot something that his trained men were missing."

"That makes sense so why you are down here playing Coffin and Gravedigger I will be upstairs getting together my own paperwork before I retire for the night."

"Skari we are going to have to vacation once my story is complete so that we can spend some time together."

"I'll be looking forward to it." Askari said as he made his way upstairs. Carle went through the diligently with a cup of hot coffee constantly at her side for the remainder of the night as she went through about twenty files until there were only ten left to search through. Around three in the morning her eyes were read, and her fingers were slightly numb from flipping through all the folders she knew it was time to end and pick back up later. After removing all her clothes, she walked back upstairs to climb in bed with Askari. A few hours later both were up prepared for the day. Carole had taken a ton of notes that she would pull from to figure out who could be behind the killings of the officers. Her element was finding and retrieving information and she was ecstatic that the information was coming together for her.

"You pulled a long one last night did you find out anything interesting in any of the files that you went through?"

"Yes, names from arrest that all the officers who were killed had made over the years. Whoever compiled these files did a great job gathering that information making it made it easy for me to go through and find the names that stuck out consistently. So, all I must do now is trace them all to see where these individuals are now and what they are up to so that I can narrow down my list. Take for instance this one name that kept popping up on all types of paperwork... wait let me find it. Here it is Lamont Jackson a.k.a n Uzi this guy has a lengthy record going back to a juvenile, but what raises a red flag is that his name is mentioned in federal paperwork as well."

"What do you mean?"

"He has been working for the government as an informant for years."

"And that is in the paperwork you went through last night?"

"Yes, you see I've been doing this so long that I know what to look for especially when it comes to government informants it is all laid out a certain way that alerts the knowledgeable eye that the individual is an informant. This guy is hardcore, yet he has put a lot of other gang members in jail. So that rules him out of the equation."

"It seems you have a solid method going on make sure you get some air before you dive back into those files again."

"You must've read my mind I am going to go on a little run to clear my head before I dive back into the files."

"I'll be gone when you get back, but I will see you tonight."

When Carole left for her run Askari quickly went through the files until he came across the one with Uzi's name. Once he found it, he ran a copy of it so that he could have it for future use. The information about Uzi made him wonder if the police had tried to send him to infiltrate his group if so, he could use it to his advantage to lure him in before killing him.

Murders had dropped significantly in Los Angeles while school attendance had spiked up from elementary to college level, a large part of this was due to refocused energy within the community. In the wake of all the chaos the past few months A.P.U.U. had finally brought summer night lights to Manchester Park a program that facilitated numerous activities for children within the park during the summer when gang violence normally reached its peak. The first day of the program was a success as the park was filled with local children who would have normally had nothing to do in the heat of the season but join a gang. The new program provided them a safe place to play as well as learn their talents by playing multiple sports. Four members of various nonprofit groups were standing in the front parking lot gathering baseball equipment from their cars before heading to the field to set up for the kids when they heard tires shrieks from a speeding white four door Cadillac that hit the brakes when it got into the parking lot a few feet from them. Before they knew it three bald head Hispanic gang members exited the car with AK 47 firing at them in the parking lot as they ducked behind their cars trying to get away from the gunfire that seemed like it would never stop as the gang members chased them down through the park gunning them down along with anyone else they could catch in the park within firing distance. The park that was filled with a new peace only a few hours ago was now left with its innocence violated as numerous dead and wounded bodies layered the sandboxes and baseball field. Shortly after in Long Beach a group of young Black females and males were headed to Kings Park to go swimming when five members of a local Hispanic gang jumped out of SUV's on them with various shot guns killing them all as the projectiles from the shotguns ripped their bodies to pieces. Reports of unprovoked murder circulated quickly through the streets as Brown on Black violence happened in every city leaving hundreds of Black people wounded and dead in the streets in manners never seen before. From Chino to Pelican Bay violence erupted abruptly from level one yards to level four yards alarms and yells to get down could be heard as echoes of mini fourteens firing into crowds of inmates could be heard throughout all California State prisons as the violence on the street was only matched by that of the prison institutions. Police officers from all jurisdictions immediately went into high alert at the news gearing up in riot gear as they prepared for the worse outcome to the string of deaths taking place in the streets. Upon hearing the news, the group sent word to their field groups to alert all the black gangs in the area to protect their families as the group would take care of the current threat that was on a killing frenzy. While word was being spread members of the group ran to put on their battle fatigues. In the war room all members of the group where in rows of single face lines with thirty members in each row ready to go. Askari knew the mafia was coming, but he did not expect for them to attack the way they did; now it was his duty to protect his people at all cost.

"Defend yourselves and protect your fellow brothers and sisters. Follow your assigned team leaders who have all been briefed on what areas they will be focusing on based on the expertise of their group. Lastly, I know some of you have lost loved ones to this senseless act of violence don't allow your feelings to dictate your combat performance neutralize the threat and keep to your objectives."

As the groups filed out of the compound heavily armed to their vehicles Askari stayed behind figuring out his next move to draw Camel out knowing he was behind the death of Shy Rock and the onslaught of murder that was taking place due to his hatred of Black people that was going to ruin all the hard work he had been doing to unite the entire community; there was also the matter of Uzi that he needed to tend to before he somehow tried to infiltrate his group amongst all that was about to take place. He had an idea where he could find Camel, so he loaded his gear into his vehicle to go find him.

Chapter 27

Red Light

The stench of gun smoke was thick in the air giving off a touch that could be felt on the faces of Askari's men as fifty groups of ten assembled to seek out various Hispanic gangs in the area for neutralization in multiple sections throughout the city. Shoot outs happened in liquor store parking lots, grocery store lots, playgrounds, and schools' yards. No area was off limits for gunfights; bodies were slain on sidewalks, apartment stair ways, and roof tops as the city of Los Angeles and neighboring cities became battle grounds. Explosions and rapid gunfire were going off every minute as Askari's groups moved with the precision of seasoned veterans finding and eliminating their targets proficiently. Vehicles were used as barricades and houses as shields from gunfire as the two sides went back and forth against each other exchanging heavy gun fire until magazines were empty, and the last breath of life were absent from bullet ridden bodies. Police were on the out skirts of the violence commanded not to intervene until given orders to do so, their duties were to protect the surrounding communities that were not a part of the carnage. With the sun setting in the horizon the police sent their helicopters into the sky to monitor the violence. Officer's orders not to intervene quickly changed quickly when a Sheriff and L.A.P.D. helicopter was blown out the sky by an RPG from a Hispanic brought over from Mexico to help in the war against the Blacks. In the darkness of the night Askari's group flipped on their night vision goggles to better combat the new threat that had begun to fire upon them. Orders from Askari were given to engage the officers as well if fired upon by them through their earpieces. Sparks of light could be seen enflaming entire alleys as gun fire from MG08 lit into police cruisers tearing them apart instantly as RPG's unloaded on S.W.A.T. vehicles inflicting similar damage. After numerous unsuccessful tries of trying to escape their S.W.A.T. vehicles without sustaining critical wounds the officers realized that they were not only out matched, but also out gunned by both sides. Chief Waters was being updated throughout the entire battle and had no choice, but to request assistance from the nationally guard a decision that pained him because he was unable to suppress a bunch of gang members in his own city.

"Pikes I can't believe that our police officers are being over ran by some gang members."

"Sir I've been telling you for the last few months that these are not common hoods running around with their pants to the ground, but highly trained individuals and what I feared most is now taking place."

"So, you knew that this would happe…." Before Waters could finish a huge explosion that caused the building to shake sent him and Pikes to the ground as the sprinkler system began to give soaking their uniforms as they tried to get to stable ground as another explosion rocked the building this time crumbling the south side of the structure.

"This is what I feared, anarchy. I knew the group would eventually attack the department when they felt threatened. "Pikes said while Waters followed behind him with a flashlight trying to find a way out of the building that was crumbling all around them.

"It looks like we are going have to jump for it the elevators are all down." Waters said shining his flashlight to the ground trying to measure the distance.

"The jump would break are legs from this distance."

"Wait, I have an idea if we tie our belts together, we can secure them on one of these loose pipes and shimmy down so that the fall want be as far. I'll go first."

Waters tugged on the belts that were tied around a piece of exposed pipe before he started to lower his self-down. When he felt he was close enough he let go dropping to the ground. He heard the crack in his ankle before he felt the pain of the fall. He had misjudged the distance in the dark.

"Fuck, I broke my god damn ankle! You might have to find another way around Pike!"

"I'll keep moving so that I can get down to you; just try to put some pressure on the ankle."

Pikes could hear automatic gun fire coming from the direction he was going in, stopping him instantly in his tracks as he heard a scream of anguish and then more screaming causing him to draw his pistol as he ducked behind some old cabinets that were turned over from the explosion. Waters was unable to find anything to tie his ankle up with forcing him to be completely still as to not agitate the wound. What the hell is that smell Waters thought to his self as a pungent odor filled his nose causing him to slightly gag as the smell entered his throat. Shortly after the smell he heard panting as if a dog was hurt forcing him to look into the dark that only allowed sight when an explosion went off, but by that time it was too late the red eyes had found his vision and the jaw was open exposing long yellow teeth that filled the creatures mouth as it neared him closer and closer before nipping at his injured left leg that was extended out. Pikes could hear the scream from Waters leaving him no choice, but to move faster to try to save his life as the screams intensified. Amadi was tearing at the legs of Waters trying to break the bones to immobilize her prey; and once her prey was helpless she went for the kill biting deep within his throat as he tried to stab the hyena with a utility knife he had in his pocket. During his death Waters thoughts drifted to Rodriguez as he took his last breath knowing exactly what happened to him now. Jelani and his unit moved on after Amadi was done feeding they had heard the explosion of the police station while they were scouting out other Hispanic hideouts when they came across a few of them trying to bring the station down with a volley of RPGs. His unit took cover while they fired upon the men killing them all before, they moved forward finding Waters who is scream lead them in his direction. Pikes arrived shortly after the unit left finding Chief Waters torn to bits in a way he had not seen since he was back in the mid-west and a coyote would get a hold of a sheep. Pikes took a deep breath before coughing from all the smoke that filled the air as he walked in front of what use to be the police station looking down Broadway which was clouded with smoke from fires that were burning un both sides of the street no matter what direction he looked in it was reminiscent of the ninety two riot, but worse the damage far exceeded the damage of that riot. Burst of gun fire could still be heard as the last of the fire fights were coming to an end leaving Pikes to wonder what the morning would bring.

***

Carole set in Askari's condo watching CNN news as they tried to get coverage of the battle that was taking place Throughout California. She could not believe her eyes at how fast things spiraled out of control. The battle outside motivated her more to try to figure out who was behind all the chaos that was happening. She immediately gravitated towards all the individuals who were released right around the time all the police killings and rapid change started to happen in the community. Once her list was compiled she did research on the individuals on the internet slowly crossing out the individuals as possible suspects do to various reason until she ran Timothy Franks name in Google and Askari's company popped up causing Carole to release a loud no! All her time talking to Askari it never came out in conversation that he received a settlement from being wrongly convicted. The investigator in her forced her to rule out all possibilities that Askari might be involved in what was going on, but all the evidence was pointing in his direction. He was the only one on the list of settlement recipients to have the resources to put together this type of army. Even though her gut was telling her it was him she still did not want to believe it so. Her suspicions turned to fear once it really dawned on her that he might be out there in the streets dead if he was involved in what was going on. Since she could not get in contact with him, she continued her investigation trying to tie all the pieces together.

***

Traffic was heavy going up the 91 east towards Riverside with people trying to scurry home to get away from the gunfire that was erupting even on side streets by the freeway. He was sure Camel was camped out waiting on further orders from the mafia. He figured if he could get to him, he could intercept his line of communication and somehow put an end to the deaths taken place. When he exited 14th street he made a couple zig zag turns onto back streets to find the location of the home his group had been monitoring before the war broke out. Seeing a group of younger Hispanics in front of the house keeping guard he was assured that Camel was inside as he parked his bike against some shrubs in the dark. Askari knew he would have to draw Camel out with a distraction, so he got up as close as possible to the house without being detected before he screwed the silencers on his FNH handgun. There were three Hispanic males in the front so he decided he needed to come from the back so that he could work up instead of back since he knew what waited for him in the front. It was about a half block run to get around to the back of the house; once he got to the back of the house he made out three more individuals all holding AR 15 which was good for him because it would be hard for them take aim if he was detected. The FNH was good for up to thirty yards because it fired rifle bullets so Askari knew he needed to get slightly closer to get a clean shot off. When he smelled their cigarette smoke he knew he was close enough to kill the men so he took aim in a crouched position doing a run through of his targets before he delivered three quick head shots to his victims which dropped them all immediately besides the thuds of their bodies hitting the ground no other sounds followed their deaths sending Askari closer to the house where he ran quickly to the side of the house to kill the men in the front which would prove a little more difficult to do. He could hear one of the men coming his way to take a leak so he holstered his gun and rolled back the sleeves of his shirt before grabbing his black combat knife; when the man came within grabbing distance Askari grabbed him by the forehead quickly exposing his neck to the blade that slit into him instantly as Askari lowered his body to the ground the blood from his neck slid down his bare arm. When he peered around the side of the house, he could see that the other two men were standing by the gate sharing a cigarette giving him the opportunity to take aim on them gaining two more head shots. Askari had disarmed all the outside security now he needed to get inside to Camel so he took the lighter of the men he had killed to the front door standing him in front of it while he imitated a knocking sound which was met by a shot gun blast from Camel.

"You fucking mayate I'll send you to play cards with the devil!" Camel screamed while trying to figure out where his target was.

It was hard to see in the house because of the shades so Askari threw a grenade into the window while ducking in the shadows taking aim for when Camel would run out the front, but instead he came running out the back firing on Askari with his shot gun that was equipped with a fifty round drum. Askari managed to squeeze off a few shots in the dark while trying to take cover not understanding how he was able to see him until he saw the night vision goggles around his face. Camel continued to chase him down firing consistently in his direction forcing Askari to flee because he was unable to get off a clean shot while being fired upon. Making a quick left Askari was finally able to get a solid position to return fire; Camel sensed that he was losing his target after he couldn't see him for a few feet causing him to fall back and take cover his self while trying to find any movement in the dark. Some of the street lights were shot out during the battles, but there was one still giving off light making it unnecessary for Camel to keep on his night vision, his patience was running short as he waited and waited for Askari to come out he was ready to get it over.

"Come out so we can finish this like men." Shortly after Camel stood up from his crotched position and placed his weapon to the side putting his hands up in the air in a beckoning gesture to come fight. Askari cleared understood the gesture Camel was making towards him and made his way in his direction with his pistol closely by his side; when he was within face to face distance Camel stepped out from behind his barrier tossing his shotgun to the side taking a boxing stance. Askari mirrored his taller opponent as they circled each other defensibly trying to find an opening. Camel long reach and boxing background in youth authority gave him a slight advantage when it came to hand speed something Askari soon came to witness as he barely dodged two quick jabs and a right hook. Every time Askari tried to come in for an attack Camel would fend him off with his quick jabs that were penetrating his defenses more and more as the two exchanged blows for over a minute nonstop. Thirty more seconds into the fight Askari realized that Camel was relying solely on punches to defend his self-triggering Askari to start incorporating kicks to the leg and body which quickly changed the flow of the fight as Camel was thrown off by the flurry of punches mixed with various kicks that were wearing him down as the two men went into the third minute of combat. Askari's eye was slightly swollen from Camels quick jab making it hard for him to see out his left eye he knew he had to end the fight before his eye was completely swollen; his opportunity came when Camel dropped his right shoulder out of fatigue exposing his chin to a right round house that sent Camel to the ground face first. Askari caught his breathe as he looked upon his opponent laid in the dirt unconscious before pulling rope from one of his pockets which he used to tie Camel's hands and legs together creating enough slack to pull him in from the road into was left of the house he was hiding in. Camel was surprised when he came to, he thought for sure that whoever won the battle would kill the other, but that was obviously not the case. Askari could not find any paper trail that would indicate what the Mexicans next move would be so he knew he would have to gather it from Camel.

"You should have put a bullet in me because I ain't telling you shit mayate."

"Camel, there is no reason for anymore funeral services our goal was never to show who was the best killer on the streets we my group wants to put an end to the violence in both of our communities."

"Never, we'll never trust your people your people are totally dysfunctional; we don't want that type of poison infecting our people."

"I agree that there are some dysfunctional behavior in the Black community, but it is being worked on vigorously by my group something that has never happened before we are eliminating those that don't want to prosper as a whole for the betterment of all."

"Even if what you say is true, I have no say so on what happens now. La Eme is in charge I just follow orders if I come to them with what you are telling me it could be looked upon as treason in which you know the penalty from what happened to Shy Rock who had more rank then me."

"You're in a tough position in which I understand, but I am sure you can figure out a way to make your comradas understand that it would be to the benefit of both sides to work together solely in the area of building community and nothing more so that our children have a future. Your hatred for my people is probably warranted steaming from some tragic event in your life for that I apologize no human being should be made to feel that they are ever below human or that they don't matter for it breeds the hate you have been living with for so long; I'm not going to kill you and the decision you make after this is completely up to you all I ask is you don't judge all my people by a few bad encounters." Askari cut the knots restraining Camel and made his way to his motorcycle. Camel stood there after Askari rode off not knowing what to think knowing he would have killed him if he had the upper hand in the situation. All his life he had lived on the edge and it wasn't until his life was almost ended that he appreciated living for another hour never in his life had he looked upon Black people with any integrity, but he had to be honest with his self that Askari carried his self like a true warrior throughout their battle changing his view immediately on how he perceived a race of people the irony to it all was that his hate ended on the same street that it had begun many years ago when he was jumped by a group of misguided 12th street Crips who were as gone then in their minds as he had become over the years it all started to make sense to him in that moment the cycle would continue as long as he kept the lie going that there was no room to repair open wounds that had been passed down from generation to generation with no solid explanation to why there was such tension between the two groups that shared so many similarities. How Race relations between Hispanics and Blacks would be after the conflict subsided lied on the words, he would give to his comarads in next few hours.

Chapter 28

Target

General Flynn had been briefed only a few hours of the situation taking place in Los Angeles before he felt it necessary to send in his intelligence team to gather information they could use before he sent in his Seal team to neutralize the combatants in the war zone. Reading over F.B.I. reports written within the last few months it did not take him long to figure out that the L.A.P.D had allowed a rogue militia group to organize right underneath them.

"General Flynn we have the photos you requested as well as Sergeant Pikes." A solider said throwing a brown folder on the round desk.

"Send him in a few minutes." Flynn immediately opened the envelope as shock spread over his face at the individuals in the pictures appeared to be South African guerillas that he had been doing surveillance on years ago before he had made general. The connection puzzled him slightly too why they would be all the way out here fighting a war in Los Angeles. While in mid thought Pikes walked in looking as if he had not slept in weeks.

"Have a seat Sergeant I know you have been through quite an ordeal within the past few days. It was fortunate my man was able to rescue from the police station before you met the same fate as Captain Waters."

"Yes, it was definitely fortunate that they had stumbled upon me. I was unaware that the military had been alerted to what was taking place."

"We had been on standby for hours hoping the local authority could suppress the kinetic activity that taking place. If I had known what I know now I would have sent my men in months ago. I just received photos of who you are up against out there in the streets and honestly, I am surprised that the death toll is not hire then it currently is. These men in these photos are members of a heavily armed guerilla group in Cape Town. This individual right here is Jelani the leader of the group along with his right hand general Akachi the hand of God, the others are known killers in Cape Town so this explain why you were out strategized over the last few hours, but what it doesn't answer is why they are in Los Angeles trying to start a war when they have been inactive since the war in Afghanistan."

"They are under the orders of an individual named Askari who feels it is duty to restructure the Black community completely by eliminating those of the race that prey on their own kind as well as outside threats."

"So, you have a terrorist group right in the heart of the city that wants to impose its views on the government and local law enforcement. We've been dealing with these issues overseas for years it was inevitable that it would eventually spread within the military always assumed it would take place in New York first before Los Angeles even though there is a lot of influence that stems from the area."

"Since you know who is responsible for this warfare are you going to try to negotiate with the group?"

"Of course not we don't negotiate with terrorist we will infiltrate and destroy this group so that you and your officers can repair your city, but I must ask before we conclude with all you have been through and partners you have lost to this group why would you even ask such a question?"

"I'm still an officer of the law and I feel that all people are entitled to a fair trial."

"Yes, civilians should have a right to a fair trial, but once that civilian picks up a weapon and goes against the grain of the government they are no longer privy to the laws set for law abiding citizens we create examples of what happens when one takes arms against the U.S. not negotiations so that more people rise up when they feel that things are not going their way where would we be if that took place? I will tell you not in America! As we speak there are four MH-6 helicopters filled with top Navy Seals headed to the garrison created by the terrorist group that formed on your watch whoever is left you can see to it they get a fair trial."

Pikes set in his chair as the General left the room staring at the pictures before him, he held the pictures in his hands shuffling threw them knowing that the individual he had spoken with was not of African descent. He had mixed feeling about what was going to happen he was against the uprising, but he understood why it happened if only the group could have taken another route.

Askari's men had taken notice that the Hispanics had fallen back as well as the officers as an awkward silence fell upon the once sleepless city that had become a battlefield continuous rapid gun fire had settled into minor crackles in the dark of those still trying to die for what they believed. Fires were ablaze everywhere throughout the city as souvenirs of what had taken place for the last few hours lay displayed in the streets that were soaked with the blood of the dead bodies that lined the streets of a city that always garnered a reputation of being a place of war. With smoke in the air Askari's men were unaware of the MH-6 flying overhead with thermo technology picking up on the heat of their weapons all they felt were the bullets ripping threw them as the shells of the 30 millimeter chain gun fell like a water fall from the MH-6 as Seals propelled from ropes onto the ground taking cover before engaging their targets. The teams attacked the same way in different parts of the city killing every group that they locked upon before alerts were sent out that they were on the ground by nearby groups that witnessed the attack and in turn started to engage the Seals once they hit the ground. Upon hearing what was happening Askari gave the code for the snipers to take position and for the ground troops to take defensive action.

"Jelani, how many groups have been hit?" Askari asked while he placed civilian clothing over his body armor.

"Abidemi, Boipelo, Chidubem, and Chike are all deceased along with their groups they were the first ground troops to be targeted by the military special units. The snipers have managed to kill a few of their men, but we are still unclear how many have actually dropped in from the copters."

"I'll send out the code for the wounded to be taken back to head quarters before the sun comes up in a few hours. I want Akachi, Ekwu eme, and you to keep fire on those troops that landed while the other groups fall back to headquarters to initiate the next phase of the plan, be safe brother."

The sun could be seen on the horizon of Los Angeles as its beams penetrated the remaining smoke lingering from the night before an in its wake it brought members of the National Guard as well as the U.S. Army who were deployed in groups of fifty or more to each of the city's affected areas. Tanks with troops hanging out them rifles in hand rolled down residential streets and once busy intersections setting up garrison while other troops were on loud speakers telling people to stay in their homes until further notice caveats were given that anyone outside would be detained or killed for acts of terrorism against the United States. People were relieved that all the madness that seemed to spur out of nowhere was coming to an end after a night of terror that seemed like it would never end. Askari's men were aware that they needed to eliminate the special unit that was sent to kill them before the National Guard and other military took further foot hold on the city's the last thing they wanted was a fire fight with the military which would be counterproductive to their goal of unity because their fight was not against the military or the United States, but the corrosion of normalcy in their community.

Ekwueme received confirmation from one of the sniper units that the special team they were tracking was two yards from them setting up communication. Once their location was penned pointed the sniper took aim killing his target before moving on to the others causing the unit of six to disperse leaving them wide open to the attack waiting on them a couple of yards off which left them helpless to the gunfire of Ekwueme unit. The gunfire alerted the other special force group who were also in the area directly in back of Ekwueme's group giving them the advantage to return the favor as they scrambled behind turned over vehicles to engage the group in a fire fight; with the shade of night gone there was little room for error for either side, but the Seals war experience proved to be give them the advantage as they used explosive and smoke grenades to draw out the novice troops to fire while other members of the group picked them off leaving Ekeueme fighting three Seals by his self after his team had been picked off one by one. Ekeueme knew he could back track so that the sniper could assist him so he through a flash grenade before he maneuvered his way back towards where the first team of Seals were setting up a communication area. The sniper was still on his post waiting for the gunfire to settle before moving position when he spotted Ekeueme being followed by three Seals two of them directly in front of his field of vision making them easy head shots the thud of their bodies hitting the ground caused the third member to look over to his right giving Ekeueme the slight advantage to squeeze off a death shot. While reloading his assault rifle he heard a movement as well close by his foot from one of the first Seals shot by the sniper who was bleeding from his left eye socket profusely before he could raises his rifle to finish the kill the Seals shot off multiple shots from his desert eagle hitting him in the chest and head before the sniper could take aim to kill him on the ground. There was one more team of Seals left, and they were aware that all their fellow members had been killed leaving them with an extreme determination to finish their mission against an enemy they had greatly underestimated. Jelani knew how special teams moved and operated from his experiences in South Africa so he knew to try to engage them head on would be asinine he would have to set a diversion to draw them out so he back tracked to one of the garrisons that the group had built for detention of gang members who were still rebelling against the mission of the group during the night time war. His unit dressed them in their fatigue and attached rifles with empty magazines to their hands with rope. Once the five decoys were set up Jelani's unit let off gunfire in hopes of drawing out the Seals who took about thirty minutes to pinpoint the gunfire and take attack position on the group sectioned in an abandon building. The Seals didn't take long to kill the men off with long range sniper fire giving their position in the process to Jelani's unit, but Jelani gave the signal for his group to stand back he wanted them to fully come from behind their covered position for the sun was fully out and they needed to get back to head quarters before being tailed by the advancing military presence. They were hesitant at first, but they had to see who their enemy was a factor Jelani anticipated on. One by one they filed out until they felt it was all clear all five of them standing over the bodies they had just killed before two of them started to search their bodies for intelligence and quickly noticed to rope binding their hands, but by then it was two late Jelani's unit closed in on them firing on them with three M134 which shook the tri pods they were stationed on leaving little that resembled a body of the Seals who couldn't escape the rapid fire of the Gatling gun powered by an electric motor a weapon that aided the group throughout the night into their final stance. They were the last unit to leave the city and return back to headquarters were they were reunited with the survivors of the night, out of the five hundred men and women deployed four hundred and five returned alive with less than half in need of medical attention. The mood was intense as the members embraced each other with emotions they had never felt before for they had been a part of history defining moment that would forever change how life would be in the ghetto for the majority of them this was the first time they had went to war and knew their actual enemy, but more so what they were fighting for; yet there was a sense of loss for the ones they had made this journey with who were no longer around in the flesh to embrace. Askari looked upon them all from his corner of the room with a warm feeling in his chest as he watched former Blood and Crips, Hoovers and Neighborhoods tending to each other wounds and showing genuine compassion for one another they had become one with themselves as well as each other these beautiful human beings were just that human beings no longer choosing to define themselves by negative damaging stereotypes, but by how they treated the next men during their walk through life. The love he had for them was strong so strong that he knew he wanted their feeling an awakening to happen in as many places around the world as possible. The war last night was only the catalyst for what was to come and be born of the rumble and decay that lay in the wake of the night before within the chaos they had managed to blow up all the liquor stores in the community along with the unneeded fast food establishments that plagued them. To the naked eye the community was damaged even more than it already was and the Blacks had once again destroyed their own community, but to the group the destruction was fertilizer on which new opportunities would be made for success and a new way of life.

Chapter 29

Regroup

Carole was frantic as she set in her husband's loft wondering about his whereabouts and safety as she watched CNN's continual coverage on the aftermath of what reporters were calling the bloodiest night of mayhem the country had ever seen. Over a thousand people where dead throughout the streets as military troops remained in the areas most affected by the uprising providing water, food, and medical attention to those in need as residents were forced to stay indoors or within the limits of their property as the military and local law enforcement continued their investigation and capture of individuals they believed were involved with the shootings. Hazmat was called in to check for any poisonous gases that may have been in the area as well as make sure dead bodies were not left to rot in the streets creating an unsafe environment. All the news reports were depressing Carole as she thought about what move to make next until her thoughts were thrown astray by the door knob twisting along with her heart as Askari walked through the door with his natural calmness not showing a smidgen of aloofness to what had transpired over the last couple of days in the streets. Their eyes locked on each other as he made his way to her noticing immediately that something was awry with his wife by the way she embraced him; scanning the room he could see that she had been keeping busy with her investigation by the stack of files piled on the table with one noticeably put aside. They held each other for a minute or so his grip tighter then hers as a plethora of thoughts and emotions encircled her mind on what to say as she battled eternally with herself on how to feel, breaking from their embrace Askari rubbed Carole's face beckoning her to have a seat on the couch.

"What troubles you Carole?"

"So many troubles me that I don't know where to begin. For starters I was worried about your safety with all the mayhem that has been taken place in the streets, but even that has been overshadowed by what my investigation has uncovered." With that Carole stood up from the couch and made her way towards the table to get the isolated folder from the table. Sitting back down hands trembling she handed the folder over to Askari. Askari scanned the papers within the folder noticing all the circles linking him as a possible suspect to the police shooting. After sifting through the papers, he placed the folder down on the couch between them.

"You are definitely a talent; your report is absolutely accurate accept it doesn't place me at any of the crimes, but it definitely provides a lead for a trail that has been nearly impossible to follow until now if given to the authorities. I hate that I have put you in such a complex situation; I can only imagine how hard this is on you my love, my wife."

"It would be foolish of me to ask why you didn't tell me Askari, for what could you have said. Hey, just so you know I run an underground resistance group in my spare time that kills corrupt police officers and gang members would you marry me. I can say what bothers me most is whether or not you didn't tell me was because you were trying to protect me or just didn't trust me?"

"Trust was never an issue for I would not have married you if I didn't trust you. With all the planning that went into creating my company and developing my group I could not figure out a way to come out and tell you. As you know it is a very delicate issue that has no normalcy to it so to place it into words in which to deliver to you has been my biggest challenge thus far. To say the least, I am thankful that you have found out for my intentions were never to keep secretes from you ever."

"Honestly, I do not view your actions as being secretive more, so I know you were trying to protect me from the being involved in which I am now because I know. In correlation to that you being here in one piece means that you group is still intact which ultimately means that this uprising has only begun; from all the planning you have put into this I know you are waiting for your next move so my only question is will it involve more bloodshed?"

"My intentions were never for things to have to come to what took place in the streets it will be a terrible stain in history that will most likely be lied about and never fully understood like most tragedies in history. When I thought about this years ago in my cell I knew what it might take to see my vision through and therefore made the decision to proceed with planning it out knowing that the results would far outweigh the loss that would and did happen if lethal force was needed. The next step is to rebuild and implement the curriculums I have been developing over the years so that a new way of living can be felt now and not later or metaphorically there has been enough of metaphoric banter the next move will be new life."

"Amongst all that has transpired I have neglected to let you know of the new life growing in me. My only hope is that our child takes the torch of the foundation their father is creating; it goes without saying that I am here to support you in any way possible."

Askari was taken aback by the news of Carole being with child. His face softened as a new feeling engulfed his soul the feeling of joy only cradled him a few times during his life all being at the forefront of his brain the movement coming together, meeting Carole, being released from prison, seeing K-Stone awaken mentally, and now knowing he had a child on the way. He moved closer to his wife on the couch to embrace her and their future child. The rest of the night was spent devising plans and the role Carole would play in the movement.

***

After a month the military presence in the cities affected by the night of war started to diminish along with coverage of the damage by news station who had moved on to the other stores taking place around the world the story of the uprising was old news now as the authorities had no actual suspects in custody assuming them all dead in what they labeled an ongoing investigation that had talking a backseat to assuring that a situation like it would never happen again by holding weekly discussion about how the community felt the rebuilding process was going. Askari had managed to secure a contract with the city that allowed him control over the renovation of the damaged areas in Los Angeles; the members of his group worked diligently night and day for months planting trees, landscaping, panting, and repairing homes and business. Old libraries were remolded and new ones put up in place that use to be occupied by liquor stores while tutoring and adult computer labs were set up throughout the city to help adults acquire their GEDs, job training, and life skills. There were numerous after school programs that were created by elders in the community as well as local churches who were constantly reaching out to the community every weekend with some type of donation drive that benefited those in need. The murder rate had dropped to zero as the gangs in the area were nonexistent it was no longer into gang bang reputations were now garnered through academics and what individuals did for their community instead of against it. The need to sell narcotics had zeroed out as new jobs were constantly being created by the new development happening everywhere in neighboring cities. Class were also given on how politics worked so that the community for once understood the power that they possessed when they worked as one politically year round on issues that effected them for the first time since the civil rights movement Black people had a sense of community again that they wanted to keep which kept them involved with every law are legislation that effected the community as a whole. Chief Pikes was held as one of the greatest to serve as Chief being credited with establishing a working relationship with the community that actual worked although Pikes knew who was truly responsible for what was taking place which was perfectly fine with him. Askari was pleased at the progress as he over saw the youth program that K-Stone ran that was preparing over a hundred youth to join the police and sheriff department through weekly activities while another group was groomed to become lawyers and politicians his long term goal was always to become self-sufficient. Relations between the Hispanic community had mended well they were also taking advantage of the opportunities that were now available to all in the community that mirrored that of communities they once envied minorities were proud of where they came from which showed on the graffiti free walls that were once stained with hate. Askari had seen Camel in passing a few times during the reconstruction process, but they never spoken words always head nods occasional smirks of acknowledgement for the work done on both sides to create what was currently taking place.

Through Carol Askari kept a detailed list of all those who came through the corners office as a result of the war and to his disappointment Uzi's body had yet to be found which meant he was dead or out in the community waiting to cause some type of havoc. A lot of thought went into how Askari was going to let his once mentee know his comrade had been an informant for years largely because he didn't want to put him in a situation where he would have to pull a trigger, yet his demeanor to the news further solidified why he had walked away from the gang lifestyle there was no loyalty or trust. He had given Askari unspoken permission to do what he must regarding ever coming across Uzi in the near future a hurtful decision despite the information that was now known by him. He couldn't find it in his self to kill Uzi his self for he still had love for his ex-comrade furthermore the K-Stone of old was no longer present in him anymore Kevin was now in control not some immature caricature that couldn't think for its self his value of human life had risen drastically over the years even more so with the birth of his own kids he had an epiphany during the birth of his first son that life was to be honored not taking away by another human being for reason outside of self-defense at the end of the day he always kept in mind who was he to take a life just because he felt a person should die for some street code or disagreement that person was still important and worth salvaging in someone else's eyes why should he be the one to take their hope for making a difference in that person's life, but these were his thoughts not to be imposed on someone else for every situation was indeed different bringing with it an impulse to do justice according to the measure of pain that each individual felt was dealt to them in the end there were hardly ever any happy ending for someone else's happiness was certainly followed by someone else's pain it was always perspective that determined peoples decision he just hoped that one day people could see the ramifications of their actions from others perspectives before they decided to make life altering choices that apologizes could not repair.

Askari was always aware that habits were the fingerprints of a person's character so it was only a matter of time before Uzi would leave prints of his whereabouts through his destructive life choices that were inescapable even in a thriving community. It didn't take long to get back to his group that Uzi was shacking up with his baby momma in the community trying to turn out old dope fiends he use to serve to when the streets were his by enticing them with their past bane of choice; through their drug counseling they were able to overcome the temptation instead opting to report the nuisance who had returned like a cancer in a healed wound. Askari knew he had to move quickly on virus like Uzi for their sick way of thinking spread quickly infecting innocent influential minds.

Chapter 30

Grow

Jelani had been watching the house Uzi was held up in from afar for the past few days so he knew he would need Amadi to keep the four pit bulls in the front yard busy so that he could get in the house to execute his target. The streets were mostly quite on Thursday nights as the week neared closer to the end the residents in the area tended to stay inside which provide Jelani the opportunity to move in the shadows of the night without being detected. He could hear the dogs barking in the front yard as they caught the scent of Amadi approaching; while they were distracted with her he made his way to the back of the house before prompting her to jump the fence into the front yard. At first the pit bulls were apprehensive about attacking the hyena for they were afraid at first site then their fear turned to rage as they tried to close in on her the first one losing its life to a bite on neck from Amadi mighty jaws that went straight through the rubbery tuff skin cracking the males neck. The other three pits took heed going at the hyena legs at once instead of head on their plan worked as two locked on to her back legs giving the third pit a chance to get a lock on her front leg directly underneath her chest forcing her to the ground as they all tried to shake the energy from her so that they could get a hold of more vulnerable areas of her body that bring a kill. The commotion outside brought Keisha to the front door to see what was going on as she opened the door Jelani grabbed her by the throat with his left hand pushing her forward back into the house as he held the FNH in his right hand extended out looking for Uzi, but he did not appear.

"I ask once where he is." Jelani said his grip getting tighter around her neck.

"At a bar across town, he just left."

Jelani released his grip as he reached in his pocket for plastic cuffs that he placed on her wrist and ankles laying her on the ground as he did a sweep of the two-bedroom house before heading outside to help Amadi who had managed to kill one more of the pit bulls, but was struggling to keep the other two from locking on as she grew weak from blood loss. Jelani ran in to help her pulling out his twelve-inch machete whacking one of the pit bulls across the face that had a hold on to Amadi's side causing it to fall weeping before he delivered four more whacks to the face that killed the pit. While this was taking place Amadi shook the last pit off locking mouth to mouth with it as the pit lounged at her in an attack that left the pit with its lower jaw completely ripped off lying in the dirt shaking. Jelani radioed for his convoy to pick up Amadi along with the dead pit bulls.

"The target is at an after hour not far from my location how do you want to proceed." Jelani asked Askari breathing heavy.

"Fall back I will send another unit to take care of him."

Jelani followed instruction climbing in the van with Amadi in his lap as the rest of the men put the pits in the back seat while another unit stayed behind to monitor Keisha in case Uzi came back to the house. Askari knew that sending men to get Uzi at the after hour would be asinine because he would start shooting immediately so he had to send one of his most lethal troops to get the target. Toy box had blossom exceptionally since she joined the group and had become quite skilled in taking out targets, but this task would be her most dangerous for she was going up against a straight killer who would shoot in a split second.

"Toy box you are needed the target will is currently at an afterhours, this will be a solo mission." Askari said over the phone.

Within minutes Toy Box was putting on her short black mini that hugged her perfectly toned body that had gotten even shapelier with all her training since joining the group. She pulled her hair out of a ponytail as she prepared to run a hot comb through it to straighten it out, she always was aware of what caught men's attention long hair and light skin. Before leaving her place she grabbed her red purse with the mini 45 automatics inside with three clips just in case even though she was confident that she would be able to get him with one swift attack because she already knew what his weakness was. She couldn't make out what was playing in the after hour, but she knew it had the fifty or more individuals up and dancing as she made her way to the back of the place where she knew her target would be. Uzi was on his third blunt of the night when he noticed Toy Box walk by; for a short minute he thought he was hallucinating; it could not be he thought to his self. Getting up from his booth he made his way to the bar to reaffirm he was not tripping.

"Don't I know you?" Uzi said his speech slightly muffled from cotton mouth.

"Stop playing you knows who I am." Toy Box said turning around on the swivel chair to face him crossing her right leg over her left one exposing even more thigh.

"Naw, I'm not playing I knew it was you, but a nigga wasn't a hundred percent, so I had to come see if my eyes were deceiving me."

"Well, are they?"

"Nope, but I thought you were on the run for that bullshit."

"I am, but with all the other stuff going on around here it makes me small potatoes."

"Right, so you still on pussy or are you fucking niggas now?"

"I see you don't waist anytime."

"Life's too short to be playing and shit. What it do?"

"Depends on what you're talking about."

Uzi reached in his pocket and pulled out a magnum condom revealing the butt of his gun in his waist band in the process to Toy Box indicating to her that she could get him before he had the opportunity to pull it all the way out. As Uzi through the Condom on the bar table Toy box reached for her purse.

"You'll need one of these too." Toy Box said reaching into her purse pulling out the pistol.

Uzi was so caught up in the moment that he assumed she was going to pull out a pill for them to pop before he realized she had a gun in her hand. Because they were in such close proximity Toy Box held the pistol close to her side as she aimed up pulling the trigger tightly hitting Uzi in the right cheek knocking him back from her towards a pole that protruded from the ground in which he grabbed a hold to trying to reach for his gun as she continued to fire at his head striking him three more times in the back of his head sending him sliding down the pole to the ground. By this time people in the establishment realized that the sounds they were hearing were gun shots causing panic to spread as they made their way to the exits. Uzi's chest was still pumping up and down as Toy Box stood over him with her high hill planted in his chest moving his body so that she could see his face that was hanging to the side from the first shots. He was now on his back chest still pumping as blood came gushing from the holes in his head a fraction of what he used to be as life poured from his miserable body yet even with death upon him his right hand contracted back and forth in an effort to reach his pistol which had slid in the opposite direction; Toy box wasted no more time as she emptied the remainder of her clip into his face and head causing him to jerk on the ground with each bullet that entered into him. Uzi was dead!

    News of Lamont's death spread quickly through the streets as well as the law enforcement agencies that had either tried to apprehend him or worked with him in the past. He had few mourners on either side. The only true victims of his death were his children who no longer had a father that only left behind a murderous reputation for them to grasp onto. His murder did serve as a calling card to both civilians and law enforcement that the group's enforcers were still amongst them ready at any moment to cleanse out any problem that threatened the peace of their community. It came as a shock too many that the enforcers of the movement were still amongst them most preferring to believe they all died that night in battle leaving only the teachers, tutors, and mentors behind of the movement.

***

Askari sat before the remaining members of his group as they finished burying Amadi in a small ceremony within the barracks that honored their fallen comrades too. The ceremony was somber for it would be the last time he would see them face to face again for years as he had made preparations to travel abroad to gather a real world knowledge that would further the advancement of the group. It would also be the last time that a lot of the members would be seeing each other as well as they too were going to spread throughout the world bringing their proven structure to other disenfranchised minorities in other parts of America and the world. As every member assembled into their rows Askari stepped up to the podium to give his last face to face speech.

"We stand united today not far removed from the battle that changed the complete social structure of how our people view one another. All of you are responsible for the success that has spread through the cities. Yes, all of you are responsible for the drop in crime, abortions among young women, and the rise of educated minorities who will come to serve these same communities in the years to come for they now see the greatness that can be accomplished by working together. For many of us this was not our first war for we have seen many in some type of way, but it was indeed the first time we knew who the enemy was that we were engaging. Let us not forget that we are here to serve for the hardest thing in this life is to not become what we so desperately despise in others. In correlation let us never forget that we are here to grow by thinking and helping others that lack the wisdom, knowledge, and understanding we now possess may God be with you in all that you pursue in life."

www.ingramcontent.com/pod-product-compliance
Lightning Source LLC
Chambersburg PA
CBHW031137160426
43193CB00008B/167